GURUS IN AMERICA

SUNY SERIES IN HINDU STUDIES

Wendy Doniger, editor

GURUS

IN

AMERICA

EDITED BY
THOMAS A. FORSTHOEFEL
AND
CYNTHIA ANN HUMES

STATE UNIVERSITY OF NEW YORK PRESS

Published by

STATE UNIVERSITY OF NEW YORK PRESS

ALBANY

For information, address
State University of New York Press,
194 Washington Avenue, Suite 305, Albany, NY 12210-2384

Production, Laurie Searl
Marketing, Fran Keneston

Library of Congress Cataloging in Publication Data

Gurus in America / edited by Thomas A. Forsthoefel and Cynthia Ann Humes.
 p. cm. (SUNY series in Hindu studies)
Includes bibliographical references and index.
 ISBN 0-7914-6573-X (hardcover : alk. paper) — ISBN 0-7914-6574-8 (pbk. : alk. paper)
  1. Gurus—United States. 2. Spiritual life—Hinduism. I. Forsthoefel, Thomas A. II. Humes, Cynthia Ann, 1958– II. Series.

10 9 8 7 6 5 4 3 2 1

In memory of

Tamal Krishna Goswami

disciple, guru, teacher, scholar, friend

you are dearly missed

Time is running out. I have perhaps another twenty years to serve. I must seriously consider how I can best utilize this remaining time. Our movement is now firmly established. Hare Krishna is a household word around the world. Yet I think that we are still largely misunderstood by others. Rooted in their own cultures and traditions, they often find our ways strange. To help them understand, we must first seek to know them better—their history, their mores, their faiths. To transmit the finer aspects of Krishna consciousness, we must first educate our own members. An intelligent learned clergy with broad educational backgrounds will then be able to relate our teachings and traditions to those of other persuasions. Both will be benefited.

Tamal Krishna Goswami
A Hare Krishna at Southern Methodist University
(Dallas: Pundits Press, 1998), 26–27.

CONTENTS

INTRODUCTION: MAKING WAVES   1
Thomas A. Forsthoefel and Cynthia Ann Humes

ONE   RAJA YOGA AND THE GURU: GURANI ANJALI OF
YOGA ANAND ASHRAM, AMITYVILLE, NEW YORK
Christopher Key Chapple   15

TWO   WEAVING THE INWARD THREAD TO AWAKENING:
THE PERENNIAL APPEAL OF RAMANA MAHARSHI
Thomas A. Forsthoefel   37

THREE   MAHARISHI MAHESH YOGI: BEYOND THE TM TECHNIQUE
Cynthia Ann Humes   55

FOUR   KRISHNA AND CULTURE: WHAT HAPPENS WHEN
THE LORD OF VRINDAVANA MOVES TO NEW YORK CITY
Tamal Krishna Goswami and Ravi M. Gupta   81

FIVE   BABA'S WORLD: A GLOBAL GURU AND HIS MOVEMENT
Norris W. Palmer   97

SIX   PASSAGE TO AMERICA: AMMACHI ON AMERICAN SOIL
Selva J. Raj   123

SEVEN   THE PERFECTIBILITY OF PERFECTION:
           SIDDHA YOGA AS A GLOBAL MOVEMENT
           Lola Williamson   147

EIGHT   OSHO, FROM SEX GURU TO GURU OF THE RICH:
           THE SPIRITUAL LOGIC OF LATE CAPITALISM
           Hugh B. Urban   169

NINE   RIDING THE DAWN HORSE: ADI DA AND THE
           EROS OF NONDUALITY
           Jeffrey J. Kripal   193

           EPILOGUE: ELEVATED GURUS, CONCRETE TRADITIONS,
           AND THE PROBLEMS OF WESTERN DEVOTEES
           Daniel Gold   219

           CONTRIBUTORS   227

           INDEX   231

INTRODUCTION

MAKING WAVES

THOMAS A. FORSTHOEFEL

AND CYNTHIA ANN HUMES

EVERYTHING CHANGES.

Mystics and storytellers in South Asia have woven this deceptively simple observation into the Indic consciousness for millennia. Hindu scriptures warn that the true nature of endlessly changing phenomenal reality can be lost to us as we thrash about the crashing waves of life. Yet the Hindu emphasis on the phenomenal fact of impermanence is tempered by the promise of something substantial, enduring, and utterly liberating beyond the very flux of life, so often likened to a roiling ocean, the "ocean of *samsara*." The phenomenal flux of mundane reality, staggering in its chaos and suffering, nonetheless motivates the journey to cross the "far shore," the quintessential Indian metaphor for liberation. Among the premier rafts for this tumultuous crossing is the spiritual teacher, the *guru*, a term that, not incidentally, also means "heavy." The word intimates the higher truth that there is something weighty, substantial, and enduring about life, a truth borne witness to by extraordinary spiritual teachers. Gurus assist in the journey to make the crossing—from the ocean of *samsara* to the ocean of awareness, from the changing flux of phenomenal reality to the far shore of liberation, from death to immortality. The far shore is the "site" for an ultimate ground that suffers no loss or change, understood variously in Hinduism to be an enduring soul, consciousness, an unchanging Absolute or a deity with form.

This book is about gurus who have crossed the far shore, but not necessarily to ultimate liberation. They have indeed crossed roiling oceans—in this case, Indian, Atlantic, and Pacific—landing upon the far shore of America. In making this passage, from the sacred land of India to the bewildering world of

1

modern day America, they may or may not have achieved the most sublime goal of Hindu spirituality, but they certainly took it upon themselves to teach it, propagate it, and cultivate a subculture dedicated to it. In doing so, they invariably have "made waves," that is, they have brought a conceptual and cultural matrix that has interfaced with a dominant American cultural matrix. Such interface has produced numerous interesting developments, which we will detail in this volume. Among these developments are reconfigurations and redefinitions of Hinduism by our subjects, a project that becomes a case study on the slippery hold of definitions.

The academic study of religion in the twentieth century has seen a lengthy, though fruitful, discussion of the category *religion*. Most scholars of religion today accept the quixotic nature of the term, agreeing on its fluid boundaries and the need to emphasize its context and frame. Most scholars and teachers of religious studies accept the provisional quality of definitions, at once constructing them for heuristic benefits while later deconstructing them in the face of diverse data. Thus, for example, to teach "religion" we paradoxically find ourselves teaching that there is no such thing as "religion." To teach Hinduism, we find ourselves teaching that there is no such thing as "Hinduism." Neither "religion" nor "Hinduism" is a frozen or absolute entity, something that stands above specific concrete cultural, political, and historical phenomena. Instead, there are religions and Hinduisms, collections of shifting but related sets of events that share certain characteristics. About these events—religions and Hinduisms—useful things can and have been said, especially by self-aware thinkers, conscious not only of their own frame of reference, but also of the goals of such framing and educating.

Once we recognize the crucial importance of historical, economic, and political contexts to the study of religion, those of us called to teach the twice-suspect category of Hindu religion often find ourselves caught in moments of cognitive dissonance. We stutter, misstep, walk forward two paces, retreat back another. Ultimately we hope there is increased nuance in our knowledge by this spiral forward, but the process is decidedly awkward; indeed, we may find ourselves in the peculiar position of objecting to our own "working definitions" of Hinduism or other sweeping categories in the study of religion. Moreover, we are painfully aware that we participate in and contribute to the very political structure that perpetuates stereotypes of the complex set of phenomena we so wish to deconstruct: the whistle-stop tour of Hinduism in our culturally mandated World Religions courses. We know the term *Hinduism* to be problematic, but we can't help ourselves: We are a product of the system, and teach within it.

To teach—not to mention to live—the complexity of events demands a certain comfort with ambiguity, and this is no easy task. Categories and concepts speak to clear lines, decisive boundaries, but, as Steven Batchelor has eloquently reminded us, there are no lines in nature.[1] Things are blurry. One finds more grey than black and white. Full comprehension often eludes us.[2] Some academics or devotees may prefer clear lines, offering a construction of particular traditions in ways that suggest decisive boundaries, marking off a set of timeless truths that capture the "real" tradition, preserved in its pristine clarity. No doubt, to claim such yields an emotional payoff—clarity resolves the difficult intellectual and emotional conflicts that a fluid universe generates. But in our view, it is disingenuous to assume stability where there is none. Moreover, the appeal to timeless truths is academically suspicious, for it often serves to perpetuate specific social or power structures: What appears to be "timeless" is, on inspection, sets of beliefs and practices emerging and being sustained by patterns of religious, social, and political conventions. In short, it is perhaps permissible for religious leaders to claim timeless truths, but not those who critically study spiritual teachers.

Our goal in this book is to monitor and assess the conceptual and cultural changes that have obtained by the arrival of significant Hindu spiritual teachers in America. The word *guru* by now has become quite familiar to many Americans. Its most basic meaning signifies any qualified teacher, regardless of discipline, in India. However, when the term applies to Hindu worldviews, overtones emerge. The guru is the adept, the skilled one, the preceptor, the saint, the destroyer of karma, the embodiment of god. And, on occasion, the guru appears to be a "confounder" too, sometimes transgressing socially constructed expectations, even those associated with guru-hood. In this book, while the teachers here all express a host of "spiritual" sensibilities, several became quite skilled in "worldly" and entrepreneurial programs as part of their program of propagation, and several have been accused of sexual impropriety. In any case, the phenomenon of the guru is one of the most prominent features of Hinduism in all its permutations. Often considered to be repositories of sacred power and the living vehicle for truth, gurus constitute a phenomenon that most Hindus would identify as important and crucial to their self-understanding as persons of faith. Indeed, the gurus in this book have sometimes been called *mahagurus*—great gurus—"great" or *maha* here usually indicating the significance of their cultural and religious impact, quality of teaching or life example, number of devotees and spiritual cachet.

Our use of gurus is the lens by which we examine religious and cultural change. It is perhaps a commonplace to note that change in religion comes from internal and external stimuli, including movements within a tradition led by thinkers and reformers and the broader cultural interface with intruding forces such as armies, migrants, and missionaries. These external forces can threaten the sanctity and safety of specific cultural "universes." When alternate universes do collide, both feel the impact of reverberating waves. In this book, we highlight a quite specific manner in which this occurs. In this case, Hinduism, whose "purity" has often been viewed as coterminous with the geographical boundaries of Bharata (the ancient name for India), has seen a remarkable migratory expansion to Europe, Africa, Asia, and North America. The recent movement to the West has been fueled not only by the migratory patterns of workers, students, and families, relocating under force of circumstance or particular personal aspirations, but the migratory patterns of gurus too, relocating with their own specific aspirations as well. This book marks what might be called the second wave of gurus in America, the first being the seminal transmission that began with Swami Vivekananda at the World Parliament of Religions in Chicago in 1893. The contours and impact of the first wave of gurus have been most notably examined by Polly Trout.[3]

We examine a recent, more contemporary, wave of gurus, noting the effects that occur when they—or their devotees—come to America bringing with them their "alternate universe." In doing so, fascinating cultural transformations have occurred, the awareness of which we hope has been stimulated by asking our contributors to consider specific questions. Concerning each tradition represented in this volume, how is the identity of the particular guru constructed? How do the gurus understand or represent whatever it is they mean by "Hinduism"? How do they adapt their form of Hinduism to a new cultural milieu? What changes can be seen in such a cultural interaction? What strategies do gurus employ to represent and/or propagate their particular representations of Hinduism? And how does that cultural milieu affect them in return? These inquiries require repeated and persistent self-examination of identity. On a personal level, the central question, as articulated by Ramana Maharshi, one of the spiritual teachers examined in this volume, is simply: "Who am I?" On a social level, the question central to this volume is still one of identity: "What do we—scholars, devotees, gurus—mean by Hinduism?" This collection of essays is the record of one set of scholars' responses, and, we hope, marks the "forward spiral" that characterizes increasing nuance to our understanding of Hinduism in America.

This volume is unique in its examination of this most recent wave of gurus in America. It is also unique in the way it brings together the contributions of scholars trained in various approaches to South Asian studies. These approaches include the methods of history of religions, anthropology, philosophy of religion, and sociology of religion. This diversity of approaches, with differing emphases on fieldwork, is a methodological illustration of one of the goals of the volume. Diversity reveals difference—and continuities. Perhaps the most unique aspect of this volume is that most of the contributors have had direct personal experience of the guru, or the guru's *ashram* or community. Several, such as Chris Chapple, Cynthia Humes, Lola Williamson, and Ravi Gupta, have been participants in the tradition embodied and taught by particular gurus. Others, such as Selva Raj, and Jeff Kripal, have had close contact with the gurus whom they have studied, which has not been without positive or formative impact. Still others, such as Tom Forsthoefel and Norris Palmer, have visited the ashram or worship communities of the gurus they have studied, also with positive outcomes. These scholars nevertheless do not let either their personal experience or their spiritual commitments prohibit their willingness and ability to engage their topics from a critical perspective, nor do they disallow their spiritual commitments to be enriched by their critical study. We hope that the interface of personal experience and academic reflection in this volume produce in our audience a similar response to that of an anonymous reader of the text for our publisher: an awareness of an honesty and vitality to our scholarship that is refreshing. We trust that this unique presentation will cross the boundaries of the academic and lay universes, in turn enriching both.

While the religio-cultural stream identified as Hinduism is vast and multifaceted, the gurus here can be classified for heuristic purposes as belonging to one of four substreams of Hindu thought and practice: Yoga, Advaita Vedanta, Bhakti, and Tantra, all easily recognized as native categories by Hindus. All four traditions share certain assumptions. For example, all four traditions share the notion of a soul, although its relationship to the Transcendent is often construed differently. Second, all four traditions note an existential human problem with the ego, and all assert that the struggle with egoism results in suffering. Third, all four share the conviction that there exists a state of unconditional bliss behind or beyond the flux of *samsara*, phenomenal, mundane reality.

While these and other Hindu traditions share certain assumptions, there are specific differences, too. The Samkhya Yoga tradition, for example, has a different answer to the notion of the human soul than most Hindu traditions. The Samkhya Yoga tradition is clearly pluralistic and dualistic; there are innumerable spirits (*purusha*) and there is matter (*prakriti*). The Yogic Path, which Christopher Chapple addresses in his essay, teaches there to be an infinite plurality of souls trapped in matter, and to remove the soul from this trap of materiality requires a discipline that calms one's mind from the disturbances of material nature to unveil the reality of the transcendent self as it is, free from egotistical imputations commonly mistaken for the true self. While many or even most ashrams in America include physical or *hatha yoga* as part of their conditioning and spiritual discipline, the Yoga Anand Ashram described in Chapple's essay is unusual in its staunch commitment to the dualistic yoga philosophy. Chapple clearly articulates the distinguishing features of classical yoga theory and practice as he discusses the life and leadership of Guru Anjali, the Bengali spiritual leader who established an ashram on Long Island based on the "royal yoga" of Patanjali, the second-century sage and reputed author of the *Yoga Sutra*. Chapple's essay also succeeds in situating the value and meaning of the guru in Hinduism and, drawing from the work of Harvey Cox and others, speaks to the psychological issues and occasional pathologies associated with an institution that gives sacrosanct status to the teacher-disciple relationship.

The work of Forsthoefel and Humes is clearly situated within the Hindu philosophical school of Advaita Vedanta, the tradition of Non-Dualism. Vedanta is one of the six schools (*darshanas*) of Indic thought. Vedanta's primary methodology has been the exegesis and analysis of sacred texts called the Vedas, especially the most esoteric texts in the Vedic corpus, the *Upanishads*. Vedanta itself is heterogeneous: Advaita is just one of three standard representations, and its most famous spokesperson and systematizer is understood to be the eighth-century philosopher, Shankara. The other two forms of Vedanta are Qualified Non-Dualism (Vishishtadvaita Vedanta), systematized by Ramanuja (1017–1137), and the Vedanta of Dualism (Dvaita Vedanta), whose great leader is understood to be Madhva (1238–1317). Vishishtadvaita and Dvaita Vedanta are devotional, privileging the practice of Bhakti, human "sharing" or partaking of the divine through the practice of love of God.

Advaita asserts that all phenomenal differences have no substantial or enduring reality. Reality is one. All temporal and finite differences are nullified upon the realization of truth. This philosophical viewpoint has proved useful in the cultural translation of Hinduism to America. How so? Advaita relativizes the cultural and even "religious" products of Hinduism, opening up Hinduism to a broader swath of humanity besides those born and raised in South Asia. Differences can be downplayed, for at its most basic, there are no differences. There is only the Real.

Forsthoefel highlights the development of such relativization in his essay on Ramana Maharshi, a teacher who never traveled beyond his native land of Tamil Nadu, let alone to America. However, Ramana's quintessential non-dualism paved the way for a migration of an *idea* swaddled in Hindu clothes. Many of the gurus who did come West either claim to be in Ramana's lineage or respond directly to his message and example. Ramana's life and teaching called into question the tendency to exclusivism in traditional Advaita, rendering coherent the universalism implied by the axioms of non-dualism. Ramana's foundation set the stage for the other gurus who did come to America. Such gurus often appealed to non-dualism as a signal strategy for the propagation and promotion of their spirituality, positing its universality, transportability, and malleability. The work of our colleagues clearly shows that Sai Baba, Ammachi, Rajneesh, and Adi Da all have drawn from Vedanta, especially Advaita, in their own pastiche of latter-day Hinduism. The premier value of non-dualism for some gurus may be less its philosophical excellence than its global marketing strategy.

Cynthia Humes highlights the relevance of Advaita to the global transmission of Hinduism as well in her study of Maharishi Mahesh Yogi, the founder of the Transcendental Meditation program. In particular, she notes the push and pull between appropriating and selling Vedanta on American terms, and subsequent attempts to clothe Maharishi's bare Vedantic meditation frame with Hindu cultural markers. Maharishi became skilled at adapting Hinduism to his

American audience, consciously marketing a spiritual program less bound to culture or ethnicity. He assertively and creatively used the universalism implied by Advaita Vedanta to thrust Hinduism into the global marketplace of ideas. He taught Americans that classical programs of renunciation bound in hoary tradition could be discarded. Instead, "cosmic consciousness," pared of its cultural baggage, could be attained by the mere recitation of a sacred mantra, learned, Cynthia wryly notes, for a minimum price. But Maharishi became more than a spiritual teacher. He is a consummate empire builder too, creating, through his subsidiaries, a line of consumer goods to be purchased, television programs, a political party that is international in scope, and recently, a new, "sovereign" country, replete with its own currency.

Maharishi's political developments are crucial to note, for only the disingenuous believe that religion and politics are absolutely separated. Both the Natural Law Party and its Indian variant, the Ajeya Bharat Party, reveal a strong neoconservatism and exclusivism with respect to other religions. But in the Ajeya Bharat Party, the jingoism is blatant and undisguised; its platform position papers rail against Western colonialism, including the very commercial and political structures Maharishi adopts, adapts, and exploits. This spiritual exclusivism holds for the superiority of Hinduism over other religions, and shows a curious development in Maharishi's program. Although he began with the universalism implied by Advaita Vedanta, he "returns" to a particularism, which steadily imbeds and validates features of Hinduism, gradually revealing it, as Humes writes, as the most accurate vision of true religion. So, while Forsthoefel's essay demonstrates how Advaita migrates well, Humes shows not only just how well it migrates, but how well it returns to its homeland, too.

Humes shows the versatile manner in which the Maharishi perpetually adapts to each situation. In South Asian terms, adapting one's message to particular time and circumstance is *upaya*, skillful means. *Upaya* as a category has been used by several of our colleagues as a heuristic device to explain (or perhaps explain away, as Norris Palmer notes) the teaching (or methodology or egregious excess) of the guru. Humes, Palmer, Urban, and even the essay by Goswami and Gupta, all advert to *upaya* as an explanatory tool for the teaching of the gurus they examined. Adapting one's message to the particular time and circumstance is the very essence of *upaya* (and seems peculiarly recognizable in our modern multicultural teaching, as we have mentioned). Our essays show the features of such adaptations to whatever might be called "classical" Hinduism, and the institutional and authority structures that developed as these gurus or their devotees established foundations in America.

The essays by Norris Palmer, the late T. K. Goswami and Ravi Gupta, and Selva Raj address guru traditions that privilege Bhakti. The devotional tradition in India emerged under a complex set of historical and cultural circumstances. The Bhakti tradition, while heterogeneous, nonetheless promoted religious experience as the decisive, most meritorious, and universalist option for spiritual progress. The passion and longing seen in the great Bhakti saints of Hinduism reveal a powerful energy ready to be tapped for spiritual progress.

Norris Palmer's essay focuses on Satya Sai Baba, the enigmatic and controversial spiritual teacher easily identified by his Afro hairstyle. Palmer's comprehensive essay includes Baba's life, ontology, and empire, all fueled by Baba's magic (some have said sleight-of-hand) and mystery as well as the fuel of the faith of his ardent devotees. Palmer's study explores the particular way that an inclusivist Hinduism emerges in the relationship that obtains between Hinduism and non-Hindu religions. Some gurus reflect a kind of egalitarian inclusivism; for example, concerning the different religious traditions of the world, Ramana Maharshi was quite clear: "All go to the same goal."[4] This attitude is not universally held by the gurus here. Instead some, including Baba, admit of pluralism while nonetheless holding that Hinduism offers the purest window to the Supreme. So, the symbolic and ritual programs of some of our subjects will include Western religious iconography and even the reading of Western religious texts in certain ritual circumstances. But such inclusivism is not always radical egalitarianism; rather, it is often an inclusivism (all religions have value) with an exclusivist subtext (while all religions have value, all find their ultimate meaning and value in Hinduism). Palmer points out that Baba, borrowing from Vedantic paradigms, is *the* Divine Presence; transcending time and space, his omnipresence therefore renders his spirituality universalist and accessible to all. This accessibility accounts for the spread of Sai Centers in the United States and Europe. The assumption of Baba's miraculous powers and omnipresence naturally leads a global audience and a global program of Sai spirituality, Baba being the other guru in this volume (the other is Ramana) who has "come to America" through his teaching, devotees, and spiritual centers.

However, Baba's agenda is also particularist and his teachings have a conservative goal, that is, reestablishing Vedic and Shastric religion. This "reinvigoration" of Hinduism back in India is especially evident in the careers of Maharishi and Rajneesh as well, whose modernizing and globalizing strategies also saw a return to particularist religion in which Hinduism emerges as the superior religious form. According to Baba, all spiritual wisdom can be traced back to India, for Bharat "was once the guru of humanity." Palmer clearly demonstrates what appear to be incompatible attitudes in Baba's approach: an openness to all persons and religious traditions and a superiority toward Indian culture and Hindu identity.

The inclusivist pluralism is clearly showed in the essays on Gurumayi, Rajneesh, Ammachi, and Adi Da. In his ethnographic approach to Ammachi, Selva Raj shrewdly observes a dynamic interchange between Ammachi's spirituality and Christianity. Ammachi's program is clearly universalist and egalitarian, one of the strongest themes that emerged in the medieval devotional traditions of India. Spiritual merit accrues from experience, not birthright. Women

and low-caste and outcaste saints are among the great models of devotion in
the Bhakti movement. Indeed, Ammachi's devotion to Krishna has been
likened to that of the sixteenth-century Rajasthani saint, Mirabai. The innate
impulse toward the divine (articulated by Guru Anjali as well) is clearly
affirmed by Ammachi, whose own universalism is seen in the flourishing
Amma centers in America and Europe. In addition to availing herself to non-
Hindus for spiritual growth, Ammachi has borrowed liberally from other traditions to speak to themes of unconditional love of the Divine Mother. Moreover, Ammachi has developed numerous cultural innovations, initiating
Westerners with "Christ" or "Mary" mantras. Raj also points out a fascinating
development in the devotional services held in the West, where certain forms
of ritual communion clearly borrow from Eucharistic models of Christian
communion.

These changes often lead to the recalibration of Hindu categories. In his
essay on Ammachi, Raj neatly addresses a hermeneutic of *darshan*, a central
event in traditional Hindu religiosity. *Darshan* is the efficacious encounter, the
exchange of sight between deity and devotee. To "take *darshan*" means to
encounter God *visibly*, whether in iconography, nature, or human form. Yet,
Ammachi's universalism not only breaks the bounds of caste and ethnicity, but
also the very method of *darshan* itself. Here, *darshan* includes a potent, robust
embrace. Such tactile *darshan* is a radical break with traditional, highly circum-
spect sensibilities of avoiding bodily contact. Another innovation is "water *darshan*," conducted at her ashram in Kerala, in which devotees receive her
embrace in a pool, ostensibly to minimize the physical hardship on Ammachi.
A further development involves the fusion of commercial opportunity and
spirituality, such as the sale of "Amma dolls" said to be charged with the *shakti*
(power) of Ammachi indicate. Finally, as with other gurus in this volume,
Ammachi has constructed a powerful institutional structure to promote her
numerous charitable and teaching organizations.

While devotion remains the supreme method in the spiritual program of
Ammachi and Sai Baba, these gurus do pepper their spirituality with a pun-
gent sprinkling of Advaita as well. This is *not* the case in the illuminating essay
by T. K. Goswami, to whom this volume is dedicated. Goswami, whose essay
was completed by his friend and colleague Ravi Gupta, looks at the theology
implicit in the "transplantation" of Krishna worship in the West. The theology
of the Hare Krishna movement is avidly monotheistic, based on the subtle philosophy of "inconceivable difference and non-difference" between the devotee
and god. Unadulterated enthusiasm, modeled by the Bengali saint Chaitanya, is
the supreme method of liberation, and this is what has been most noticeable
about the Hare Krishna movement in America and Europe. However, this tradition does not at all operate from a premise of non-dualism, and instead
counts "differences," notably the divine excellences of Krishna, as supremely
salvific. Additionally, cultural patterns are also accorded certain sacrosanct

status, with the literal home of Krishna, Vrindaban, being the human realm that best captures and models the divine realm. This means that A. C. Bhaktivedanta Swami, the missionary of Krishna worship to the West, needed carefully to address what Goswami and Gupta call the Krishna against culture, the Krishna of culture, and, following classical Gaudiya philosophy, a Krishna that both distinguishes and affirms the two. His theology reveals the premier value of Krishna worship over all other cultural and religious programs, and yet, owing to his subtle nuances, he could not condemn in absolute terms either Indian or non-Indian culture. Indian culture, especially in Krishna's homeland of Vraj, models the heavenly realm, and non-Indian culture has value insofar as its resources can be used to promote Krishna consciousness. Despite the inherent conservativism of Bhaktivedanta's theology, he nonetheless cultivated radical innovations in the interface between Hinduism and America, namely, the ongoing use of English in services, the valuation of women's spirituality and leadership, and the possibility for non-Indians to be Brahmins.

The essays of Lola Williamson, Hugh Urban, and Jeffrey Kripal turn to three gurus within the Tantric fold, a complex religious matrix that emerged in India perhaps as early as the sixth century. Steeped in secrecy and fueled by its own version of non-dualism, Tantra is often viewed as radically iconoclastic and transgressive, shattering conventional categories and social mores with the aim of breaking through all mental constructs and organizing filters to an awareness of reality as it is. This tradition "used" all energies to provoke and promote such goals, and, under specific ritual circumstances sexuality itself was such a vehicle. One must note the condition of such sexual activity: *specific ritual circumstances*; in "classical" Tantra, this was not a sexual romp. Tantra is fundamentally a soteriological, not sexual, path. Its countercultural methods aim for the collapse of boundaries and a breakthrough to the non-dual Absolute. Both Rajneesh and Adi Da drew from a central assumption of Tantra—that sexual energy itself can be a vehicle for non-dual experience—but the history of those gurus and their movements shows all too clearly the egregious excesses that can be effected in the name of spiritual wisdom.

Lola Williamson's essay elucidates the history and development of the Siddha Yoga community based in upstate New York, centering on the direction of its current leader, Guru Chidvilasananda, or Gurumayi. Also drawing from the Tantric tradition, among others, the Siddha Yoga community very much shows the "Americanization" of Hinduism in upstate New York. Williamson charts this out, while also demonstrating how Siddha Yoga has become a "global *sangham*," with a vast network of technical and institutional helpers to support it. Williamson explains how the Tantric notions of the transmission of *shaktipat*, the transfer of energy between guru and disciple, are modified to facilitate the guru's global reach. In the newly imagined universe of Siddha Yoga, *shaktipat*—traditionally, a rare and tactile experience—is now transmitted "by will" over long distances through the international electronic media that serves Siddha Yoga.

Williamson notes other developments in Siddha Yoga's adaptation of "Hinduism" as it has interfaced with America. Abandoning traditional emphasis on renunciation and even liberation, Gurumayi instead has openly encouraged single disciples to get married, and she has also encouraged her married disciples to bear children. Additionally, to facilitate the movement's expansion, she initiated an annual singles dance with the express aim of matchmaking. These transitions are a remarkable departure from traditional Hindu emphases on radical renunciation embodied by the *sannyasi*, one who has "cast down" all with the goal of liberation. Gurumayi has intentionally modulated the urgency and intensity for liberation by nurturing a communal lifestyle with the more modest goals of morality and good living, experiencing the power of the guru within the world.

If Gurumayi adapts communal lifestyles to facilitate the creation of generations of Siddha Yoga families, Urban's essay clearly shows the adaptive style of Rajneesh to celebrate the unconventional individual. Born a Jain, Rajneesh modeled his ashram and message primarily on Hindu texts and practices, but ultimately claimed to be "Osho" (a Japanese Buddhist term for master). In some sense Rajneesh might be considered an ultra existentialist (he began his career as a philosophy professor), pressing his listeners to break through their constricting thought forms in order to come to their truest authenticity, in this case, an identification with absolute consciousness. While Rajneesh drew from Hindu models of devotion, replete with saffron clothes, bead necklaces (*malas*), and iconic photographs, Rajneesh's decisive style was radically fluid, arguing for a "religionless religion" that rejected all institutions even as, Urban notes, it borrowed freely from a wide array of traditions (most of the gurus examined in this volume employed the same strategy). Rajneesh ultimately refused to be locked in any conceptual boxes. He used Tantra—itself a universalist philosophy, finding homes in Jain, Buddhist, and Hindu traditions—to chart out his own unique fusion.

According to Urban, Rajneesh shrewdly developed Neo Tantra in the West, knowing that it supported two of the most central concerns of late capitalist consumer culture: sex and money. Rajneesh's claim to be the messiah America was waiting for may strike one as supreme arrogance, but, given the Western obsessions with individualism and sensuality, Rajneesh may have indeed offered precisely what many Americans seek. While many of the gurus reviewed in this volume have built empires of one sort or another, Maharishi's remarkable entrepreneurial spirit is probably best matched by Rajneesh. As if conjuring a Tantric version of the Protestant work ethic, Rajneesh made the accumulation of material wealth the expression and manifestation of his charisma. Urban notes the history of Rajneesh in America, the fall of his empire, and his return to India as Osho. While a host of spiritual activities are supervised through the Pune center, Rajneesh, after his death, has been trans-figured from sex guru to an icon for a high-tech global and business enter-prise. Urban closes his essay with a careful analysis of the interface between economics and religion in the global market.

Jeffrey Kripal's essay on Adi Da points to the logical extension of non-dualistic thought: Just as it can appropriate and subsume other cultural forms, it can be appropriated by others. Jeff examines the life and thought of, as he comments colloquially, a "white guy" from Long Island. Adi Da (born Franklin Jones) is an American guru who borrowed heavily from Hindu categories, especially Tantra, as he attested to non-dual truth. There is a coherent logic to the appropriation of Hinduism by an American spiritual teacher, no matter how much such appropriation may aggravate some South Asians who consider it cultural theft. The logic is the very principle that emerged in India (and else-where for that matter): non-dualism. If non-dualism is true, then in absolute terms it does not matter one whit if a white guy from Long Island "rips off" Hinduism. If non-dualism is true, there is no white guy, no black guy, no male, no female, no Hindu, no Christian, no "one" but the One. The logic of non-dualism terminates not only in the spread of Hinduism in America by these gurus, but the emergence in America of gurudom with teachers such as Adi Da. As with Rajneesh, Da's method included the shock tactics of "crazy wisdom," which embraced confounding conceptual and moral categories in an attempt to expand one's consciousness of the one true Real.

While Kripal's essay explores the life and career of Adi Da and the notion of "American Tantra," the subtext of his essay is the relativizing logic of non-dualism. Kripal's essay is a fitting end to our "gathering of gurus," for it shows what can happen when alternate universes collide: Change occurs, morphing takes place, and cultural adaptations flourish. At first glance, these changes seem surprising, but a sustained gaze reveals the inner logic of cultural negotiation in a world of permeable boundaries. In Adi Da's case, a white guy from Long Island dons the accoutrements of Hinduism, follows the logic of non-dualism, and claims his stance as a guru. If the flap of a butterfly's wing somewhere in the deep forest has its own decisive reverberation (as physicists tell us), how much more the mutual penetration of cultural systems?

This volume emerged from a panel at the national meeting of the Ameri-can Academy of Religion in 2001. Daniel Gold's response to the original papers, marked with synthetic and astute observations, has been amplified and serves as the epilogue here, and we are grateful for his contribution. *Gurus in America* addresses key questions about the nature of the guru, the diverse histo-ries of each guru and movement, the varied constructions of Hinduism, and the complex process of cultural interaction. It is our hope that this unique view of a number of significant cultural and religious frames contributes to answering the questions that emerge from the most recent wave of gurus to the United States. Crossing the far shore to America, these gurus have indeed "made waves." It is precisely these waves, the conceptual and cultural repercussions of their impact, that we register and assess here.

NOTES

1. Stephen Batchelor, *Buddhism without Beliefs* (New York: Riverhead, 1997), 76.

2. David Knipe beautifully captures the "uncapturable" in India with the epilogue in his book, *Hinduism* (San Francisco: Harper, 1991). Knipe comments on a photo of a dark, gnarly tree, from which hang a number of burlap bags. Having no unequivocal sense for the meaning and purpose of the tree in that village, the photo, for Knipe, "hangs here as a reminder of how much of Hinduism I do not understand (152)." Such a statement is a model of humility.

3. Polly Trout, *Eastern Seeds, Western Soil: Three Gurus in America* (Mountain View, CA: Mayfield, 2001). Trout focuses in the main on a "first generation" of gurus in America: Swami Paramananda (1884–1940), Paramahansa Yogananda (1893–1952), and Jiddu Krishnamurti (1895–1986). See also Anthony Copley, ed., *Gurus and Their Followers: New Religious Reform Movements in Colonial India* (New Delhi: Oxford, 2000).

4. *Talks with Sri Ramana Maharshi*, 9th ed. (Tiruvannamalai: Ramanasramam, 1994–1996), 114.

ONE

RAJA YOGA AND THE GURU

Gurani Anjali of Yoga Anand Ashram, Amityville, New York

CHRISTOPHER KEY CHAPPLE

ONE DISTINGUISHING FEATURE of spiritual life is the need for a guide or preceptor. While the specific texture of spiritual life differs among religious traditions, it is safe to say that, differences notwithstanding, the spiritual teacher provides a map for a deepened spirituality. The teacher in effect marks the path toward "home," that is, the most complete expression of human fulfillment in the context of the sacred.

In the Indian tradition, the teacher or spiritual preceptor takes on sanctified status, as indicated by the term Guru-Deva, "divine teacher" or "teacher of divinity." The *Yoga Sutra*, a text on meditation dating back nearly two millennia, claims that all teachers have been instructed by a special unencumbered soul (*ishvara*) who has been untouched by afflictions or attachments. The idealized teacher symbolizes a state of perfection, and from that vantage point can offer counsel and model techniques for meditative acuity.

The *Guru Gita*, a text of 182 verses that appears in the *Skandha Purana* (ca. sixth to eighth century CE) on the relationship between the teacher and the student, lists many benefits that accrue from following the instructions of the preceptor, including good health, long life, happiness, and prosperity. Two modern classics attest eloquently to the quest for and commitment to following one's guru: *The Autobiography of a Yogi* by Paramahamsa Yogananda (1946) and *Be Here Now* by Baba Ram Dass.

The spiritual preceptor within Indian religious traditions generally grounds his or her teaching in a textual tradition. In addition to drawing on an authoritative theological source such as a written text or a particular chanting sequence, the guru also provides direct instruction in meditation techniques and often gives personal counseling or advice. In some instances this can be conducted in a mass conveyance of *darshan*, particularly if the movement is quite popular. Often a guru will deputize key disciples to assist in this aspect of the work.

This chapter will first discuss the development of the guru tradition in the United States, and then shift to a personal narrative regarding the author's relationship with Gurani Anjali, a teacher from Calcutta who established a small meditation center in Amityville, New York, in 1972 for spiritual direction within the path of classical yoga. Drawing from literature on the advantages and disadvantages of the guru-disciple system, the chapter will close with some reflections on the theology and psychology of the guru tradition.

DEFINING THE GURU

One of the most well-read books on the topic of finding and following one's guru is Baba Ram Dass's *Be Here Now*. This widely read book was published in 1971 and has sold nearly a million copies by the time of its forty-third printing in 2001. Although not generally recognized as fitting with the realm of academic scholarship, *Be Here Now* was in fact composed by Richard Alpert, a former Harvard professor of psychology whose guru bestowed on him the name Ram Dass, "servant of Lord Ram." Richard Alpert found his guru Baba Neem Karoli while traveling in India and remained devoted to his teachings even after Karoli's death in 1973. Ram Dass writes:

> At certain stages in the spiritual journey, there is a quickening of the spirit which is brought about through the grace of a guru. When you are at one of the stages where you need this catalyst, it will be forthcoming. There is really nothing you can do about gurus. It doesn't work that way. If you go looking for a guru and you are not ready to find one, you will not find what you are looking for. On the other hand, when you are ready the guru will be exactly where you are at the appropriate moment.[1]

The famous guru Paramahamsa Yogananda described such a moment in his autobiography, when Shri Yukteshvar appeared to him on the street in Banaras.[2] Their "chance" encounter forever altered Yogananda's life, and eventually led him to establish the Self Realization Fellowship in Los Angeles. However, not every disciple personally meets his or her guru; Ram Dass notes that "[t]here have been many saints who realized enlightenment without ever meeting their guru in a physical manifestation."[3] In such instances, devotion to a chosen deity (*ishta deva*) as mentioned in the *Yoga Sutra* might substitute for the actual presence of a living spiritual preceptor, and a community of fellow believers will help form the support network required to keep balanced on the path.

In the Hindu faith, the guru can become identified with divinity. For example, Ramana Maharshi, another *mahaguru* (great guru) examined in this book, once claimed, "Guru, God, and Self are One."[4] While this statement is perhaps best understood from the viewpoint of non-dualism, other traditions in India clearly affirm the divine status of extraordinary teachers as well. For example, it is not uncommon to see graffiti in India that proclaims "Gurudeva," an expression that clearly imputes divinity (*deva*) to the spiritual teacher. Within the context of India, this makes sense. The conventional world occupies continuous space with the spiritual world. Special places and natural objects such as trees, stones, groves, and river systems are said to possess spiritual power (*shakti*), which abounds, permeates, and pervades what otherwise would seem ordinary. The attribution of divine qualities flows freely in India, where one's parents are proclaimed to be God, a wife's husband is said to be a God, and one's teachers are proclaimed to be God. However, we must consider what is intended by the term *god*. The religions born in India do not share the eschatological worldview of the prophetic monotheisms. They do not predict the final end of the world, only an occasional downturn in the cycle of epochs (*yugas*). Nor do they announce the coming of a single messiah, as hinted in Judaism and certain sects of Islam, and believed in Christianity. Rather, divinity comfortably finds a home in India's saints and in the epic stories of the *avatars*, heroic figures sent forth by Vishnu, the Lord of Preservation, to restore order to a world in chaos. The continuity in the Indian worldview between spirit and nature allows for certain places and individuals to be seen as infused with divinity.

FINDING THE GURU

In writing about the role of the guru, I must confess that I am not a neutral or objective assessor of this phenomenon. In the late '60s and early '70s, while still in high school, I set out on a spiritual quest. I was involved with Quakerism and religious theatre, performing at church services regularly with Wakefield Players, a troop recognized by the Episcopal Church. I augmented this with a bit of Zen meditation as learned from Philip Kapleau and some Yoga that I picked up from the Sikh community also known as 3HO: Happy, Healthy, Holy. In 1972, as I was setting off to college, I had an important dream, wherein Meher Baba introduced me to a gracious Indian woman. I had been reading his voluminous *Discourses* slowly over the period of that summer and from it I learned the foundational vocabulary of Indian philosophy. Of Persian descent, Meher Baba had a profound awakening experience in 1913 at the age of nineteen. In 1925, he took a vow of silence that lasted until his death in 1969. He communicated through the use of a letter board, wrote several books, and traveled throughout the world. He wrote about the spiritual significance of dreams noting that "Masters have not infrequently first contacted aspirants by appearing in their dreams."[5] I was thus prepared to experience what turned out to be a remarkable number of profound dreams that summer.

In the fall of 1972, I set off to the State University of New York at Buffalo. During my first semester, a fellow first year student told our philosophy class about a woman named Anjali, her yoga teacher in Amityville, Long Island, New York. Intrigued, over Thanksgiving break I visited the newly dedicated Yoga Anand Ashram, located in what had been the hayloft of an old barn, and Anjali's house, a nineteenth-century tenant farmhouse in the midst of Massapequa's sprawling suburban tract homes. Anjali served us soup as we sat around her oak table discussing the *Bhagavad Gita,* which I was studying with the International Society for Krishna Consciousness at the university. She spoke of her dedication to the yoga path and the power of spiritual practice (*sadhana*) in self-transformation and self-discovery. She encouraged me to read from a sacred text each day.

After returning to Buffalo, I remembered one of my significant dreams from the summer. Meher Baba was pulling a plow down Genesee Street in my hometown of Avon, and led me to an old farmhouse where I met a gracious Indian woman dressed in white. We discussed spiritual matters around an oak table surrounded with books by Kluckorn and other anthropologists. I realized that the dream had come true! After further visits during my first year of college, I decided to transfer to the State University of New York at Stony Brook to continue my studies. I moved right after the end of the spring semester, got a job working in a pool factory, and embarked on a course of rigorous spiritual training.

The yoga path as taught by Anjali followed the theology and practice of Patanjali's *Yoga Sutra* (ca. second century CE), and referenced popular teachings such as that found in the sixth chapter of the *Bhagavad Gita.* Like Samkhya, yoga ascribes to the perspective that each life holds its own trajectory and that each person shapes his or her own circumstances either through actions influenced by the past or through concerted effort in the present. One does not look to an external god to effect changes in one's life nor, strictly speaking, to another person for anything more than guidance and inspiration. Each individual shapes and controls his or her own destiny through the practices of *sadhana.* The guru (or in this case, the Gurani, a feminized Bengali form of the word), sets forth the principles and procedures for spiritual practice, but the doing lies in the hands of the doer. No one other than oneself can bestow spiritual accomplishments.

The solitary nature of the yogic quest allows for multiple styles of spiritual practice. Depending upon the personal history and proclivities of each practitioner, yoga can take many different forms even within the context of a shared community. Patanjali outlines dozens of practices in the *Yoga Sutra*, from chanting the names of God (*japa*) to careful adherence to ethical precepts to various types of concentration and meditation. All these practices seek to allow a person to restructure and redirect one's intentions and desires. Within the ashram, some individuals loved chanting and the recitation of God's names, a practice associated with the yoga of devotion, *bhakti yoga*. Others reached deeper levels of purification through selfless action or *karma yoga* (for example, through work in our vegetarian restaurant!). Others gravitated toward study and reflection, with many pursuing undergraduate and graduate degrees in philosophy and religion, in the style of *jñana yoga* (the yoga of knowledge, which privileges study and reflection to gain enlightenment). To some degree, nearly all engaged in "cross training," as it were, expressing their *sadhana* through song, work, and study.

Anjali, known by the late 1970s as Gurani Anjali or Guruma, generally taught one class a week and conducted a meditation service each Sunday morning. She trained a core group of people known as pillars or *dharmins* who helped out with the business aspects of the ashram and taught beginning yoga classes. She also composed scores of songs, and many of her meditation talks have been transcribed.[6] Her message through song and the spoken word emphasized selfless service, purifying the senses, and honoring the lives of great spiritual leaders, including Jesus and Martin Luther King Jr.

Born and raised in Calcutta, Anjali began teaching classical Patanjali Yoga on Long Island in the 1960s. Her instruction consistently avoided specifying a single name for the supreme deity. This inclusivist, pluralist approach made her teachings accessible to suburban New York clientele as well as remained true to her own lived pluralism, for she had been married to a Jew for several years. At the time of her own initiation as a girl in India, her guru bestowed upon her the chosen deity (*ishta deva*) of Jesus, not unusual in Brahmo Samaj–influenced West Bengal. She, in turn, bestowed on her first initiate the deity Krishna, and did not necessarily specify a chosen deity for subsequent initiates.

Within the context of the ashram ritual life, deities were of little or no importance, aside from Agni, the deity manifesting as the ever present flame kindled with ghee upon the fire altar (*havan*). Aside from her own personal devotions and the devotions she encouraged among her first initiate, she preferred to refer to the goal and purpose of yoga as ascending to higher levels of consciousness, and would often talk about the *maha purusha* or great soul. However, despite her unwillingness to specify the name of God, she spoke often of love, of devotion (*bhakti*), and of Mirabai, the sixteenth-century Rajasthani princess who rejected all social expectations in her ardent passion for Lord Krishna. Anjali clearly drew inspiration from Mirabai while developing a method of spiritual practice for those who studied yoga under her guidance. In fact, within nine years of founding the ashram, Gurani Anjali published forty-four songs, each expressing profound devotion and spiritual yearning. One such song, "Someone is Calling," speaks to the yearning that often accompanies the spiritual quest:

> Someone is calling, Someone is calling, Someone is calling us
> Someone is calling, Our hearts are yearning, Someone is calling me
> Someone is calling, Our hearts are yearning, Someone is calling you and
>   me
> The world is hearing, Our hearts are yearning, Someone is calling me
> Without the cymbals, Without the trumpets, Without the sounding of
>   the drum
> We hear the calling, Our hearts are yearning, Someone is calling me

This song recognizes and praises that capacity within the human being to be called to a higher purpose. Her songs reveal a clear philosophical anthropology, indicating that spiritual yearning is a fundamental feature of human experience. She asks the singer to recognize the immediacy of this innate longing by claiming that the specific individual is being called, indicated by the word *me*. Then, recognizing the universality of this spiritual impulse, she claims that we are all in fact being called, and that the world itself can hear this invitation for conscious evolution. However, this "upward movement" happens in silence. Only the heart can hear. No cymbals, trumpets, or drums beat or blare forth to announce this sacred invitation, only the whispered silence in the heart issues this call.

Theologically, this theme of the unheard sound finds precedent in the *Rig Vedic* hymn of creation, which talks of the one breathing without air and proclaiming that even the sages and gods in heaven do not really know definitively about the origin and nature of the world. Gurani Anjali sings to that unseen seer of the *Upanishads*, the uncreated and uncreative *purusha*, the Yogi in sacred isolation (*kaivalyam*), idealized by the sage Patanjali as the liberated soul free of all karmic impressions.

Guru Anjali's songs often advert to *Samkhya Karika* (ca. third century CE), a text that encapsulates the metaphysical assumptions of the yoga and Samkhya schools of Indian philosophy. These schools affirm a realistic dualism of soul and matter; that is to say, while an ontological superiority is granted to spirit, the physical world is not at all illusory as some have interpreted in Shankara's Advaita Vedanta. The physical world in fact is the vehicle or instrument for liberation while also being the proximate cause for suffering (for even the most sublime mental and physical satisfactions are fleeting). Indeed, Patanjali writes in words that very much evoke the teaching of the Buddha, "all is suffering for the sage" (*Yoga Sutra* 2.15). By this he means that attachment to impermanent events inevitably produces suffering. Realizing this, the sage transcends it.

To express the mystery of the dualism of soul and matter, Samkhya often appeals to a famous metaphor in the *Mundaka Upanishad*. Two birds sit in a tree; one is silent, the other active, busily pecking at fruit. The former is the soul, the silent witness to phenomenal events, and the latter is the embodied ego, bearing and "eating" the fruit of ego-driven impulses and activities. This tension is further symbolized in the *Samkhya Karika* as an eternal and mysterious dance between material activity (*prakriti*) and consciousness (*purusha*). The following song of Guru Anjali clearly refers to this:

> I know that you are watching me
> In the silence you are watching me
> I know that you are watching me
> So I'll dance, yes I'll dance, yes I'll dance
> This dance for you, alone
> Yes I'll dance, this dance for you, alone
> I know that you are there beside me
> Ever silently beside me
> I know that you are close to me
> Silently watching, watching me
> When I am caressed
> In the arms of ecstasy
> The joy becomes the pain I bear
> Then I know you are watching, watching me

Here we see Anjali's metaphysic clearly informed by Samkhya Yoga philosophy. The soul is the seer of all activity of the mind-body complex, and therein ultimately lie the seeds for freedom. The mind-body complex establishes a host of ego-identifications either validated or invalidated by experience. But this process is inevitably frustrating, as if we are perpetually riding a roller coaster of success and failure which either affirms or insults our various ego-identifications. Guru Anjali and the yoga system both indicate that we are more than such identifications: We are the unseen seer of all phenomenal events. And yet the pain we experience in our more limited perspective paradoxically is to be celebrated, for it is exquisitely instructive, ultimately serving as a "slingshot" into deeper self-knowledge. In this sense, "experience" becomes the greatest guru of all, for embedded within it are the conditions not only for suffering but eventual liberation. In this regard, there is a clear telos to experience in Samkhya Yoga; mundane experience, with its fascinating array of pain and pleasure, tends ultimately toward liberation.

The theme of pain and its instrumental role in Samkhya continues in the following song, entitled *Purusha*:

O *Purusha* bound from within / without
Looking without from within
Form drifting by
Silently absorbed in the play
Curtains rise and they fall
To be or not to be
Purusha bound from within / without looking on
No wonder the pain is never too painful
The joy never complete
No wonder the pain never too painful
The joy never complete
Spring showers
Summer heat
Autumn breezes
Winter cold
O *Purusha* bound from within / without looking on
Forms drifting by
Silently absorbed in the play
Curtains rise and they fall
To be or not to be
Purusha bound from within / without looking on
No wonder the pain is never too painful
The joy never complete
No wonder the pain is never too painful
The joy never complete
Purusha bound from within / without looking on
Om Satyam Shivam Sundaram

This song contains a wistful celebration of the irony of life highlighting the presence of the world in its beauty and agony as constitutive and necessary for the spiritual quest. In the philosophy of Samkhya Yoga, we in fact *must* exhaust our phenomenal experience, burning up all the habituated egotism associated with it. Pain then becomes a mere phenomenal event, to be witnessed along with every other phenomenal event. In this case, there is pain, but no suffering. Suffering obtains from attachment to egocentric identifications. The process of "burning up" these identifications occurs through meditation. Meditation stops the mind and allows the witness to emerge. Here, yoga ("yoke," "unite"), while often construed as a method of "attaching" oneself to the divine, is very much about "detaching" oneself from the spinning drama of mental and physical events.[7] Suffering has value, however, as premier catalyst for the spiritual life. In the last song I will quote, Anjali sings about the process of meditation. She again acknowledges that people are moved to meditate because of the burdens of life. Anjali often mentioned in her talks that Mirabai took up the spiritual life because of the agony she experienced at the hands of her in-laws. Just as Mirabai was driven to ecstasy in the context of persecution, so also the yogi reaches for the transcendent because of the pains that come from affiliation with the phenomenal world, illustrated in this song, *Meditation*:

> There is a place called meditation
> Brought through deep concentration
> Born of the afflictions
> There's a place called meditation
> Beyond the senses
> Beyond the mind
> Beyond the body
> Beyond you and me
> In this place
> There is no fear
> The heights are soared beyond the stars
> All those that have been there
> Have taken rebirth
> Born of the silence
> Words cannot express
> A place called meditation

Singing praise to the meditation process, she creates a meditative space for reflection on the power of silence that can be felt at a song's end. This silence is the "still point of the turning world" that T. S. Eliot speaks of in his own extraordinary poem, *Four Quartets*. The practice of classical yoga aims to calm the mind precisely in order to arrive at that sacred still point.

I had always felt a keen draw to classical yoga philosophy, and in 1972 I had successfully found my guru, Anjali. During our undergraduate years, through graduate school, and for our first years of employment, my wife and I participated in yoga training under the guidance of this remarkable woman. We entered life in the ashram with great energy. While with Gurani, we helped to establish a vegetarian restaurant, co-managed a bookstore, helped with editing and publishing her book *Ways of Yoga*, and supported the spiritual and ritual life of the community, which generally numbered no more than one hundred people.

During the 1970s, relatively few Asian Indians had settled on Long Island, and nearly all the people in the ashram were representative of the local demographic: largely Jewish and Christian, mainly white, with some African Americans participating from time to time. Most were in their late teens and twenties; including veterans, high school dropouts, college students, and some older housewives. Anjali was firmly committed to offering yoga to people from all walks of life. Rather than re-crafting a purely Asian ashram, she chose to deemphasize the "Hindu" aspects of the tradition. Though she often read from the *Upanishads* and assigned to us memorization of entire sections of the *Bhagavad Gita* and the *Yoga Sutra*, she was as likely to refer to the Bible or Jesus or the practices of Judaism and Islam in her lectures and meditations. Education led her from Calcutta to New York, and a variety of circumstances brought her to Long Island. She established the ashram after teaching yoga through night classes at the local school district.

One of the central issues of this volume is the interface of "traditional" Indian cultural assumptions within a Western cultural context. The edges of this interface at Yoga Anand Ashram were no more evident than in gender roles and relationships. Gurani's commitment to inclusivity extended to both genders. Guruma worked with both men and women at the Yoga Anand Ashram. Yet from time to time, she would follow the Indian convention of asking the men to sit on one side and the women on the other, or the men in front and the women in back. These formalities were periodic and sometimes puzzling. She would often make allusions to Hindu folk wisdom regarding gender, joking that men are always searching, and that women ultimately hold great power because of their creative powers. Women, she would say, are active, like *prakriti*, the creative principle in Samkhya. Men are watchers, not doers, and need a woman to keep them engaged and moving. While such representations clearly issue from a South Asian cultural context, especially in the Samkhya philosophical worldview, her practitioners at times became confused: she sometimes advocated traditional gender roles, but particularly through her own example, she generally flaunted social gender norms, more from a place of fearlessness than of pride or aggressiveness. She taught the women of the ashram how to wear saris, and designed a simple tunic and *salwar* outfit for the male "pillars," those individuals who chose to share in her vision and dedicate their life to assist her in creating, upholding, and maintaining the ashram. The pillars were all encouraged to wear combinations of yellow and green, with the yellow representing *purusha*, the sun, and the male gender, and green representing *prakriti*, the material earth, and the female gender.

Guruma's own guru had been a storefront yoga teacher in Calcutta called Krishna. After several years of living in the United States, she visited her old neighborhood in India, but could find no trace of her teacher's operation. By contrast, Guruma proved to be a whirlwind of extraordinary creative activity, accomplishing a great deal in her lifetime that endures after her passing. She built from scratch a spiritual organization that has lasted more than three decades, and an array of businesses, including an art gallery, a bookstore, and a restaurant. She also established a women's organization named Shakti Sangam, which continues to meet and discuss women's issues and women's spirituality.

To make the ashram attractive and meaningful to the local Long Island clientele, Anjali arranged feasts and festivals that did not reflect the Hindu holiday cycle but were adapted from her own growing intimacy with the climate and local flavor of Long Island. She would occasionally tell stories of her own training, but she did not maintain any active links with India or other spiritual organizations. Though many conventions within the ashram clearly found their inspiration from India, Anjali did not seek to attract Indian devotees. In the tradition of the *raja yoga* lineage, Anjali had become a truly independent guru, standing alone in sharing her unique interpretation of spirituality to disciples.

THE CALL TO DISCIPLESHIP

I welcomed the invitation to contribute to this book as an opportunity to reflect on my experience in the context of the overall context of the guru-disciple tradition. What attracted me to Yoga Anand Ashram? In his 1977 book *Turning East: Why Americans Look to the Orient for Spirituality and What That Search Can Mean to the West*, Harvard Divinity School theologian Harvey Cox explores several paths of alternative religious experience and outlines six "types" who join such communities. The six reasons are a search for friendship, to "experience life directly," to be delivered from "overchoice" by an authority, to live a more simple or natural life, to escape male domination, and for environmental reasons.[8] Religious communities of whatever faith might provide some fulfillment of the six needs listed by Cox. Most, however, will offer some approach or avenue to a religious experience that transcends the somewhat conventional or psychologized needs articulated by Cox.

Upon reflection, three of Cox's categories clearly did not fit my situation: I had plenty of great friends before my ashram life, I did not crave an authority figure to mandate the details of my life, and I did not feel particularly oppressed by male domination. My own reasons did include three of the six: a quest for immediacy, simplicity, and ecological integration, and I will explain below how my ashram experience moved me toward those three areas, as well as attempt to articulate some additional reasons, drawing from personal experience, to explain the allure of the guru-disciple relationship. Notably absent from Cox's list are the two prime reasons given in Indian texts as to why people pursue a religious quest: desire for knowledge (*jijñasa*) and desire for liberation (*mumukshu*).[9]

The path taught at Yoga Anand Ashram grounds itself in classical or *raja* ("royal") *yoga*. Patanjali's *Yoga Sutra* defines yoga as "the restraint of fluctuations in the mind" (*yogas-chitta-vritti-nirodhah*). After defining five different states of mind, Patanjali gives more than two dozen techniques for bringing the mind to equanimity or dispassion (*vairagya*). This dispassion allows one to conquer thirst, the core cause of suffering. Patanjali lists several dozen methods to accomplish yoga. These techniques range from reflection on auspicious dreams to different styles of meditation, breathing techniques, postures, devotionalism, ethical behavior, and clear thinking. In one way or another, all these methods were employed in the course of Gurani's yoga training. The result would fit into Cox's first category: an ability to experience life directly. According to yoga psychology, past actions (*samskaras*) cloud a person's ability to see the world clearly. The practices of yoga purify a person's karma, allowing one to see things as they are, to stop expecting or projecting, and move into a mode of acceptance and absorption (*samadhi*). The final goal of yoga is described in various ways, including becoming "like a clear jewel" (*Yoga Sutra* I:41), the destruction of all karmic seeds (*Yoga Sutra* I:51), becoming the pure seer (II:20), gaining sovereignty over all states of being (III:49), dwelling in a cloud of *dharma* (proper behavior, duty, righteousness) (IV:29), and, finally, pure isolation (*kaivalyam*), defined as steadfastness in one's true nature and the power of higher awareness (IV:34). Some have criticized the philosophy and practice of yoga as a form of escapism. In my experience, yoga can only be understood through rigorous self-analysis and self-correction. To me, yoga has been more of a confrontation of oneself than an escape from oneself.

Ram Dass has written that the guru serves as a mirror that reflects back to oneself one's state of mind and level of attachment. In a very informal style, he explains the guru as follows:

> He has no attachment either to life. Or death. And: if he takes on your karma it is your karma. That he should take on your karma. Simple as that. You see: You are the guru . . . and *that's* what you finally know when you are hanging out with one of these guys. You hang out with yourself because there's nobody at home there at all. So to the extent that there's hanging out (in the interpersonal sense) all you can be seeing are your own desires. He is a perfect mirror since there's nobody there.[10]

For the first three years after the initial excitement of beginning yoga training, the process of self-reflection was quite painful. I struggled with seeing thoughts and behaviors of mine that—while not pathological—were uncomfortable, and I sought purification and improvement. At times, Gurani would mirror to me my own expectations and attachments. For instance, after one singing practice she praised everyone else in the room, but ignored me. For me, accustomed to being rewarded for good behavior, this was devastating. Then I realized the source of my attachment, and I struggled through the foul mood that overwhelmed me and surrendered into an unspeakable place of acceptance. Simultaneously, I felt the concern and compassion of her desire for me to rise to a higher state and I felt my grade-school-engendered search for praise and acknowledgment loosen. It was a transformative moment.

The second aspect discussed by Cox entails simplicity. In his book, Cox includes an extended critique of spiritual consumerism. Citing Veblen's famous essay on conspicuous consumption, he describes a "new gluttony" that, in the twenty-five years since the publication of his book, has only increased. Cox observes that religion—even "Oriental" religions—has become big business, and he satirically refers to this phenomenon as "Enlightenment by Ticketron."[11] Eventually, Cox suggests that true spirituality for America should be found within biblical roots, citing the commercialization of non-Western faiths as one reason. In my experience, however, the ethics of yoga explicitly address Cox's concern with gluttony.

The most systematic aspect of Patanjali's system includes eight discrete practices: disciplines, observances, yoga postures, breath control, inwardness, concentration, meditation, and *samadhi* or absorption. Disciplines (*yama*) and observances (*niyama*) constitute the ethical core of Patanjali's eightfold system. At Yoga Anand Ashram, students in the applied method (*sadhana*) classes are given a discipline and/or observance to practice for the week. The first time I heard about this practice was in conversation with Carole Zieler in the Student Union at the State University of New York at Buffalo. She said that she had received her *sadhana* in the mail, and she was to practice nonviolence or *ahimsa*, which meant, among other things, that she needed to find cookies made without eggs! I became intrigued with the detail of this practice, which was my first introduction to dietary orthopraxy. Several months later after moving to Long Island, I entered a *sadhana* class, and each week brought a new challenge. How could I make my life more austere? We routinely observed a weekly day of fast and weekly day of silence as an aspect of austerity (*tapas*). But what more could be done? We worked at not walking off with little things such as pencils and or hording intangible things such as time while practicing not stealing (*asteya*), another of the five ethical disciplines in the first stage of Patanjali's eightfold path. Truthfulness (*satya*), another discipline, was always a great challenge. How could I resist the temptation to exaggerate? Was my being in the world fully authentic? Though my wife and I shared these practices with one another, the bulk of our days were spent on a university campus where such topics were not appropriate to bring up in conversation. So we cultivated a life of ethical introspection rooted in Patanjali's yoga while engaged in our studies and campus jobs, enjoying the company of our fellow yoga students while in class at night and on the weekends. In little and big ways, we forged a different path than that dictated by the dominant culture, which was promoting disco dancing and the hustle. Perhaps the biggest culture gap came with the practice of non-possession (*aparigraha*). For our teacher, this meant avoidance of debt. In India, lending policies have historically been draconian. Until recently, even houses were paid for with cash. We came to value and stretch our meager resources and live a truly simple lifestyle that has carried over to a certain extent in our adult years.

The other aspect of my relationship with my guru that merits mention pertains to Cox's sixth category, pertaining to those who "had turned to some version of an Eastern tradition as the result of a concern for health, ecology and the conservation of the planet's dwindling resources."[12] Having been raised in an intensely rural environment, I carried an innate aversion to settling in the country's largest and most densely populated metropolitan region. In the ritual life of the ashram, however, I found a sense of comfort and connection with the rhythm of nature. Compared to the tropical climate of Calcutta, Anjali observed great beauty in New York's changing seasons. She initiated festivals in honor of each of these changes and eventually asked me to serve as the ritualist or *pujari* to organize these events. As *pujari* of the ashram, in addition to organizing the seasonal festivals, I was responsible for blessing the ashram each sunrise and sunset with the *Gayatri Mantra*, maintaining the flowers and fruits on the altar (*havan*), making certain the incense was lit during Sunday morning meditations, and, on two occasions, officiating at weddings.

Anjali would tell us stories about the power of the monsoon rains, and encourage us to fully experience the extremes of heat and cold that characterize the weather on Long Island. During the Christmas season, she designed Deva Devi Ratra, a festival in honor of great sages from Buddha to Zoroaster to Jesus. Acknowledgment was made to the power of the sun at each equinox and solstice. In the summer, we would gather for a picnic, replete with volleyball and other traditional summertime pastimes. In the winter, we would sing late into the night and light candles in honor of the world's great sages. In fall, we would share poetry and prepare food in the style of a New World vegetarian harvest. In spring, the festival would celebrate the return of the flowers and the warm weather. Though none of these festivals bear much similarity with the traditional religious celebrations in India, Anjali saw these to be important events for raising the consciousness of her American students. As she often emphasized, she had to invent new traditions reflecting life on Long Island.

Additionally, our yoga training included an intense study of the five great elements, or *mahabhutas*. Over a period of several months we dedicated a space of time each day to gazing and reflecting upon the power of the earth, then the power of water, of fire, of air, and finally of space itself. This set of concentrations (known in Buddhism as the *kasinas* and in Brahmanism as *bhuta shuddhi*) brought me into that sought-after immediacy, a connection with the fundamental aspects of reality that can be found regardless of the specificity of one's environment. Having been a connoisseur of the sweeping vistas of the Finger Lakes and the glimmering sunsets of the cloud-studded western New York landscapes, I remember commenting to a fellow yoga student that the little bit of median strip along the Grand Central Parkway in Queens included it all: green earth, moist soil, glimmering sunlight, grasses swaying in the breeze. This simple observation brought all my years of wandering through fields and forests into the immediacy of a parkway moment, and helped release my nostalgia and wistfulness for being elsewhere.

In addition to working with the elements, we were also given *sadhana* that included concentration on the sensory process and sustained observations of animals. I would revel in seeing Anjali interact joyously with her own dogs. She seemed simply to merge with the consciousness of animals; they would respond to her quiet signals with alertness and eager compliance. Our trainings in the elements, the senses, and animals, combined with an ongoing practice of *ahimsa,* served to anchor some of my later scholarship, which has focused on issues of ecological concern.

FINDING THE GURU WITHIN

As my life in yoga matured, my relationship with the guru also changed. When I first came to the ashram, I was in awe, a bit dumbstruck by the power and gracefulness of this woman who had dedicated herself to building a refuge where people from any and all walks of life could learn the joys of yoga. As mentioned earlier, she made a spiritual home available and open to anyone. Some of us were college students, some of us were college educated. Others (many others) were high school dropouts who were drifting through life. She treated all of us equally. I received no special praise for my chosen career in scholarship (though I was told later that she was happy for my work on behalf of elucidating yoga). In fact, much of her time was taken up with helping people in great need: cancer survivors, people recovering from various types of addictions (or at least attempting to), and people who were sad and lonely. Her generosity seemed endless. And yet I also saw a human side, as she dealt with her own family issues and worked at finding a balance between motherhood and ashram management. As she became humanized in my eyes, I not only came to a deeper appreciation for her seemingly boundless energy, but I gradually came to a fuller recognition of my own gifts and calling in life.

An added duty I held as *pujari* was to greet the car when the Gurani would arrive to speak, open the door, and escort her upstairs. To my great surprise, after several months (or years?) of this routine, one day she hopped out, ushered me into the car, closed the door, and then went through the formalities of opening the door for me! It was all in great fun, but also signaled a lighthearted change in our relationship.

Achievements along the yogic path were marked by various rites of passage. After several months or years in the beginners' class, one would move into a more advanced class, generally taught by Anjali or her assistant director, who was a graduate student studying Indian philosophy. All students were encouraged to study the Sanskrit language. Additionally, several dozen students entered Pillar training, an intense preparation to accept more responsibilities within the ashram. For instance, all *pujaris* have been Pillars. Special ceremonies were held to acknowledge the completion of Pillar training, including a small ceremony for my wife and me after we had moved to California. Gurani Anjali passed away in 2001. During her lifetime, Gurani bestowed her final initiation on only four people: Padmani, Indu, Viraj, and Satyam. In this ceremony, each individual received a special *mantra* and a new name. Though neither my wife nor myself received this honor, our lives have been enriched beyond description by having the opportunity to grow into maturity with her blessing. She modeled a wonderful style of teaching for both of us: Meet people, know their needs, be bold, be tactful, be fun. Her life also spoke to us in lessons unsaid. We learned to be busy but to avoid being overextended, an accomplishment not realized until our move from New York to California. Anjali, reflecting her commitment to Samkhya philosophy and its emphasis on individual souls, commented frequently that "we come alone and we go alone." Our physical parting from the ashram after twelve years of constant involvement shocked the community, but did not result in ostracism or resentment. We felt our inner growth propelled us to a new environment. We continue to benefit from and give back to the world some of the wonderful lessons we learned from our teacher.

INAUSPICIOUS ENCOUNTERS

Not all the lessons learned in life are happy lessons. Though I of course encountered my share of power struggles and internal jealousies and sometimes confusing administrative decisions in the ashram, in the process I learned a great deal about the structure of organizations and about human nature. Not all people have pure intentions. Unfortunately, spiritual communities can sometimes become a trap, particularly if an individual does not have the fortitude to integrate ethics with power. After college, one of our acquaintances, Fred Lenz, who had studied with a different New York City Hindu guru, announced to us that he had learned how to lecture, mesmerize his listeners, and attract followers. He had also learned how to obtain free publicity. He preceded us in our move to California and though we never saw him again, some of my university students in Los Angeles were his disciples. His photograph was even displayed with Yogananda and Krishnamurti in the Bodhi Tree Bookstore, the spiritual center of West Hollywood! In his ten or so year career as a guru, he amassed millions of dollars, beautiful houses, and enjoyed relationships with hundreds of women. Having known Fred fairly well, we were surprised and skeptical. We knew that he used flattery to gain followers and had faked a book on reincarnation. Sadly, our intuitions proved correct. After a scandal, he was driven from California back to New York. He committed suicide on Long Island in 1998, drowning with his dog in his beloved Conscience Bay after overdosing on barbiturates.[13]

Was Fred a sad aberration, or is there something inherently flawed in a system that accords divine status to its leaders? The *Guru Gita*, a medieval text in praise of the guru tradition, states in verse 13 that "the water of the Guru's feet (has the power) to dry up the mire of one's sins, to ignite the light of knowledge, and to take one smoothly across the ocean of this world." This attitude toward the guru is wonderful and essential for the disciple. Devotion to a guru allows one to adopt the ultimate role model. The guru symbolizes the best of all human possibility. According to the *Yoga Sutra*, all gurus have been instructed by Ishvara, the supreme teacher who has been untouched by karma or its afflictions. By ascribing divine qualities to the teacher, the disciple creates for himself or herself a new standard for excellence, a paradigm to be emulated. Feelings of deep love and respect often accompany this devotion or *guru-bhakti*. But what does it do for the guru? If the guru can withstand all the adoration and the rigors of being constantly on call, as can be seen with several contemporary teachers, then everything will feel safe. But in some cases, things have gone terribly wrong, as with Fred Lenz.

Some critics will seemingly condemn gurus categorically, as found in the work of Anthony Storr. Though he acknowledges that some gurus are saints, he also writes that some are simply mentally disordered. Storr attributes a form of narcissism to all gurus, saying that they "retain this need to be loved and to be the centre of attention together with the grandiosity which accompanies it."[14] He goes on to note that the guru "remains an isolated figure who does not usually have any close friends who might criticize him on equal terms." He cites Gurdjieff, Rajneesh, and Ignatius of Loyola as prime examples. Though he does not impugn the basic notion of the validity of religious transcendence and the need for spiritual leadership, he feels compelled to present a typology of pathological behavior. Jeffrey Masson has attempted to do a similar analysis in his discussions of Shri Ramakrishna and Gurdjieff.[15] Jeffrey Kripal created a great controversy when he attempted to find psychological causes for Ramakrishna's visions,[16] and Joel Kramer and Diana Alstad devote an entire volume to the dangers of blindly following authoritarian mandates.[17] A critical reevaluation of the guru-disciple relationship is being attempted, with, in the case of Kramer and Alstad, the suggestion that the institution be replaced by more democratic, relational structures.

Despite a generally positive assessment of gurus after a rather harrowing experience in the 1980s, Georg Feuerstein cautions about "crazy-wise adepts and eccentric masters":

> To the extent that they can help us free ourselves from the blinders with which we block our Reality and conceal ourselves (or our Self) from ourselves, we would do well to heed their message. At the same time, I feel, they are relics of an archaic spirituality that, sooner or later, will be replaced by a more integrated approach to self-transcendence. This new approach will be sustained by teachers, including holy fools, who place personal growth and integrity above the need to instruct, Reality above traditional fidelity, and compassion and humor, above all role-playing.[18]

Interestingly, he cites Ramakrishna as an example of a guru who established friend-like relations with disciples, and commends Sri Aurobindo for encouraging frank debate among his followers.

The literature on the controversial aspects of the guru tradition is quite extensive, as the bibliographies in any of the books cited will indicate. Our own teacher expressed a slight sorrow at her situation from time to time, saying: "It is lonely at the top," "Heavy is the head that wears the crown of thorns," and, "Even the therapist sometimes needs therapy." Standing by the vow to help others can be beautiful and liberating, but it can also become burdensome. Having witnessed the comportment of many spiritual leaders or gurus of the Hindu, Buddhist, Christian, Jewish, and Jaina faiths, I feel compassion for them because of the great burdens they have assumed. Driven by an inner calling to be of service to others, they run the risk of placing their own well-being in peril.

REVISITING THE GURU TRADITION

Do the counterexamples of Fred Lenz and others and the hesitations put forth by the various scholars mentioned above in any way invalidate the tradition of spiritual leadership? I would argue not, based on my own experience. Without the commitment of men and women willing to serve others, the world will even more rapidly fall into the consumer-driven pit of gluttony. We need heroic figures such as the environmentalist Julia Butterfly, the young woman who sat for months high in the tree called Luna, to do the unexpected, to demonstrate that the human being can ascend beyond the humdrum existence to embrace a higher cause. We can learn from others, as long as our intentions are clear and we hold sight of our own dignity. A guru or spiritual advisor must be grounded in creating a safe place that acknowledges an underlying spiritual equality. When this space serves as the ground, then the work of spiritual introspection can begin. On the one hand, the guru has the difficult task of respecting the student; on the other hand, the guru needs to devise techniques and seize opportunities to awaken the student and move him or her to transcend the constraint of their ego-defined self. For me, this training was not always pleasant. It was, however, clear that *sadhana* was given not to enhance the status of our teacher or even our organization, but for the purposes of my own purification. By exerting one's will and creativity, one advances along the spiritual path. As long as one seeks to please the teacher, no growth can be effected. Ultimately, the boundary between teacher and student, guru and disciple, needs to melt.

The guru tradition arose within the context of a highly hierarchical society. In traditional India, one's status in the family and caste determines one's expected behavior. Obedience to one's parents and elders, rather than any questioning of authority as found in the United States, is the norm. As noted above, texts such as the *Guru Gita* extol the need to submit to the authority of a higher teacher. Seeming inequalities can be seen throughout the traditional, pre-independence society that stem from this assent to hierarchy, from special privileges accruing to people of high caste to sometimes crude treatment of women.

Some organizations have questioned the usefulness of continuing the guru-disciple tradition, such as can be seen in the institution of a complex governance board for the International Society for Krishna Consciousness and the replacement of Amrit Desai as head of Kripalu, a large yoga center located in the Berkshire Mountains of Massachusetts. However, will these changes diminish the guru tradition? William Cenkner makes the following potent observations about the centrality of the guru to the Hindu tradition:

> The guru occasions the immediacy of the religious experience of the devotee. For the faith-filled devotee, he [sic] is the center of mystery. The sacred center of Hindu life is the living guru . . . his followers experience him as the restorer of the *dharma* order. . . . The guru is the center of sacredness. In his company the scriptures, idols and even liberation paths pale in importance. . . . The guru is the context wherein an individual gathers spiritual resources in order to encounter mystery; likewise, the guru is mystery itself in the faith experience of some devotees.[19]

Though Cenkner primarily refers to India's thirteen-hundred-year-old Shankaracharya tradition, he also includes within his definition of gurus the many new teachers and religious leaders who fall within the rubric. Daniel Gold, in his study of north Indian saints (*sants*), notes that "the redemptive power of *sants* of the past is made available through the living guru. His words convey their instructions, explain the meaning of scripture, and make known the will of the highest divine."[20] However, at the same time, Gold comments on the human qualities of the guru: "The earthly embodiment of the guru known to close disciples is a living, changing person whose behavior may seem continually paradoxical, and his outer worship is performed through practical service that is often unpredictable and almost always most mundane."[21] The mercurial nature of the guru seems both to reflect his or her humanity and mysterious allure.

Theology in India seems well equipped to accommodate the notion of *gurudeva*, viz., the idea that divinity can be revealed through one's relationship with a living teacher. Persons generally approach such an individual with an understanding that the spiritual path requires at least two elements: a desire to learn and a desire for liberation. The Advaita Vedanta text *Atmabodha* begins by suggesting that persons on the spiritual path should already be of "diminished sin due to their austerities, peaceful, and free from attachment." In the traditional context, a guru often ascends within the confines of a preexisting organization with a number of social controls in place. This is not always the case in the West. In the American context specifically, as noted by Harvey Cox, people might more readily approach a guru from a different sort of need. In some instances, disciples might be seeking to replace a weak relationship with authority or a desire to be "re-parented," a phenomenon that I witnessed within the ashram and other spiritual organizations with a strong leader in charge. I have seen some of my own university students drawn to spiritual teachers in an attempt to undo damage incurred during childhood. By devoting themselves to a new mother figure or new father figure, they hope to return to an earlier state of innocence and unload whatever had burdened them in their younger years. Gurani Anjali spent a great deal of time with some of the more psychologically needy of her students and, in some instances, I have seen some lives transformed by her care and attention. However, some persons did not find that the practice of Yoga met this specific need and moved on rather quickly. Such a situation complicates the job of the guru, whose training does not necessarily include being able to assess the mental health of his or her disciples.

The guru-disciple relationship remains one of the most complex and dynamic of possible interpersonal encounters. For me, it gave focus and grounding to my life. Combined with the good guidance of various professors and a wonderful family, my experiences within a traditional ashram context have been formative, informative, and transformational. I see in my own university a desire for many faculty members to mentor their students, to guide them into appropriate career paths, to give them advice from time to time on personal issues. Though seemingly less hierarchical, it seems that even in such a seemingly mundane context as a university, the precepts and intentions of improving others through instruction and examples can be found in abundance.

NOTES

An earlier version of this chapter appeared in Norvene Vest, ed., *Tending the Holy: Spiritual Direction Across Traditions* (New York: Morehouse Publishing, 2003), 32–44.

1. Baba Ram Dass, *Remember Be Here Now* (San Cristobal, NM: Lama Foundation, 1971), 4.

2. Paramahansa Yogananda, *Autobiography of a Yogi* (Los Angeles: Self-Realization Fellowship, 1946), 92–97.

3. Dass, *Remember Be Here Now*, 5.

4. Ibid., 7.

5. Meher Baba, *Discourses*, 7th ed. (Myrtle Beach, SC: Sheriar Press, 1987), 180.

6. See Gurani Anjali, *Ways of Yoga* (Amityville, NY: Vajra Printing and Publishing of Yoga Anand Ashram, 1993).

7. For an extended discussion of yoga metaphysics and objectives, see the first chapter of Mircea Eliade, *Yoga: Immortality and Freedom* (Princeton: Princeton University Press, 1990).

8. Harvey Cox, *Turning East: Why Americans Look to the Orient for Spirituality and What That Search Can Mean to the West* (New York: Simon and Schuster, 1977), 95–100.

9. Sankaracarya, *Atmabodha*, trans. Swami Nikhilananda (New York: Ramakrishna-Vivekananda Center, 1970), 1.

10. Dass, *Remember Be Here Now*, 65–66.

11. Cox, *Turning East*, 129–45.

12. Ibid., 100.

13. Beth Landman Keil and Deborah Mitchell, "The Yuppie Guru's Last Seduction," *New York Magazine*, 1999.

14. Anthony Storr, *Feet of Clay: Saints, Sinners, and Madmen: A Study of Gurus* (New York: Simon and Schuster, 1996), 211.

15. See *The Oceanic Experience* for his critiques of Ramakrishna and *My Father's Guru* (Reading, MA: Addison-Wesley, 1993) for the intriguing story of his family's relationship with Gurdjieff.

16. Jeffrey Kripal, *Kali's Child: The Mystical and the Erotic in the Life and Teachings of Ramakrishna* (Chicago: The University of Chicago Press, 1998).

17. Joel Kramer and Diana Alstand, *The Guru Papers: Masks of Authoritarian Power* (Berkeley: Frog, Ltd, 1993).

18. Georg Feuerstein, *Holy Madness: The Shock Tactics and Radical Teachings of Crazy-Wise Adepts, Holy Fools, and Rascal Gurus* (New York: Paragon House, 1991), 259.

19. William Cenkner, *A Tradition of Teachers: Sankara and the Jagadgurus Today* (Delhi: Motilal Banarsidass, 1983), 186–87.

20. Daniel Gold, *The Lord as Guru: Hindi Sants in North Indian Tradition* (New York: Oxford University Press, 1987), 213.

21. Ibid., 44–45.

TWO

WEAVING THE INWARD THREAD TO AWAKENING

The Perennial Appeal of Ramana Maharshi

THOMAS A. FORSTHOEFEL

THE EVER-BURGEONING LITERATURE on mysticism has assessed, scrutinized, evaluated, and critiqued the so-called perennial philosophy, most notably articulated by Aldous Huxley, which holds for common religious experience at the heart of all religions, "superficial" cultural patterns and practices notwithstanding. The mountain of that literature is indeed large, and I have added my own modest contribution to it elsewhere; in this essay, however, I shall focus on the perennial appeal of Ramana Maharshi, a modern adept of Advaita Vedanta, to Indian and Western thinkers.[1]

Ramana never identified himself as a *mahaguru*—or even guru, for that matter. Moreover, most of the gurus featured in this volume flourished in the last twenty or thirty years, and Ramana died in 1950, having spent nearly his entire life near or at the base of Arunachala, a sacred hill in the South Arcot district of Tamil Nadu. A review of Ramana's life and impact is important for this volume, however, because his life and thought, reflecting a strict form of non-dualism, set the stage for later gurus who actively and creatively marketed Hinduism to the West. Indeed, Advaita Vedanta, long held with fascination in the West, has proved itself to be a most efficient philosophical instrument to serve the transmission of Hinduism to the West.

The "perennial" appeal of Ramana Maharshi should be understood in two ways: first, Ramana's life and example seem to have met with continuing praise by scholars and devotees alike during his lifetime and in the years since his death. No exposés, no *Karma Colas*, no deconstructions of his life have appeared or are likely to appear in print. Instead, of the many sincere or fraudulent gurus that have captured the West's attention, Ramana's life and teaching have struck many scholars with a similar reaction: This person is genuine, which is an admittedly elusive quality to determine in someone, but which remains a quality that needs to be considered as we review the persuasive force of religious experience. Moreover, the host of spiritual qualities manifested by Ramana also contributes in large measure to his continuing appeal among thinkers and spiritual adepts. An examination of the outcomes of spiritual practices—an evaluation of the quality of human presence—may promise communion in the face of very difficult philosophical differences. Although a "meeting of the minds" may at times be impossible if one hopes for a pristine resolution of all conflicting metaphysical claims, a meeting of the heart may offer the best hope to realize what Wilhelm Halbfass called the "unfulfilled potential" of interfaith dialogue.[2]

And yet there is another way to construe his perennial appeal, a way that implicates the controverted debates in the philosophy of religion over a "core" mystical experience at the heart of all religions. In this case, the source of Ramana's perennial appeal lies in his paradigmatic experience of realization and his repeated insistence that such experience is accessible and available to all, regardless of cultural or social conditions. This appeal and call to liberating experience—represented here as a universal, transcultural phenomenon—proved eminently attractive to Indians and Westerners holding slightly different interests, and it must be situated against the backdrop of broader philosophical and cultural agendas that have emerged in the East and in the West since the Enlightenment. Both Halbfass and Anantanand Rambachand have written illuminating studies on the notion of experience in recent discourse on Indian religiosity, highlighting the ambiguities and rhetoric in the use of the ubiquitous term for liberating experience in Advaita, *anubhava*.[3] My own study of the Vedanta probes the cognitive dimension of religious experience by using contemporary debates in the epistemology of religious experience to examine the nature and scope of *anubhava* in classical and modern Advaita.[4] Here, I wish to draw from that research and argue that the deeply inward or internal methodology of Ramana Maharshi accords well with the thought of certain thinkers in the East and the West who favor the notion of a transnational, transcultural "mystical" experience at the heart of all religions.

The claim for the immediacy and universality of such experience typically characterizes the perennial philosophy, a philosophy that has stimulated much critical debate, such as that of Steven T. Katz.[5] My agenda here is not to argue for the correctness of perennialism, but instead to show that Ramana's life and teaching implicate a perennialist position, one that has proven to be compelling to thinkers and disciples both in India and in the West. This worldview is of considerable social and philosophical significance in an era of shrinking worlds and filmy boundaries, for it permits or even requires the relativization of culture in favor of something supposedly deeper or more essential. The universalism implied by non-dualism and articulated by Ramana and other Advaitins genuinely contributes to the globalization of whatever it is we call "Hinduism" or at least this particular stream of Hinduism. In "sublating" culture in favor of non-dualist truth, Ramana unself-consciously contributed to the transmission of Hinduism in the West catalyzed by Swami Vivekananda at the Parliament of World Religions in 1893. Ramana's own call to the universal inward path to awakening relativized all cultural patterns, including those of orthodox members of the priestly caste (*Brahmins*). Such a view is the polar opposite of Bhaktivedanta, whose philosophy of culture is lucidly articulated by the late T. K. Goswami and Ravi Gupta in their chapter in this volume.

The perennial philosophy, while a decidedly minority view in the Western academy, nonetheless remains an important, if problematic, theory. Perennialism attempts to account for the diversity of religious experience by positing a common core to mysticisms across cultures. Katz and many others have rejected such hegemonic speculation as historically and philosophically flawed; indeed, Paul J. Griffiths rejects the perennial philosophy outright as incoherent.[6] Still, the position is not without its advocates. The work of Robert Forman, for example, has attempted, with some success, to amend the difficulties of the perennial philosophy by reframing it as a "perennial psychology."[7] The contemporary nuances of Forman and his colleagues notwithstanding, the teaching and reflections of Ramana clearly implicate an important version of the perennial philosophy, one that contributed in no small way to the transmission of "Hinduism" to the West.

Ramana Maharshi's appeal crosses numerous cultural boundaries, and his personal example and teachings have been used, for different purposes and in different contexts, by Indian and Westerners alike. On the one hand, Ramana embodied the supreme excellence, the highest ideal represented in so many epic accounts, mythologies, and philosophical texts in the history of Hinduism. Such an example provides, for Indians with apologetic interests, a counter-example to the Western and missionary critics of Hinduism. At the same time, Ramana's experience and teachings represent an inclusive universalism, highly attractive to some Westerners also inclined to perennial philosophies, ecumenism, or interfaith practice. What demands close scrutiny, however, is the method of accessing such saving experience, for not only must the experience itself be available cross-culturally, but the method itself must also "translate" well across cultures. And this is the case in Ramana's version of Advaita, which privileges an inward, self-directed, self-guaranteeing method of liberation. Borrowing from contemporary Anglophone philosophy, Ramana's soteriology suggests an internalist epistemology of religious experience, a method of religious knowing that emphasizes self-awareness, internal states, and privileged access on the part of the knower. This method's counterpart is sometimes called externalism, which denies internalism's premises and instead affirms the validity of reliable belief-forming mechanisms external to the agent. These mechanisms, which include perception, inference, and testimony, recall classical Indian epistemologies and their analyses of these and other mechanisms of producing knowledge. The question, whether posed in the East or West, is whether and how far these "mundane" epistemological processes can be applied to religious knowing. Both William Alston and Alvin Plantinga have written creatively and critically on internalist and externalist epistemologies and their potential application to the warrant or justification of beliefs that follow religious experience.[8] Plantinga has argued that the epistemological framework of internalism has been largely dominant in the West since Descartes. I would suggest that Western thinkers, spiritual figures, and seekers, self-consciously or unself-consciously operating out the introspective model so classically exemplified by Descartes, will find the methodology and promise of Ramana's "inward quest" compelling, especially as it favors self-validating experience over and above restrictive and limited time-bound tradition.

Concerning Ramana's version of Advaita Vedanta, it is probably misguided to identify Ramana as an Advaitin at all, since Advaita Vedanta represents an entire cultural and institutional matrix that minimally consists of text, tradition, and teacher. All of these, in turn, constitute a kind of "external" circuitry, that is, a complex set of socially established belief-forming mechanisms that inform and shape traditional Advaitin programs of liberation and their subsequent verbal outcomes. Ramana, although a brahmin, seemed unaffected by the cultural and social differences that often are, paradoxically, implicated in formal programs of renunciation in India. In this he deeply internalized the truth of non-dualism, which finally renders innocuous all cultural and social distinctions, especially that of caste and stage of life. For Ramana, the truth of the eternal Self, the deepest truth of our being and our destiny, radically revitalizes all social patterns. Outcastes, women, and non-Hindus were welcomed in his presence, and he repeatedly revalorized traditional eligibility (*adhikara*) for spiritual training in terms of mental fitness, dismissing traditional cultural criteria for eligibility such as gender, caste, and stage of life. Above all, *sannyasa* "is only the renunciation of the I-thought, not the rejection of external objects;"[9] for Ramana, rather than being a formal religious institution, *sannyasa* is a mental state; it means "renouncing one's individuality, not shaving one's head and putting on ochre robes."[10] Such a program, strengthened by the premise of non-dualism and the inward thread of inquiry, can thus be practiced and realized in any place and in any context. For Ramana, we are already liberated; it is who we are here and now. To the question whether one should wander in the forest or remain at home, Ramana replies with a typical rejoinder, "You are to remain in your true state."[11] Our "true state" is here and now, available to any person, regardless of caste, gender, stage, nationality, or religion. Though it is beyond the scope of this chapter, Shankara's Advaita Vedanta, while obviously also functioning in terms of non-dualism, nevertheless accords considerable emphasis to socially established doxastic practices, in the main affirming orthodox patterns of culture and renunciation. These externalist emphases actually lock Advaita to a local context. But Ramana, neatly weaving non-dualistic theory with a decisive internalist epistemology of religious experience, liberates Advaita from its local context, allowing for a genuine universalism to emerge, which in part accounts for his appeal to various thinkers in the East and in the West.

RAMANA'S EXPERIENCE AND ITS APPEAL

Ramana Maharshi was born in 1879 in Tiruchuri, a village not far from Madurai in the south Indian state of Tamil Nadu. While he had little or no formal religious training, he was raised in a brahmin household in India, in which it was virtually impossible not to have at least a minimal acquaintance with some forms of Hindu religiosity. Ramana's parents were Smarta Brahmins, an orthodox community that tended toward Advaita Vedanta for its conceptual framework, and their family deity was Shiva. According to B. V. Narasimha Swami, one of Ramana's early biographers, a family priest occasionally conducted domestic devotional rites (*pujas*), and Ramana's father, Sundaram Ayyar, occasionally visited the local temple and hosted evenings of spiritual reading.[12] Although much of the family religiosity appears conventional, it is important to note that Ramana had at least a notional understanding of traditional Indian religious symbols and categories to which he could later refer.

Venkataraman's childhood years do not reveal any outstanding insight into his destiny. Although endowed with a prodigious memory and a keen intellect, he was apparently indifferent to studies and preferred sports to academic pursuits. Narasimha Swami notes that Venkataraman "drifted" into conventional Shaiva worship without experiencing any extraordinary emotion or insight.[13] All this changed forever during a crisis he experienced in 1896, an event significant not only for the impact it made on his life but in its universal implications as well. Gripped by the fear of death, he came to visualize his mortality intensely, as if literally experiencing death and expecting some sort of decisive annihilation. He did, apparently, experience a death: the death of his limited ego. At the same time, however, he experienced what he interpreted to be the transcendent Self. Ramana recounts:

> The shock of fear of death made me at once introspective and introverted. . . . The material body dies, but the spirit transcending it cannot be touched by death. I am therefore deathless spirit. All this was not a mere intellectual process, but flashed before me vividly, as living truth, something which I perceived immediately, without any argument.[14]

After this transformative experience, which I shall soon address, Ramana quickly found the mundane patterns and habits of conventional life wanting, and he eventually left his home and traveled to Tiruvannamalai, being drawn to Arunachala, a sacred hill in South Arcot district said to be an embodiment of Lord Shiva. After arriving in Tiruvannamalai in 1896, he remained there until his death in 1950.

For more than twenty years, Ramana maintained silence, not in obedience to a vow, but to sustain quiet absorption into the Self and deepen his transformative experience. He spent these years in two hermitages on Arunachala itself, Skanda Ashram and Virupaksha Cave. By 1915 the "Brahmin swami" was well known in South India, and a steady stream of devotees began climbing up Arunachala to sit in his presence. In 1922 he came down the hill and an ashram was constructed at its base for Ramana and his disciples. One of his early disciples, Ganapati Shastri, insisted that the young guru be called Bhagavan Ramana Maharshi, the name by which he was known for the rest of his life.

Ramana's paradigmatic experience and his subsequent teaching are significant, for they represent a version of Advaita Vedanta abstracted from traditional monastic structures, thus sidestepping, at least initially, issues of institutional authority and traditional legitimization. We observe that a particular crisis—at once compelling and universal—provoked Ramana's search for truth and propelled him inward. This fundamental process of introversion or introspection ultimately resulted in Ramana's realization and became the paradigm for future aspirants to liberation. The premier method of accessing this font of "experience" is inquiry, or *vichara,* a focused inward penetration allowing access to the ultimate source of the limited ego, what Ramana calls the 'I-I'. Repeatedly, Ramana called his disciples to "dive within" to discover this source. His preferred method for this process involved reflecting upon a quite specific question fundamental to all human searching: Who am I? According to Ramana, reflective meditation on this question eventuates in a felt experience of the deeper source of one's empirical ego, the eternal Self. He insisted that the question, "Who am I," is the "principal means for the removal of all misery and the attainment of supreme bliss."[15] In the end, this is the only question necessary for realization and leads to a "wordless illumination of the form 'I-I'." This question is the direct means for "destroying the mind," a process of quieting all mental chatter and melting competing ego identifications into the one true Self. Thus, he urges the aspirant to still the mind, with its many mental protests, with the "inward turning" of inquiry. The goal of this process is to experience the divine Self within, to *know*, but not to *think*. The knowledge gained from such experience is direct, immediate, and alive: for Ramana this experience was an encounter with "living truth" and no "mere intellectual process." Consideration of a saint's representation of his or her transformative experience must be viewed as a fruitful site of inquiry for philosophers of religion, for even if that particular experience is currently unavailable to us, Ramana's own reflections on it need to be considered in order to explore the prospects of a "knowing beyond knowledge," an experience of knowing, but not thinking. Such knowing recalls *prajña* in the Buddhist context, what Robert Thurman has called "transcendent genius" or "superknowledge." Significantly, Ramana claimed to have had a direct experience of such knowing, incontrovertible precisely because he experienced it. He then spent the rest of his life deepening this experience and calling inquiring disciples to experience it themselves.

Direct experience becomes the source of Ramana's authority, surpassing traditional programs of legitimation. This is made clear in a brief exchange with Olivier Lacombe, the French Indologist, who once asked Ramana if his teaching followed Shankara's. Ramana, who rarely referred to himself in the first person, replied, "Bhagavan's teaching is an expression of his own experience and realization. Others find that it tallies with Shankara's."[16] With this statement, Ramana at once distances himself from Shankara and establishes his authority on personal experience. No lineage renders his teaching authoritative, but, rather, his own experience does.

This theme is often repeated by his disciples, no more enthusiastically than by D. M. Sastri, a disciple of Ramana who translated and commented on Ramana's *Upadesha Saram*, a slim volume that expresses Ramana's essential teachings. Sastri writes concerning Ramana's enlightenment, "His Experience was prior to and superior to any scriptures."[17] A statement such as this surprises one for its philosophical naiveté, but we see it repeated, with slightly more sophistication, by T. M. P. Mahadevan, the first director of the Radhakrishnan Institute of Indian Philosophy at the University of Madras. In his introduction to Ramana's *Vicharasangraham*, Mahadevan explains that the text is fundamentally based on Ramana's "plenary experience"—Mahadevan's favorite phrase for liberation—and all references to scriptures or sages are "offered only as confirmations of the truth discovered by Bhagavan himself in his own experience."[18] Though both Mahadevan and Sastri seriously underestimate the role of culture in religious experience, their views are indicative of the tendency to interpret Ramana's experience as transcending all social and cultural constructs. Ramana's life and teaching thus represent a particularly modern form of spirituality whose appeal in part lies in the promise of an immediate experience of the divine, uninflected by cultural forms and therefore available to all, regardless of culture or society. It thus neatly accords with the perennial philosophy that enjoyed much currency in the twentieth century and still resonates strongly in popular culture, if not in academic circles.

Ramana insisted, in no uncertain terms, on the need for personal experience to establish and to confirm liberation. This demand of course follows on his own experience of realization. In response to a question on the usefulness of reading books on the Vedanta, Ramana said, "[Y]ou can go on reading any number of books, but they can only tell you to realize the Self within you. The

Self cannot be found in books. You have to find it for yourself, in yourself."[19] Elsewhere, he insisted, "Mere book learning is not of any great use. After real-ization, all intellectual loads are useless burdens and are to be thrown over-board."[20] Indeed, Ramana, writes, "there will come a time when one will have to forget all that one has learned."[21] The reason for this, following the premise on non-dualism, is that no words, categories, or concepts can apprehend the limitless self. In this, Ramana stands squarely in the Indian apophatic tradition seen as far back as in the *Upanishads* and of course affirmed by Shankara in the *Brahma Sutra*. The ubiquitous, plenary self is beyond all name and form; how-ever, to affirm this is no mere intellectual assent, but an affective knowing. Ramana insisted that felt experience constitutes supreme knowledge, not dis-cursive reasoning. "Thoughts must cease and reason to disappear for the 'I-I' to rise up and be felt. Feeling is the main thing, not reason."[22]

This turn to experience has a particularly modern feel to it, no matter how distant Ramana may have been from historical processes in Europe and even in India. His turn to experience, apparently cultivated in isolation in Tiruvannamalai, nevertheless accords well with historical developments that emerged in Europe and India in the past century or more. We know that Enlightenment critiques of dogmatism and metaphysical speculation led apolo-gists to emphasize feeling or experience as the essential element of religion. Schleiermacher's emphasis on a direct, unmediated experience of the infinite as the primary moment of religion began a trend in the academic study of reli-gion later developed, with their own particular nuances, by William James, Rudolf Otto, and Mircea Eliade. The emphasis on experience is picked up by others, such as Aldous Huxley and Huston Smith, as part of a broader agenda to discover a common essence in mysticisms across cultures as well by other thinkers committed to interfaith dialogue.

At the same time, the turn to experience has also had its appeal to Indians. Ramana's call to an immediate experience of the Self, apparently unbound by culture and tradition, accords well with versions of neo-Hinduism, which have constructed and reconstructed Hinduism for various apologetic and political purposes. Ram Mohan Roy, Dayananda Sarasvati, Ramakrishna, and Vivekananda each represented their particular version of Hinduism either to purify the egregious excesses of priestly or popular Hin-duism and/or to propound the "true" Hinduism, which was every bit the match for and even superior to Western religious traditions. This transcendent universalism had its immediate "spiritual" embodiment in the Ramakrishna Mission, with monasteries emerging in various parts of India and the West constructed very much along the lines of Christian monastic institutions. It also had its "intellectual" embodiment in institutes such as Mahadevan's, which generated much outstanding scholarship in Indian philosophy, but which also clearly reflected an Advaitin bias; most of the texts produced under Mahadevan were critical editions of Sanskrit texts by classical Advaitin thinkers who were much less well-known than Shankara. The inference, of course, is that the most important or most valuable component of Indian philosophy is Advaita Vedanta.

Nevertheless, the impact of the life and thought of Ramana, with its repeated and insistent call to immediate realization, certainly does echo, as Lacombe's question suggests, the philosophy of Shankara. At the same time, it recalls the vision of Ramakrishna, thus neatly paralleling the Bengali mystic's universalism, this time from South India. These adepts propounded an immediate, non-dual realization, and in doing so, directly or indirectly represented a universalist spirituality of commanding appeal both for Indians operating out of the agenda of a neo-Hindu renaissance and for Westerns convinced of the ubiquity of mystical experience. The emphasis on direct, immediate experience represents a critical plank in the versions of neo-Hindu apologetics, such as is found in the works of Sarvepalli Radhakrishnan, T. M. P. Mahadevan, R. Balasubramanian, and A. Sharma. Each of these scholars has represented Advaita as the quintessence of Hindu spirituality and has, either in scholarly or popular works, emphasized "direct experience" as the exalted feature of Hinduism. Radhakrishnan, for example, writes that Hinduism presents "an intimate inseparability of theory and practice" in which "every doctrine has been turned into passionate conviction, stirring the heart of man and quickening his breath, and completely transforming his personal nature."[23] According to him, Indian philosophy shows its superiority over the "objectifying spirit" of Western analytical philosophy by its call for an "intuitive apprehension" of truth over rational argument; as he writes, "Reason is not useless or fallacious, but it is insufficient. To know reality one must have an actual experience of it. One does not merely *know* the truth in Indian philosophy, one *realizes* it."[24] This statement neatly parallels, as an abstract claim about Indian philosophy, Ramana's claim about his transformative experience at the age of sixteen. Recall, he said that this event was "no mere intellectual process," but something that flashed before him, "vividly, as living truth."

The rhetorical use of experience, in this case with a direct appeal to Ramana as the sage who quintessentially embodies non-dual realization, is seen in Arvind Sharma's recent book, *The Experiential Dimension of Advaita Vedanta*. Sharma, professor of Hinduism at McGill University, considers Ramana to be the chief spokesperson for what he calls "experiential Advaita," much as Shankara is the chief spokesperson for "doctrinal Advaita." The conclusion of Sharma's analysis clearly suggests the perennial appeal of Ramana. He writes, "For the natural consequence of an experiential presentation of Advaita Vedanta is to disengage it from its cultural contingencies and its religious baggage. What is left is something which we as human beings may appropriate or choose not to, depending on our judgment of it."[25]

We can read the two-fold "perennial appeal" of Ramana in Sharma's statement. First, the life and example of Ramana reveal a compelling human presence, clearly meeting with favorable review by thinkers East and West. But more subtly, Sharma's statement also reveals an appeal to the perennial philosophy, the notion that there exists a universal and shared "mystical" experience, finally pared of all cultural trappings. Here, however, Sharma qualifies this view by suggesting that the "common core" of mysticism is to be found not only at the heart of all religious traditions, but at the heart of all human experience. Sharma's perennialist reading of Ramana thus hardly limits the prospects and possibility of liberating experience to any geographical or cultural area. Such universalism and its implied metaphysics of experience holds that consummate experience is decisively available to non-Hindus and non-Indians as well. Its philosophical framework is thus inclusive as well; persons from other cultures are included or invited. Space is made for the Westerner to participate in traditional *sadhana* and other spiritual practices. But in another sense, inclusivism can also mean that the metaphysical vision of these saints includes, comprehends, or even surpasses that of other traditions. It is this last interpretation that occasionally fuels a neo-Hindu or neo-Advaita apologetic, though Ramana himself appeared to be entirely aloof of any considerations of the "Hindu Church Triumphant." Instead, his own experience and its metaphysical assumptions suggest a "cool" perennialism at the root of all religions, that is, Ramana appeared to show little emotional attachment to his "theory of religions," much less willingness to engage in polemics over it. Responding to the diversity of religious traditions, he affirmed, rather simply, that "their expression is the same. Only the modes of expression differ according to circumstances."[26] Elsewhere, he adds, concerning distinctions of East and West, "All go to the same goal."[27] Ramana's perennialism here is hardly in vogue, at least among contemporary scholars of religion in the West. But it is entirely in keeping with his non-dual metaphysic; we are the Self; differences are only circumstantial modifications. In the end, he says, "the highest state is the same and the experience is the same."[28]

In this appeal to direct experience, free from cultural trappings, there are parallels to Jiddu Krishnamurti (1895–1986). Krishnamurti was also a South Indian Brahmin who came to his realization through an unusual event, strikingly absent of complex theoretical infusions. Like Krishnamurti, Ramana adopted a method of inquiry to enlighten disciples but with fewer intellectual digressions. Although less known than Krishnamurti, Ramana's appeal was broader and extended beyond the elite and educated classes in India and in the West that were drawn to Krishnamurti. Indeed, as Gavin Flood notes, Ramana's teachings have inspired many other gurus, including the low-caste Bombay *bidi* (tobacco leaf) roller, Nisargadatta Maharaj.[29]

While there is much to examine in the life and thought of Ramana themselves, my interest here is the reaction to Ramana from the circle of Western scholars and religious figures who have encountered him. A brief survey of some recent and not-so-recent responses to Ramana's life and work highlights the unusually positive reaction to him on the part of Western scholars and religious figures. Klaus Klostermaier, for example, considers him to be "among the greatest and deepest spiritual influences coming from India in recent years," and notes that even after his death, the ashram in which he lived "is somehow charged with spiritual power, emanating from him."[30] Heinrich Zimmer wrote a study on Ramana in 1944 that included a foreword by C. G. Jung. In addition to painful hyperbole ("In India he is the whitest spot in a white space," etc.), Jung writes simply that Ramana "is genuine and, in addition to that, something quite phenomenal."[31] Jung's enthusiasm for Ramana's spirituality is consistent with his own intellectual agenda, which includes his own version of perennial philosophy. Although his interpretation of Ramana's life and thought favors the perennial view that a single unified experience is at the core of mysticisms across cultures, Jung nevertheless tends to a cultural dualism, importing romantic notions of the "spiritual" East as contrasted with the "materialist" West. According to him, Ramana's example is an important resource for the West, increasingly threatened by a lack of consciousness in a culture of commercialism and technology.[32] Indian saints such as Ramana and Ramakrishna are modern prophets recalling to the West "the demand of the soul."[33]

Zimmer's student Joseph Campbell also appeals to the perennial philosophy in evaluating Ramana and Ramakrishna. Sages such as these have, as he writes, "renewed the ineffable message perennially, in variable terms, which philosophers classify and *adhikarins* transcend."[34] This statement is fascinating as much for its location in Zimmer's book as for its perennialist declaration; it is the last sentence in Campbell's appendix, which follows Zimmer's text, serving to underscore both Zimmer's and Campbell's perennialism.

While it is perhaps no surprise that Jung and Campbell, both advocates of the perennial philosophy, were impressed by Ramana, a more recent tribute is somewhat surprising. No less than the late Agehananda Bharati, who, it is clear from his writings, suffered fools poorly, also agreed that "Ramana Maharshi was a mystic of the first order."[35] Bharati was a German who donned the ochre robes of a Hindu renunciant and later became a prominent, if occasionally grumpy, anthropologist of religion. His book, *The Light at the Centre*, is a conceptually astute analysis of "mysticism," which carefully assesses the conditions leading to and following from what he calls the "zero experience" or "consummative experience." While disputing the contention of disciples that Ramana was in perpetual cosmic absorption (*samadhi*), Bharati accepted as genuine Ramana's claims to non-dual realization. Despite questions concerning the social circumstances of Ramana's spiritual career, Bharati nevertheless affirms that "Ramana was an exceptional mystic."[36] And while Ramana has always drawn the positive attention of Indian scholars,[37] leading Western spiritual figures drawn to him include the late Thomas Merton (1915–1968), Bede Griffiths (1907–1993), and Dom Henri Le Saux (1910–1973).

Merton's attraction to Ramana is difficult to assess. Only indirect references to Ramana are found in his *Asian Journal*, though the editors offer considerable interesting and useful annotations. Still, the fact that Merton mentions locations associated with Ramana and the name of Mouni Sadhu, an early Western disciple of Ramana, suggests that he had more than a superficial knowledge of Ramana's career and impact. Elsewhere, however, Merton spells out his assessment of Ramana's teaching; in a review of Arthur Osborne's edition of Ramana's collected works, Merton writes, "It is a teaching which recalls Eckhart and Tauler, but according to the Maharshi absolute philosophical monism is beyond doubt. His teaching follows in the pure tradition of Advaita Vedanta. What is important to us above all is the authenticity of the natural contemplative experience of this contemporary 'Desert Father.'"[38]

Merton's interest in Ramana seems to follow on his growing interest in Eastern versions of non-dualism, which served to nourish and to complement his long-standing interest in Christian apophatic traditions. His journal is rich with references to Shankara and the important Advaitin manual, *Vivekachudamani*, a text that Ramana himself valued, so much so that he translated it into Tamil. In addition to these academic references to non-dualism, Merton's journal records a particularly vivid "peak" experience, a moving account of his visit to the sleeping Buddha at Polonnaruwa. Though it is difficult to ascertain precisely what happened there, his journal suggests that the event was an epiphany, which could be construed in terms of non-dualism. Merton himself uses the Buddhist terminology of *shunyata* or emptiness to capture the epiphany's essence.[39]

Bharati's and Merton's assessment of Ramana insist on the authority and authenticity of direct non-dual experience. These assessments and positive valorizations are also seen in the reflections of Bede Griffiths and Dom Henri Le Saux, both of whom increasingly adopted Advaitin paradigms to inform their own spiritual experiences. Griffiths was an English monk who, in his words, traveled to India to "find the other half of my soul."[40] He eventually assumed the leadership of the Shantivanam ashram founded earlier by Le Saux and Jules Montchanin. Griffiths wrote numerous books and gave considerable impetus to the interfaith dialogue movement as well as to the Christian ashram movement in India. Concerning Ramana, Griffiths wrote, "Perhaps the most remarkable example of Advaitin experience is that of Ramana Maharshi."[41] He considered Ramana's transformative experience to be "authentic mystical experience, that is, an experience of the Absolute."[42] Using the idiom of Advaita, Ramana, according to Griffiths, was a *jivanmukta*, one who is liberated while alive. Griffiths then engaged in a comparative analysis of Ramana's mystical theology, offering parallels, as Merton, to various Western apophatic theologies, including those of Dionysius, Meister Eckhart, Ruysbroeck, and Saint John of the Cross.

Comparisons of such mystical theologies may yield considerable fruit when carefully unpacked, but Griffiths does not engage in such systematic analysis. Still, what seems evident in each of the figures mentioned so far is that a first or secondhand acquaintance with Ramana's life or work seems to provoke a visceral reaction concerning his authenticity. This is nowhere more so apparent than in the writings of Dom Henri Le Saux, the French Benedictine monk who began a Christian monastic foundation in South India and eventually took *sannyasa* or renunciation under the name of Abhishiktananda. In his writings, Abhishiktananda makes noteworthy references to Ramana, all of which affirm the compelling power of Ramana's life and experience. Concerning the effect of Ramana's presence at the ashram, he writes, "Above all there was the presence—that of the Sage who had lived in this very place for so many long years, that of the mystery by which he had been dazzled and which had been so powerfully radiated by him. It was a presence which overarched and enfolded everything, and seemed to penetrate to the core of one's being, causing one to be recollected at the centre of the self, and drawing one irresistibly within."[43] Abhishiktananda himself gives an account of Ramana's life in his book, *Saccidananda: A Christian Approach to Advaitic Experience*.[44] More significantly, in this book he offers an account of the mechanism by which realization occurs; it is the "inward quest,"[45] a phrase that suggests the internalist epistemology of religious experience discussed above.

Other writers have testified to the extraordinary life and example of Ramana, often in the same florid style that we saw in Jung and Le Saux. Paul Brunton (1898–1981), the prolific British writer who contributed in no small measure to the Western fascination with the "mystical East," also met Ramana in his travels, and like Abhishiktananda, was profoundly transformed. He writes with a certain grandiloquence of his encounter with Ramana, "It is impossible to be in frequent contact with him without becoming lit up, as it were, from a ray from his spiritual orb."[46] But the language of these—for its emotional force—invites a return and scrutiny of the life and thought of Ramana. A more sober but nonetheless positive assessment of Ramana's life and example is found in Francis X. Clooney's recent book, *Hindu Wisdom for All God's Children*: "People like Ramana testify to the continuing power of the non-dualist conviction that there is only one true self."[47] In addition to these favorable estimations, Ramana's life and thought have influenced contemporary Western gurus as well, such as Andrew Cohen and Andrew Harvey.[48] In Santa Cruz, one Western guru, Master Nome (as in "no me") leads the Society for the Abidance of Truth (SAT), which holds Ramana's teaching as the very axis of its spiritual life.

Finally, I may add my own testimony. In the course of my language and philosophy training in India, I stayed at the Aikiya Alayam Research Center for Inter-faith Dialogue in Madras, led by the late Ignatius Hirudayam, SJ, who himself embodied a profound human excellence, the fruit of a lifetime of prayer and meditation.[49] Hirudayam modeled confidence and peace as he liberally drew from the wisdom traditions of India to complement the mysticism of St. Ignatius Loyola. In the course of a conversation with him, I was struck by his immediate and unqualified praise for the "Hindu saint" of Tiruvannamalai, and soon afterward I took up his suggestion to visit Ramana's ashram. While there I found myself quite moved by the quality of "presence" that does indeed seem to linger so many years after his death. After returning to the United States, I happened upon Klostermaier's observation in his *Survey of Hinduism*, and his comment very much resonated with my own experience at the ashram. This apparently shared sensibility led me to investigate other reactions to Ramana's life and teaching and, more specifically, to consider what accounts for such an appeal.

Examining the appeal of Ramana is worthy of consideration, especially when that appeal is fueled by theoretical or political needs, whether those of perennial philosophers or neo-Hindu apologists. Moreover, such an appeal begs for further scrutiny by philosophers of mysticism who argue over the prospects and possibility of "pure consciousness events." This ought to be all the more intriguing insofar as Ramana has been held to represent the clearest form of Advaita in this century: he is the "sage of pure experience." It is this theme that accounts for his appeal both to Indians holding apologetic interests and to Westerners interested in mysticisms across cultures. The call to "pure experience" becomes particularly compelling to thinkers and spiritual figures consciously or unself-consciously operating from the Enlightenment emphasis on experience as the essence of religion. This conceptual backdrop partially explains the appeal of Ramana to the West. The report and example of so-called "pure experience," uninflected by cultural patterns, remains for many a compelling source of inquiry, but not always for abstract theorizing. Ramana's unique experience and subsequent teaching have provided an important resource for students and scholars interested in studies of mysticism, metaphysics, and interfaith dialogue. These efforts, with differing degrees of "hermeneutic self-awareness," become part of the process of deepening intercultural, interfaith understanding, as they themselves become objects of reflection and analysis.

But the turn to "experience" in the West since the Enlightenment also reveals an epistemological shift to internalism. Such a method can be implicated in programs of "religious knowing," and it constitutes much of the creative agenda of thinkers such as Alston and Plantinga to advance such programs of scholarship. The internalist epistemological zeitgeist in the West also accords well with the deeply inward, internal epistemology of religious experience of Ramana. And, if most of us are, as a colleague once said, "unself-conscious internalists," then the subset of those interested in religious knowing will find strong appeal in internalist epistemologies of religious experience. Moreover, while Rambachand is quite correct in emphasizing the "external" elements in Shankara's epistemology of religious experience, there is little doubt of the strong internalism of Ramana, who repeatedly called his listeners to "dive within" to experience their true nature, their original state (*sahaja sthiti*). "Self-inquiry" promoted by the penetrating question "Who am I?" stimulates the "inward quest," which eventuates in self-realization. In advancing this program of religious knowing—a knowing beyond knowledge—Ramana at the same time profoundly relativized or modified traditional Hindu categories or practices, the result being a construction of Advaita universal not only in theory but in practice. While Ramana never stepped foot in the West, his non-dualism helped to liberate Advaita from its local context, thus supporting and facilitating the transmission of Hinduism from India, a transmission catalyzed by Vivekananda and established in creative ways by the contemporary gurus examined in this volume.

NOTES

1. A version of this chapter was originally published under the title "Weaving the Inward Thread to Awakening: The Perennial Appeal of Ramana Maharshi," *Horizons* 29, no. 2 (2002): 240–59. I have made revisions to it to align it more properly with the goals of this volume, but much of the article remains intact; hence I've retained the same title.

2. Wilhelm Halbfass, *India and Europe: An Essay in Philosophical Understanding* (Albany: State University of New York Press, 1988; reprint, Delhi: Motilal Banarsidass, 1991), 402.

3. See chapter 21 of Halbfass, *India and Europe*, and Anantanand Rambachand, *Accomplishing the Accomplished: The Vedas as a Source of Valid Knowledge in Shankara* (Hawaii: University of Hawaii Press, 1991).

4. Thomas A. Forsthoefel, *Knowing Beyond Knowledge: Epistemologies of Religious Experience in Classical and Modern Advaita* (London: Ashgate, 2002).

5. Steven T. Katz, "Language, Epistemology, and Mysticism," in Steven T. Katz, ed., *Mysticism and Philosophical Analysis* (London: Sheldon Press, 1978), 22–74.

6. Paul J. Griffiths, *Apology for Apologetics* (Maryknoll, NY: Orbis, 1991), 45–59.

7. Robert K. C. Forman, "Introduction: Mystical Consciousness, the Innate Capacity, and the Perennial Philosophy," in Robert K. C. Forman, ed., *Innate Capacity: Mysticism, Psychology, and Philosophy* (Oxford: Oxford University Press, 1998), 3–41.

8. See especially William Alston, *Perceiving God* (Ithaca: Cornell University Press, 1991); Alvin Plantinga, *Warrant and Proper Function* (New York: Oxford University Press, 1993); and his *Warranted Christian Belief* (New York: Oxford University Press, 2000).

9. Ramana Maharshi, *Vicharasangraham* (Tiruvannamalai: Ramanasramam, 1994), 14.

10. Arthur Osborne, ed., *The Teachings of Sri Ramana Maharshi* (Tiruvannamalai: Ramanasramam, 1993), 91.

11. Ibid., 96.

12. B. V. Narasimha Swami, *Self Realization: The Life and Teachings of Sri Ramana Maharshi* (Tiruvannamalai: Ramanasramam, 1993), 11.

13. Ibid., 15.

14. Ibid., 21.

15. Maharshi, *Vicharasangraham*, 12.

16. Osborne, *The Teachings of Sri Ramana Maharshi*, 9.

17. D. M. Sastri, "Preface," *The Maharshi's Way: A Translation and a Commentary on Upadesa Saram* (Tiruvannamalai: Ramanasraman), i.

18. T. M. P. Mahadevan, "Preface," *Self-Enquiry (Vicharasangraham) of Bhagavan Sri Ramana Maharshi* (Tiruvannamalai: Sri Ramanasramam, 1993), iv.

19. Osborne, *The Teachings of Sri Ramana Maharshi*, 5.

20. Ibid., 6.

21. Ramana Maharshi, *Who Am I?*, trans. T. M. P. Mahadevan (Trivuvannamalai: Ramanasramam, no date), 14.

22. Osborne, *The Teachings of Sri Ramana Maharshi*, 35.

23. Sarvepalli Radhakrishnan, "General Introduction," in Radhakrishnan and Charles Moore, eds., *A Sourcebook in Indian Philosophy* (Princeton: Princeton University Press, 1957), xxiv.

24. Ibid., xxv.

25. Arvind Sharma, *The Experiential Dimension of Advaita Vedanta* (Delhi: Motilal Banarsidass, 1993), 101.

26. *Talks with Sri Ramana Maharshi*, 9th ed. (Tiruvannamalai: Ramanasramam, 1994–96), 67.

27. Ibid., 114.

28. Osborne, *The Teachings of Sri Ramana Maharshi*, 67.

29. Gavin Flood, *Introduction to Hinduism* (Cambridge: Cambridge University Press, 1996), 271.

30. Klaus Klostermaier, *A Survey of Hinduism* (Albany: State University of New York Press), 395–396.

31. Heinrich Zimmer, *Der Weg zum Selbst: Lehre und Leben des Indischen Heiligen Shri Ramana Maharshi aus Tiruvannamalai* (Zurich: Rascher Verlag, 1944). Zimmer's book includes a biography and German translations of Ramana's Forty Verses on Reality and *satsang* (spiritual gathering) conversations. Jung's quote above is reprinted as the foreword to C. G. Jung, *The Spiritual Teaching of Ramana Maharshi, Shambala Dragon Editions* (Boston and London: Shambala, 1988), ix.

32. Jung, *The Spiritual Teaching of Ramana Maharshi*, x–xi.

33. Ibid., x.

34. Joseph Campbell, "Appendix A: The Six Systems," in Joseph Campbell, ed., *Heinrich Zimmer, Philosophies of India*, vol. 26, Bollingen Series (New York: Pantheon Books, 1951), 614.

35. Agehananda Bharati, *The Light at the Centre: Context and Pretext of Modern Mysticism* (London and the Hague: East-West Publications, 1976), 29.

36. Ibid., 89.

37. For example, Arvind Sharma and T. M. P. Mahadevan, the late chair of the Radhakrishnan Institute for the Advanced Study of Philosophy at the University of Madras.

38. Thomas Merton, review of editor Arthur Osborne's *The Collected Works of Ramana Maharshi* (London: Rider, 1959), *Collectanea Cistersciensia*, 27.1 (1965): 79–80; "C'est une doctrine qui rappelle Eckhart et Tauler, mais chez le Maharshi le monisme philosophique absolu ne fait pas de doute. Sa doctrine est dans la plus pure tradition de l'Advaita Védantiste. Ce qui nous importe surtout à nous c'est l'authenticité de l'éxperience contemplative naturelle chez ce "Père du Désert" contemporain." English translation above is mine.

39. Thomas Merton, *The Asian Journal of Thomas Merton*, Brother Patrick Hart, James Laughlin, and Naomi Burton, eds. (New York: New Directions, 1968), 233–36. Klaus Klostermaier cites excerpts from these passages as a sidebar titled, "Thomas Merton's Enlightenment," in his book, *Buddhism: A Short Introduction* (Oxford: One World, 1999), 186.

40. Bede Griffiths, *The Marriage of East and West* (Springfield, IL: Templegate, 1982), 7–8.

41. Bede Griffiths, *Christ in India: Essays Towards a Hindu Christian Dialogue* (Springfield, IL: Templegate, 1984), 205.

42. Ibid., 206.

43. Abhishiktananda, *Guru and Disciple* (Delhi: ISPCK, 1990), 2.

44. Abhishiktananda, *Saccidananda: A Christian Approach to Advaitic Experience* (Delhi: ISPCK, 1974), chap. 2.

45. Ibid., chap. 3.

46. No page given. Brunton's prose comment is found under a photo of Ramana.

47. Francis X. Clooney, *Hindu Wisdom for All God's Children* (Maryknoll, NY: Orbis, 1998), 32.

48. Flood, *Introduction to Hinduism*, 271. See also Andrew Rawlinson, *The Book of Enlightened Masters: Western Teachers in Eastern Traditions* (LaSalle, IL: Open Court, 1997), 489.

49. On Hirudayam, see Francis X. Clooney, "Three Mentors in India," *America*, March 2, 1984, 161–65.

THREE

MAHARISHI MAHESH YOGI

Beyond the TM Technique

CYNTHIA ANN HUMES

NINETEENTH-CENTURY Hindu Renaissance leaders openly offered Vedantic wisdom to the West. Western Transcendentalists, Unitarians, and Spiritualists offered their own wisdom and, enjoying the dialogue, picked and chose which aspects of Oriental thought they wished to appropriate to fold into what they deemed to be a "universal religion," the essence of which could be discerned in religions throughout the world. Much like Romantic philosophers of the nineteenth and early twentieth centuries, Maharishi Mahesh Yogi, the founder of the Transcendental Meditation Movement, has preached that there is an Absolute Being that is the source of all life, all intelligence, and all creativity.[1] This Being may be discovered by any and all through a wide variety of religious and spiritual programs.

Western appropriation of Vedanta continues today, intersecting and at times lending itself to the service of interested New Age dabblers. Paul Heelas explains that the central tenet of the New Age affirms that a significantly better way of life is dawning; its *lingua franca* is "Self-spirituality," requiring that each individual make contact with the spirituality that lies within.[2] In contrast with its precursors—the nineteenth- and early-twentieth-century Romantic appropriators of Hinduism and other Oriental faiths—Heelas notes that the New Ager has become "detraditionalized," that is, not locked into a specific religious or spiritual heritage:

> New Agers are averse to traditions, with their dogmas, doctrines and moralities. Yet New Agers continually draw on traditions—shamanic to

Buddhist. The solution to this seeming paradox lies with the fact that
New Agers are perennialists. . . . Having little or no faith in the external
realm of traditional belief, New Agers can ignore apparently significant
differences between religious traditions, dismissing them as due to historical contingencies and ego-operations. But they do have faith in that
wisdom which is experienced as lying at the heart of the religious
domain as a whole.[3]

New Agers emphasize "spiritual technologies" that can be drawn out of the
perennial wisdom found sporadically in various traditions.[4] They employ them
selectively in service of all manner of goals, for among all but the purists (i.e.,
those who might reject anything deemed "unspiritual"), most New Age adherents incorporate all human desires holistically. Thus, all human impulses,
including sexual gratification, materialist pleasures, friendship and companion-
ship, unity with nature, and the quest for enlightenment, are ennobled and
divinized as aspects of the great cosmic unity.

Maharishi's movement can be credited with furthering many of these
New Age beliefs, but I argue that its ultimate rejection of alternative spiritual-
ity and insistence on maintaining the purity of Vedic knowledge situate
Mahesh Yogi and his movement securely in the folds of what most would call
Hinduism.

American Hindu transplants manifest themselves in a variety of ways,
some of which can be elucidated by adapting categories suggested by Jan Nattier in her study of American Buddhism.[5] Nattier explains that in general,
Buddhism has been taken in by America in one of three ways: as import, as
export, and as baggage. By Import Model, Nattier refers to the type of Buddhism espoused by those who have sought out the faith, either by journeying
to Asia and then returning with it, or by reading Asian books and then adopting concepts. Export Buddhism, contrarily, is disseminated through missionary
activities whose impetus comes from outside, and thus includes the practices of
Asian religious evangelists. Baggage Buddhism is simply brought to the United
States as part of the cultural practice of Asian immigrants.

Nattier reports that American Buddhists of the Import variety fall into a
specific demographic constituency: they tend to be well educated, financially
comfortable, and overwhelmingly European American. Nattier thus sees
Import Buddhists as members of an "Elite Buddhism," whose most striking
feature is its emphasis on meditation, but whose distinctiveness is "not its heavy
emphasis on meditation but its scanting of other aspects of traditional Buddhism," such as monasticism and "activities that are best described as "devotional." Nattier concludes, "Elite Buddhists, many of them still fleeing the
theistic traditions of their youth, have little patience with such practices."[6]

This particular spin reveals Elite Buddhism to be not simply an Asian
religion transplanted to a new environment; rather, Nattier explains, Elite

Buddhism in the United States is a "curious amalgamation of traditional Buddhist ideas and certain upper-middle-class American values—above all individualism, freedom of choice, and personal fulfillment."[7] These American values
are "non-negotiable cultural demands," and Elite Buddhists' insistences on
them have "reshaped Buddhist ideas and practices in significant ways, yielding a
genuinely new religious 'product' uniquely adapted to certain segments of the
American 'market.'"[8]

In general, Nattier's categories work well for describing much of American Hinduism and the TM Movement. Initially, Maharishi's treks in the United
States would correspond to the category of "Export Hinduism." Maharishi
responded to his disciples as a fairly traditional guru, offering to all interested
guidance, prayers, and what he claimed was his own guru's meditation practices. Some of his followers developed strong modes of devotion to Maharishi.
As he came to understand Western values and desires better, Maharishi sought
to strip away those aspects Americans felt uncomfortable with, and instead he
marketed a less devotional, less ethnic type of spiritual development, shedding
excess "baggage," as it were. Uttering specially selected mantras for twenty
minutes twice a day, Maharishi promised that the individual could experience
Absolute Being in Cosmic Consciousness without all the cultural baggage. The
technique could be learned easily and quickly, for a minimum price. Because
Westerners more responsive to his American message eventually sought him
out, and most initiates learned about TM from Maharishi's books and how to
meditate from other Westerners, the majority of TM-ers correspond to Nattier's Import category. Those who undertook TM as simply a technique to not
only improve sleep and work, but also fulfill their nondevotional desire for self-
realization, fit the description of the New Ager described by Heelas, as well as
the demographics of "Elite Hindus" modeled on Nattier's categories of Buddhism. Such TM technique initiates privileged individualism, freedom of
choice, and personal fulfillment, but shorn of the undesireably devotional
aspects common to a "religion."

Maharishi Mahesh Yogi has crafted what many would identify as a highly
influential Hindu global theological perspective through his Transcendental
Meditation Movement. In the West, he has achieved this influence in part by
denying the "Hindu-ness" of his teachings, and at least for a time, their religiosity as well. In so doing, he thrust the reach of his Advaita Vedantin interpretations and many standard cultural markers of Hinduism into a global
context.

In this chapter, I will examine selected themes in Maharishi's adaptive
strategy by focusing on just three localized instances: his formative years in
India, TM in the United States, and his triumphant return to India and establishment of an alternative world.

I first acquaint the reader with Maharishi's personal background, intellectual and cultural heritage, early reception in his home country, and his stated

goals in the West. I demonstrate how his secular scientific training helped shape the philosophical and ideological warrants for his movement, which I believe to have remained constant throughout the past fifty years. In "Science Moving West," I discuss his early reception in the West, noting some of the movement's most prominent leaders, their impact, and their process of forming TM centers around the world. I reveal here how Maharishi's innovative approach to mantras, authority, and teaching underscores a profound pedagogical innovation from his guru's teachings. I close with a brief discussion of the 1976 lawsuit that stalled the brisk rise of the TM Movement in the United States. In "Religion Turning East," I discuss how Maharishi urged his Western disciples to become renunciants, graduating from TM-Sidhi[9] techniques to Maharishi Ayur Ved and beyond, resulting in the creation of the Natural Law Party, an international political party based on Maharishi's philosophy, active in at least eighty-three countries as of this writing, and the establishment of his own Country of Global Peace. The turn eastward was not well received among all. I illustrate how many disciples took to the virtual universe to "unstress" collectively about Maharishi. At the root of much of the criticism is the successive unveiling of Maharishi's message. I conclude by questioning how Maharishi's shifts—from science to Veda, from stripped down TM technique to full-fledged Vedism—raise issues regarding self-definition and his strategies to extend his Vedantic message and movement into a global context.

MAHESH BECOMES A MAHARISHI

Maharishi Mahesh Yogi's guru was Swami Brahmananda Saraswati, a *Shankaracharya*, or an authoritative spiritual teacher modeled on the great philosopher and guru, Shankara.

In the eighth century, the "original" or *Adi Shankaracharya* decided to take steps to preserve the purity of his non-dual or Advaitin teachings. During Shankara's time, the Advaitin philosophy based on the *Upanishads* was taught to disciples by enlightened gurus, without the benefit of any monastic organization. Shankara is credited with establishing four monasteries (*math*) of higher learning in the four cardinal directions of India: Jyotir Math in the North, Shringeri Math in the South, Govardhan Math in the East, and Sharada Math in the West. Each center would be led by a teacher of Shankara, or *Shankaracharya*, whose role was to preserve the Advaitin teachings, provide effective leadership, and ensure appropriate succession of control over the four centers of learning.

Yet despite these protective measures, at times there were lapses in a Math's leadership, and for more than 165 years, there was no *Shankaracharya* at Jyotir Math (ca. 1776–1941).[10] Dharma Maha Mandal, representing religious people and scholars from North regions, initiated a search to locate a suitable candidate for the position.[11] The group had long heard of an ascetic famous for his solitary life in a cave far off the beaten paths of north India. Born some seventy years before in a Mishra *brahmin* (priest caste) community near Ayodhya, Uttar Pradesh, Brahmananda Saraswati was initiated into renunciation in 1906 by his guru, Swami Krishnananda Saraswati. He fulfilled the requirements of a *Shankaracharya*: to be a lifelong celibate and Brahmin by birth; to demonstrate profound knowledge of scriptures; and to be a Dandi Swami who respected the caste system and upheld the principles of Advaita Vedanta. After being urged to accept the post for years, Saraswati finally agreed to become *Shankaracharya* of Jyotir Math and he was installed on April 1, 1941.

For twelve years, until his death at eighty-four years in 1953, Brahmananda sought to re-enliven Advaitin teachings among the masses by traveling all over North India. His message, based on his own experience and long study of scripture, was very simple, rooted in devotion, and yet consistently honoring the Advaitin philosophy. Within just a decade, tens of thousands of people had become his disciples, and the primacy of Jyotir Math as a site of Advaitin philosophy was reestablished.

Mahesh Prasad Varma was still a college student when he met Brahmananda Saraswati in 1940. The apocryphal meeting is well known; Maharishi himself recounted it on multiple occasions, and later TM teachers repeated it to new meditators. Once when I shared some material I was working on about Maharishi and "Gurudev," viz., Brahmananda Saraswati, with Jerry Jarvis, a major figure in the United States movement's early days, he was disappointed with my account of Brahmananda's and Maharishi's relationship. He told me I had left out a major part of the story, as I had omitted Maharishi's first glimpse of the man whom he would call simply, "divine teacher," or *Gurudev*:

> When Maharishi first went to meet Brahmananda Saraswati, he was told, "wait there." He had to wait for some time outside the door. Just then, a car came from around the corner, and the lights illuminated the end of the porch, and lit up the figure of a sitting man, completely silent and non-moving. Maharishi knew instantly in that flash of light that this man would be his guru. He wanted to be with him right away, but Gurudev said to him he must finish college first, so Maharishi finished college. Gurudev, in the meanwhile, became *Shankaracharya*, but when he first met him [Brahmananda], Maharishi did not know this would happen.[12]

I had known this story for many years from having been a practitioner of Transcendental Meditation myself. Others in the movement commonly mentioned it, and the omission was deliberate because it was so common, well known, and in some ways, too hagiographic. Yet for TM practitioners' own self-understanding, I realized from Jerry's reaction to such a barebones account that the story of the two men's meeting is intrinsically significant. The story of Maharishi's first auspicious sight or *darshan* of Brahmananda Saraswati reveals that

Mahesh was attracted instantly to Gurudev, and not because he was a *Shankaracharya*. Second, he felt called to a spiritual life at this man's direction. Third, despite his inner impulse driving him toward the guru, the story underscores that Mahesh nevertheless remained in school at Brahmananda's orders, graduating with a bachelor's degree in physics from Allahabad University. And significantly, all of these aspects—his instant attraction, devotion to Gurudev, obedience to the master, and the primacy his guru placed on his gaining a secular educational background in science—would have tremendous influence on Mahesh's later teachings.

Mahesh remained devoted to Brahmananda Saraswati from 1940 until the great master's death in 1953. For many of those years, he had served Gurudev personally as a clerk. In that capacity, Mahesh met many famous persons who visited the great *Shankaracharya*, and some photos record Mahesh by Gurudev's side. Mahesh was then known as Bal Brahmachari Mahesh, referring to his identity as a celibate student (*brahmachari*) since childhood (*bal*, child). It remains unclear to what extent Mahesh was initiated into the ascetic circles of Jyotir Math. While many of Mahesh's followers claim he was a member of the *kshatriya* or ruling warrior caste, and many books written about TM and Maharishi reiterate this, Mahesh has made no such claim. Rather, Maharishi's name—Varma—and most Indian sources identify him as a member of the *kayasth* or educated clerical caste prior to becoming a monk.

This caste factor is significant. The *kayasths* are a learned caste with a long and fascinating history of attempts at self-definition. The *kayasths* are famous for having served as the clerical arm of the Muslims who came to rule North India prior to the British occupation of North India. A sector sought in the nineteenth century to identify themselves as descendents of the Emperor Chandragupta, thus giving rise to some people's claim of their *kshatriyahood*. Especially during the 1920s and 1930s, *kayasth* leaders sought to "*sanskritize*" caste rituals, that is, emulate higher caste religious behavior, as well as twice-born culture, specifically, abstaining from alcohol. Their high level of education but ambivalent caste status lead to the kind of scoffing evidenced by this remark, attributed to Brahmananda Saraswati, "Nowadays, *kayasths, vaishyas*, oil sellers, and even liquor merchants put on the different colored garb of a holy man (*sadhu*) and are eager to make many disciples of their own. In this way both the guru and disciple will have their downfall. What I am saying is in accord with the sacred codes (*shastras*), I am not telling you my own mental construction."[13]

Yet a *kayasth* was not barred from spiritual teaching. Brahmananda recounted how "the great King Janaka Videha was a very great wise man, but because he was a *kshatriya*, he never tried to become a guru." Even when the Brahmin Sukadeva was sent by his father Vyasa to Janaka to learn wisdom, Janaka refused, saying he was not authorized to teach him. "Then Sukadeva said, 'You are a *kshatriya*, so to give charity is your *dharma* [rightful duty]. The *shastras* have given you permission to give charity; give *brahmavidya* (the knowledge of *Brahman*, viz., ultimate reality)[14] to me as charity."' Janaka agreed to do so, but Brahmananda Saraswati asserted, "After listening to this, Janaka seated Sukadeva on a higher seat than his own, worshipped him, and in the form of charity, gave him the knowledge of *Brahman*. But Janaka did not make him his student to teach it. This is the ideal of those capable people who protect the limits of the *shastras*."[15]

Enlightened people of varying castes can teach *brahmavidya*, and once a person becomes a yogi, caste is a moot point (Sri Aurobindo and Paramahamsa Yogananda, for example, were both *kayasths*) but the title of "guru" and the ability to accept disciples is reserved for males of the Brahmin caste, and so, as an agent of orthodoxy, *Shankaracharya* Saraswati preserved the teaching that guru-hood is restricted to the Brahmin male.[16]

I believe these strictures were formative for Mahesh's self-understanding, and that they directly affected how he would teach. I have never found any reference in which Mahesh claimed to be anything other than a teacher, one adept in yoga (*yogi*), or a seer of truth (*rishi*), all titles permissible to his caste. Thus, while one may quibble (as his detractors often do) that no learned elder bestowed such titles as *maharishi* or *yogi* on Mahesh, there is no scriptural rule forbidding such honorifics for Mahesh Varma. Mahesh utilized very specific strategies as he climbed to the pinnacles of teaching success, without the safety net of the guru mantle, to stay true to his guru's orthodoxy.

Mahesh came to teach his guru's method of "deep meditation," seeking to avoid a basic misconception prevailed in India: Meditation required mind control, which involved holding onto the mantra.[17] At the 1955 Great Festival of Kerala (*Kerala Maha Sammelan*), "Bal Brahmachari Mahesh" affirmed that his guru had taught that all could be enlightened: "Everybody can have, should have and must have, the great privilege of enjoying the glories of the soul, the glories of the glorified aspect of everybody's life. Caste, creed or nationality is no hurdle in the realm of the soul or on the royal road to it. Soul is the individual property of everybody."[18]

Conspicuously, Mahesh alluded to metaphors and direct allegories to Western scientific concepts, even as he invoked a "science of the soul":

> The spirit or soul is the basic motive force of our existence and spirituality is the science of that motive force. The material science of tody [*sic*] speaks highly of atomic power. Today the political power of a nation depends upon its resources of atomic energy. But we in India know that the atomic energy is not the basics [*sic*] motive power of our existence. It can only be called the basic motive force of material existence, because it is found to be very gross when compared with the powers of our mental and spiritual existence. That is the reason why India laid more importance on the field of the soul which is the ultimate motive power behind

our life in all its aspects; spiritual, mental and physical. That is the reason why India always regarded the science of the soul as the best and most useful of all sciences. This is the reason why His Holiness has called spirituality as the backbone of India.[19]

Since 1955, Mahesh has not wavered in his subordination of Western science to India's superior "science of the soul," nor has he moved away from his assertion, "The theory of Mantras is the theory of sound. It is most scientific and natural."

Although signing his name as "Bal Brahmachari Mahesh" in *The Beacon Light of the Himalayas* pamphlet, Mahesh is referred in one segment of the same as "great seer" or "Maharshi." Within the next year, others would begin referring to him as *Maharshi Mahesh Yogi*. In December 1957, Maharshi Mahesh Yogi was one of several sages invited to speak at a religious festival held in Madras called the "Congress of Spiritual Luminaries." Mahesh announced his bold plan to bring the "wisdom of the Vedic tradition" to the entire world, "I'm inspired to start a Spiritual Regeneration Movement." According to TM Movement oral hagiography, the audience applauded for about ten minutes, and even while the applause was still going on, the Congress's organizer asked Mahesh why he hadn't told him he was going to announce this campaign. Mahesh responded, "I didn't know I was going to do it."

By 1958, many of the formative characteristics of Mahesh Varma's teachings were in place. First, he espoused the conservative Advaita Vedanta lineage of the north Indian *Shankaracharya* tradition, and he taught none other than the original message of Shankara himself: "Remember, it is nothing new that the Adhyatmic Vikas Mandal of Kerala is saying today. . . . It is the same age-old voice of eternal peace and happiness for which India stands out from times immemorial. It is the same age-old voice of eternal peace and happiness which the child of Kerala, the pride of India, Shri Sankara gave out to the world more than two thousand years ago."[20] Second, Mahesh claimed that his simple technique of *mantric* meditation was the gift of Guru Dev, and it allowed anyone to access the true self or *atman*, which was none other than Godhead or *Brahman*: being, consciousness, and bliss. "Although nothing is new in the realm of the soul the experience of it which was thought to be very difficult has now become very easy under the grace of Guru Deva. . . . Kerala Maha Sammelam is raising a voice that under the universal benevolence of Shri Guru Deva, MIND CONTROL IS EASY, PEACE IN DAILY LIFE IS EASY AND EXPERIENCE OF ATMANANDAM (Bliss of the Self) IS EASY."[21] All of the world could be understood through the superior Indian science of the soul, whose subject is a field of knowledge even more subtle and fine than the smallest of atoms. Mahesh's special gift would be his ability to reinterpret phenomena by linking these two branches of world knowledge: the encompassing Vedic science, which subsumes Western science.

In 1955, Mahesh declared that he would regenerate spirituality not just in India, but the entire world. Mahesh soon received financial backing for travel, gathered his few belongings, and set out on his first world tour, teaching what he then called "Deep Meditation." Inserting an additional "i," he became "Mahar(i)shi Mahesh Yogi," and undertook initiation of disciples, but always in the name of his guru Brahmananda Saraswati, not his own. By interpreting Western knowledge through an Advaitin lens, Mahesh Varma would preserve the purity and primacy of Shankara's teachings, as enlivened by his master Brahmananda Saraswati.

SCIENCE MOVING WEST:
MAHARISHI IN THE UNITED STATES

In the United States, Maharishi's first adherents were predominately spiritually inclined, as autobiographies by early American followers such as Helena Olson[22] and Nancy Cooke de Herrera show.[23] Yet despite the basis for his audience's attraction to him, all early sources I have uncovered simultaneously reveal Maharishi's confidence that the benefits and effects of meditation could at least partially be proven by scientific observation.[24]

Maharishi himself lectured to potential meditators beginning in 1959-1961. After he conducted screening and approved the hopefuls, he began initiation into the *mantric* meditation with a devotional ritual (*puja*) whose focus was Brahmananda Saraswati and the *Shankaracharya* lineage. Initiates were given a specially suited mantra, and taught how to practice meditation.

Maharishi's theory of the nature of mantras affected his innovative teaching approach. Meditation was "effortless" by its very nature, because the mind tends to wander toward what attracts it, and the most attractive focus is inward. When one used the correct mantra as it should be, uttering it effortlessly without concentrating the mind on it, the mind, floating free of being focused on relative concerns, would be attracted inward. In his speeches to the laity, Guru Dev had explained how the mantra worked in a very theistic way, consistent with Hinduism and the *Shankaracharya* tradition in general. The personal gods evoked within and from the mantras were intercessors for the meditator, and the power resident in the mantra. In Maharishi's 1955 speech, he mentions a connection with personal deities in the mantras, and occasionally one can find similar references in later works. However, more commonly he describes the mantras working automatically. Metaphors of machines abound, similar to Tantric explanations of mantra. Maharishi's scientific description would develop even further when tied to another innovation: the creation of cadres of "teachers" and "initiators."

Since Maharishi did not claim guruhood for himself, becoming a guru was obviously not a requirement for others to teach TM. Indians, Maharishi felt, tended to emulate the West, so if he could convince the West of the merits of his approach, he would in turn buttress his authority in India. By the fall of 1959, Maharishi announced that he would train a cadre of "teachers" who could deliver the message about TM, who in turn would work with "initiators," teaching appropriate mantras based on specific criteria to those interested.

Beulah Smith was the lone American to act as an initiator until 1966. Jerry and Debby Jarvis joined Maharishi's inner group in the United States, becoming "meditation guides," able to assist those already initiated, at a three-week course held in November 1961. Jerry Jarvis was chosen as the principal teacher during this time period in the United States to give the seven lectures required before Beulah Smith initiated students. Jerry Jarvis recounted to me that it was almost by accident that he stumbled onto a new clientele for Maharishi's message. One day, a young man approached him and said he had a group of friends who wanted to learn TM at El Camino College in Manhattan Beach. Jerry was so inspired by their eager reaction that he completed the first three or four lectures in just one night. He came back and finished the last three lectures the second night, and thereafter, the practice of holding just two introductory lectures came about. Not only were college students eager to be initiated, but they were also willing to go to India for teacher training as well. Other countries saw how the United States had turned to college students, and they began to target that group as well. After becoming an initiator himself in 1966, Jerry subsequently become the most successful TM teacher and initiator ever, initiating literally thousands of young people.[25]

While many historians of the sixties recount Maharishi's involvement with the Beatles as the formative turning point to TM's gaining popularity among Western youth, in fact the opposite was true. The Beatles became interested in Maharishi precisely because he was already well known in England among the youth there from his publications and appearances.[26] Maharishi built on his successful outreach to sixties youth by focusing on training TM teachers, all to help accomplish his goal of bringing Vedic wisdom to the entire world.

Unlike his guru, Maharishi preferred to postpone teaching Western initiates those philosophical aspects central to Advaita but less appealing in the West, such as caste, reincarnation, or the social place of women. When asked about past lives, for instance, Maharishi would answer (somewhat humorously), "reincarnation is for the ignorant."[27] Teaching about the central concept of *maya*, viz., the illusory characteristic of the world of transmigration, was reserved for the advanced TM student. This stance is in direct contrast to Brahmananda Saraswati and other Advaitin teachers, whose potential converts commonly expressed at the onset of their spiritual path a disenchantment with the illusory world and a desire to seek release from rebirth.

Perhaps most significant, discussion of the goal of meditation shifted profoundly. In less than a decade of outreach, by the early sixties Maharishi ceased talking openly about "enlightenment" per se, instead describing the goal as becoming aware of Transcendental Consciousness. Eventually, although it was alluded to briefly in introductory lectures, Maharishi decreed that extended discussion of the attainment of Cosmic Consciousness should take place only after initiation, so that people would have had practical experience of Cosmic Consciousness through meditation first. Maharishi discovered people were far more interested in using meditation to reduce stress or for self-improvement— better academic performance, business results, or social life.

In 1970–1972, Maharishi sought to distance himself from the nomenclature of "Hinduism," or "spirituality," even as he laid the groundwork for providing more advanced Vedic training for his key disciples. The Science of Creative Intelligence (SCI) was the new name for the same Advaitin teachings Maharishi had been giving all along, that is, the TM group's philosophy or worldview, which would facilitate his plan to spread Advaitin wisdom throughout the world as "science," without the resistance invited by labeling his message "Hindu," or "religious."

The Science of Creative Intelligence became part of a systematic campaign, beginning around 1970, to shift focus away from appealing primarily to the spiritually inclined, which then comprised a relative minority, toward the masses, whose predilections lay in the pragmatic New Age technique of the mantra. Yet he did not abandon his special followers, whom he sought to teach more sophisticated techniques and deeper Vedic truths. He mandated celibacy for his "skin boys" (a group that included none other than pop self-help guru John Gray), so-called for their role in placing the antelope skin on which Maharishi was to sit.

Due to the interconnectedness of all beings, the benefits of TM extended beyond the individual performing it, claimed Maharishi. If TM reduced stress in the individual, then the newly de-stressed individual affected others who were still under stress, providing a cooling or calming function in society as a whole. So when a 1974 study purporting to prove that cities in which at least one percent of the population had learned Transcendental Meditation experienced marked decreases in crime rates, Maharishi confidently asserted that this "Maharishi Effect" was not only predictable and scientific, but had ushered in the dawn of The Age of Enlightenment.

The hierarchical system of support for his burgeoning movement differed dramatically from traditional Advaitin models: Maharishi had come to adapt Western models of education and metaphors of secular government. Maharishi established "capitals" of enlightenment and inaugurated the accredited Maharishi International University in Fairfield, Iowa, in 1974. MIU taught standard liberal arts fare, but incorporated TM as well as aspects of the Science of Creative Intelligence.[28]

TM crested on what is often called in the movement the "Merv Wave," or the 1975 spike in popularity marked by the famous incident when Merv

Griffin and other famous Hollywood types spoke openly about the benefits they found from TM. Members of the movement were positively giddy from riding their leader's ascendancy to such soaring heights. Even the United States government became a TM customer. Popular books extolled the virtue of TM. The assertion that no change in lifestyle was required was a major selling point, which was not lost on marketers or observers of TM. Denise Denniston and Peter McWilliams, for instance, wrote a rhetorical FAQ in their 1975 best-seller, *The TM Book:*

> The TM program is not a religion? I've heard it was just some Western-ized form of Hinduism.
>
> No, no–it's absurd to assume that just because the TM technique comes from India it must be some Hindu practice. . . . The TM technique is a scientific discovery which happens to come from India. . . . The TM program does not involve any religious belief or practice—Hindu or oth-erwise. . .
>
> Does TM conflict with any form of religion?
>
> No. People of any religion practice the TM technique. . . .
>
> No change of life style?
>
> There is no need to change in any way to start the TM program. There are no pleasures you must abandon, nor any new traditions you must uphold.[29]

The year 1976 was a shockingly steep fall from grace for the TM move-ment. That year, Maharishi introduced the TM-Sidhi program. The new tech-niques were based on a classic text of Hindu philosophy and practice, the *Yoga Sutras* of Patanjali. The power of this *mantric* practice was such, Maharishi claimed, that accurate performance could result in "Yogic Flying," for example. Although Maharishi maintained that meditation was science moving West, the courts decreed otherwise, stating that Transcendental Meditation was a reli-gion. A New Jersey law court effectively put the brakes on TM's ascendancy in the United States. By declaring TM and its teaching as "religious," the *Malnak v. Yogi* lawsuit stymied Maharishi's attempt to mainstream his technique in the United States as science, and dismantled the TM program's efforts to establish meditation in secondary schools, jails, and to a lesser extent, the workplace, with the support of the American government.[30] Since then, TM has made a comeback of sorts, with some governmental sponsorship of initiation, but I concur with Jerry Jarvis, who told me that he thought this lawsuit was the most significant setback for TM in the United States.[31]

With the courts having declared TM to be a religious practice, the move-ment directed its momentum inward and made a swift retreat to Maharishi's deep Vedic roots. Back in the sixties and early seventies, mainstream TMers had meditated for forty minutes a day and then gone about their normal routine, assured that their chosen path involved no change in lifestyle beyond whatever the person might choose for themselves, in keeping with the rhetoric found in the book by Denniston and McWilliams. By the eighties, it was clear that to *start* the TM program no lifestyle change was required, but to continue along the path to Cosmic Consciousness, numerous new commitments were expected. McWilliams himself later expressed to me deep disappointment in discovering this. Those members who demonstrated enduring interest and commitment to TM became the focus of increasingly intense efforts to translate that commitment into additional consumption, and the product was remarkably authentic Hindu main courses.

RELIGION TURNING EAST AND THE NEW RAAM RAJYA

Signaling the transition from the sciencified to the Vedicized, the standard Science of Creative Intelligence program popularized in the late sixties and early seventies was melded in the late seventies and eighties with new theories based squarely on the Vedas, the traditional Hindu core of Sanskrit scriptures. Dedicated Western disciples of Maharishi were taught to adopt the cultural warrants, religious markers, and deep philosophy of Advaita Vedanta to secure the highest promises of TM.

But for the careful consumer, this shift could have been predicted by reading Maharishi's earlier writings. In the preface to his work on the *Bhagavad Gita*, Maharishi claimed Shankara was misunderstood; people mistakenly thought him to be nondevotional, but Shankara's principle of devotion is founded on transcendental consciousness. Indeed, both knowledge and devotion find their fulfillment on the "fertile field of transcendental consciousness,"[32] or *samadhi*. Direct experience, Maharishi insisted, was the starting point to inculcate virtue. Thus, the TM technique, which leads to the direct experience of *samadhi*, is a first step; through its ongoing practice, the disciple progresses into greater embodiment of Vedic virtues.

Maharishi's Vedic Science sought to provide the eager devotee with a fuller range of human knowledge, restored and re-enlivened from Maharishi's wisdom gleaned from Brahmananda Saraswati's teaching of the Vedas: healing and "long life" (*ayur*), classical Indian music (*gandharva*), astrology (*jyotish*), building design (*sthapatya*), and ritual (*yagya*).[33] New programs emerging from a "Vedic University" became extremely popular.

As early as 1955, Maharishi had claimed India to be the source of a superior "science of the soul." The new forms of ancient "science" were none other than common features of Indian life that have been routinely categorized as "Hindu" practices: secret techniques to become "flying" Sidhas; food supplements and expensive *ayur-veda* treatments; strict diets according to diagnosed body types; "life supporting" music dictated by *gandharva veda*; dwellings built in accord with *sthapatya veda*; *jyotish* astrological consultations, and *yagyas* performed out of sight by priests to avoid calamity. In the nineties, the Maharishi Yoga SM Program emerged, presaged years earlier by a booklet of postures (*asanas*) compiled by Arthur Granville. Just one decade after the Merv Wave of 1975, the TM movement had been utterly transformed from offering an easy "technique" to offering a full range of components of an idealized Hindu lifestyle. Knowledge borne of TM's *samadhi* was quickly stepping into practical life under Maharishi's constant direction.

Care is necessary, for at any moment, a disciple could take a wrong turn, of course, and Maharishi vigorously sought to preserve the purity of the teaching. In just one instance of this preservation, he prohibited interaction with the TM apostate Deepak Chopra. In happier days, Maharishi referred to Chopra publicly as "Dhanvantari of Heaven on Earth," a heavily symbolic title ennobling Chopra as well as Maharishi and his minions.[34] Their famous falling-out led to Chopra's uprooting himself and his herbs from cold-hearted Boston and replanting both in a tiny and tony San Diego suburb. With the takeoff of his bestseller, *Ageless Body, Timeless Mind*, Chopra and his operations threatened the well-being of his former guru's business world.[35]

The success of Chopra did not go unanswered by TM officials. On July 16, 1993, the "Maharishi National Council of the Age of Enlightenment" wrote to all TM centers in the United States. Not only had Deepak Chopra left the movement but, "Dr. Chopra has said that the Centers, Governors, Teachers, Sidhas and Meditators 'should ignore him and not try to contact him or promote him in any way.'"[36] The council went on to say,

> Accordingly, we should discontinue promoting him, his courses, tapes and books (including *Creating Health, Return of the Rishi, Perfect Health, Quantum Healing, Unconditional Life*, etc.). Since he is no longer affiliated with our Movement in any way, if you happen to hear that Dr. Chopra is coming to your area to lecture you should in no way try to contact him or organize for him. This is extremely important for the purity of the teaching.
>
> The pure and complete knowledge of Maharishi Ayur-Ved will now be available to the whole population in the United States and Canada through the courses Maharishi is preparing. . .

Two weeks later, Dr. Chopra wrote a letter to dispel "rumors and misunderstandings." "I am not really sure what is meant when people ask me if I've left the Movement," he wrote. "I still practice TM and the Sidhis, and will continue to recommend them and refer people to the Centers and Clinics." He said he would be pleased to hear from anyone "who feels the need or desire to contact me."[37] Chopra now provides Ayur Vedic procedures through his own seminars and institution (La Jolla's Chopra Center for Well Being), offers his own Primordial Sound Meditation, and sells his own food supplements, "all at former students' requests," and at a considerably lower price than correlative Maharishi Ayur-Ved products.

This issue over Maharishi's monopoly of spiritual services mirrors a commercial tradition most Americans would recognize: supposed "quality control issues" in a franchiser/franchisee relationship. McDonald's, for example, requires its franchises to order food products and paper goods solely through their parent company. Maharishi also requires his franchisees—teachers, meditators, and governors, and so on—to use his products, and his alone. Indeed, he even requires his teachers to sign statements of loyalty—a contract—to him. He has gone to court to protect his trademarked wares and monopoly rights, which extend to the mantras used in TM—all of which can be found in a standard *mantrakosha*, or "treasury of mantras."

Yet to compete against incursions into his domain, ostensibly "to ensure the purity of the teaching," Maharishi deftly offers counter-products should competitive teachings or spiritual products arise. To counter Chopra's "Primordial Sound Meditation," Maharishi offers Maharishi Vedic Vibration Technology, a competing service that promises "to awaken the body's own intelligence" to relieve chronic disorders.

Might Maharishi's strategies function as a kind of "product differentiation"—that is, does his insistence on only Maharishi-approved products help his line of wares be perceived as higher quality, even if no real difference exists? In their literature, Maharishi's companies make explicit claims that only his products are truly superior and can meet the needs of the spiritually savvy consumer. Are competing products, such as the meditative techniques passed down by other disciples of Guru Dev and renegade teachers such as Deepak Chopra and Shri Ravi Shankar, for example, capable of achieving similar effects? Are these measures to assure quality—the purity of the Teaching or the Big Mac or Amrit Kalash—or is it a marketing ploy to make additional profit selling the goods that are prescribed as necessary components?

During the *Malnak v. Yogi* crisis, a two-page memorandum was sent to "All Departments" by Lenny Goldman regarding the "proper use of term: Transcendental Meditation." Goldman describes how the World Plan Executive Council (WPEC) was in the process of seeking to register as "service marks" in all countries around the world all terms identifying movement activities, such as Transcendental Meditation, Science of Creative Intelligence, TM, and SCI. The success of registration applications depended on their proper use; accordingly, he describes a service mark as "a word, phrase, or design which distinguishes the source of a particular service from other sources." By associating these terms with WPEC's services, he continues, people enrolling in programs can be assured they come from the same source. This recognition, he explains, serves the following important functions: "1) It helps and protects the public; a) by distinguising [sic] our services from others so that people make easy and accurate choices; and b) by serving as a guarantee of consistent quality. 2) It helps us to advertise our services."[38]

While it is tempting to ascribe a mundane and cynical motive to this, a philosophical warrant exists in support of this strategy. One cannot simply heed the Self and one's own assessment of goods and services in lieu of a Master's discretion, as the Elite Hindu or New Ager might feel empowered. Whereas before the mid-seventies "Guru Dev" was on every TMer's lips, the emphasis shifted so that virtually everything Maharishi touched bore his name: it is Maharishi who can determine appropriate goods and services.[39]

Even for those who accepted their teacher's authority to decree what to buy and what to do, by the 1980s Maharishi had created so many structures to support his ambitious goals that he was unable to spend personal attention on each organization, including MIU and the American TM hierarchy. According to interviews with former TMers who remained loyal through the implementing of the *sidhis*, the primary reasons for attrition were not just the launching of so many new programs and products, or the insistence on loyalty to Maharishi alone, but the rise of bureaucratic authoritarianism that developed in the eighties—characterized by a by-the-book ethos, and disavowal of criticism. In the development of his hierarchy, Maharishi implemented a patriarchal order, which—while not a caste system per se—preserved the Hindu concept of some people being more "advanced" than others, based on notions of karma and spiritual attainment. The American bureaucrats encouraged bizarre titles and jargon, favoritism and divisiveness. By the nineties, waves of meditators had left the TM movement.

Technological innovation led to what I term "High Tech Unstressing," playing on the word Maharishi uses to describe complaints or manifestations of dissatisfaction that are "natural" outcroppings of the meditation process.[40] Simply put, legions of former TMers have taken to the World Wide Web to "unstress"—they point out numerous discrepancies between what they were initially taught and what they later came to learn. Maharishi's attempt to put the Veda in the words of Western science and only gradually reveal ultimate truth (however neatly that coheres with his philosophy of teaching Advaita and yoga) not only failed to convince most Elite Hindus whom he attracted, but led to direct accusations of fraud.

Such charges are exacerbated by current developments, which are openly lampooned on sites by former TMers. Not content with providing the individual with a panoply of Vedic tools for mere self-transformation, in 1992 Maharishi helped create a full-fledged political entity called the Natural Law Party, which aims to achieve world transformation. Fueling the party rhetoric are premises about the universe, mankind, and social relations that have traditionally been labeled "Hindu," but which are promoted by the party in the United States and other Western countries as secularized "natural law."

Yet comparing documents written in English and in the Hindi language, the party rhetoric has a profoundly different flavor when tasted in India. There, the Indian corollary to the "Natural Law Party"—the *Ajeya* or "unconquerable" *Bharat* "India" Party—makes no pretense about its intentions: jettisoning "alien education, alien medicine, alien defense, alien economics, alien foreign policy, and alien laws," and urging the success of the "Indianization of India." The Ajeya Bharat Party's mission is to promote and create a state grounded in knowledge of the laws of *prakriti,* the Hindu concept of materiality or "nature."

Even the establishment of a political party in more than eighty countries in the 1990s did not satisfy Maharishi, who could not wait for the Natural Law Party, in all its various incarnations, to work through all of the world government's permutations to fulfill his ambition of Raam Rajya—the idyllic rule of the great mythic god-king, Raam, which is the true heritage of India:

> Motivated by the persistent failure of national administrations throughout human history, and the pressing need for a more effective system of administration, on the 7th of October, 2000, Maharishi inaugurated the Global Country of World Peace. The Global Country of World Peace, founded upon the discovery of the Constitution of the Universe, is offering the complete science and practical programs to achieve perfection in administration—problem-free government—in every nation.[41]

The "sovereign ruler," "King," or "Raja" of this utopia is "Dr. Raja Raam Nader." "His Majesty" Nader, born Anthony Nader, is credited as "the world's foremost neuroscientist, who discovered that the human physiology is a direct, material reflection of the field of consciousness, the field traditionally known as Veda, which in the language of modern physics is the Unified Field of all the Laws of Nature."[42] The significance of this discovery is that "through proper education, every individual can have direct access to the Unified Field—the source of all the laws of nature governing the Universe—in the simplest form of human awareness."[43] And most crucially, "Access to this Unified Field brings mastery over Natural Law, his majesty has been credited with saying, remarkably in unison with Maharishi's original theses in South India over forty years earlier."[44] Protected by an "invincible shield" created by the sustained protective meditation of thousands of "yogic flyers," this new world order exists by virtue of Maharishi's decree, and is maintained by his followers through their shared willingness to believe.

And yet, when all is said and done, even the perfectly managed Global Country of World Peace cannot operate on faith alone, which is why Maharishi proclaimed the theme of the year 2002 to be "the launch of a truly global currency—the Raam. This currency is designed to play an integral role in Maharishi's global programme to remove poverty from the poorest nations of the world, and help restore the dignity of self-sufficiency and sovereignty for every nation, while taking the world economy out of the grip of capitalism."[45] TM followers are urged to become citizens of this new country, and support its aims with their donations and currency conversions. Clearly, TM has come a long way since its heyday as a program of chanting a meaningless sound to get better grades and less stress.

CONCLUSIONS

Contrary to Sai Baba, who moved from the particulars of Hindu/Indian religion to a more universalist stance, Maharishi began with a universalist stance, rooted in the technique of *samadhi* through Transcendental Meditation, and has moved to an ever more particularist stance, gradually imbedding the Hindu/Vedic religion year by year as successive unveilings of the most accurate vision of true religion, allowing knowledge to step into practical life.

Specific segments of TM organizations were able to exploit the American predilection for self-help and self-improvement schemes by promoting TM to students and business people as a means to reduce tension and increase productivity, rather than as a Hindu spiritual movement with its attendant baggage. A hybrid of Eastern and Western sensibilities, the American TM package predating the mid-1970s focused on meditation and its attendant promises of self-fulfillment, shorn of any residue of undue spiritualism, just as Import Elite Buddhism is noteworthy in its "scanting" of other aspects of traditional Buddhism. In the 1960s, Maharishi claimed TM improved relationships, job performance, beauty, and spirituality. He declared his method to be perennial, transcultural. He argued that anyone, espousing any religion, would benefit from his "technology" of mantra. Maharishi promised a better way and even dared to found "Capitals of the Age of Enlightenment." TM was supported by personal experience and, since the early seventies, empiricism and numerous scientific studies.

But the TM Movement did not end as this form of Elite Hinduism, cousin of the New Age. In the mid-seventies, Maharishi began training senior staff in advanced techniques. By 1977, Maharishi officially focused his attention on more advanced groups of people who underwent TM-Sidhi techniques. With the advent of the Sidhis and his lofty World Plan programs, Maharishi changed the rules of his own game, even the playing field itself. He still claimed empirical support for his product and theories, but gradually he incorporated many facets commonly understood as "Hinduism," distinguished from the old, unimproved Vedic wisdom by his unique spellings and trademarks. In this sense, the TM Movement that evolved into Maharishi's later programs resembles an even more ethnic Hinduism than that which he first exported: Not only is it Hinduism, but it is a specific incorporated brand of Hinduism.

Defying the New Age embrace of sexuality, Maharishi urged favored followers to practice chastity and suggested the preferable path of becoming a celibate monk or nun. He incorporated Indian cultural habits, "baggage" ranging from dressing in specific colors, speaking in certain ways, reading only accepted books, avoiding certain astrological occurrences, and avoiding inauspicious architectural design. And despite New Age deemphasis of devotionalism, he prohibited free choice in "guru-shopping," insisting that followers either love him or leave him.

This transition from a nondevotional, meditation-based Import Hinduism to a full-blown example of baggage-laden Export Hinduism is at the heart of the controversies swirling around Maharishi. Maharishi's initial insistence on TM's nonreligiosity or Hindu character has led to charges of deception and hypocrisy. Since Maharishi refuses to label his transformed movement a religion, much less Hinduism, those involved are faced with cognitive dissonance. When is a path to enlightenment, which sponsors rituals to deities and is based on meditation that deploys the names of gods, not a religion? When is a "great seer"—a "*maharishi*"—and an adept of *yoga*—a "*yogi*"—who greets people with salutations of "*jai guru dev,*" and insists on disciples' loyalty to him alone, not a "guru" himself?

While New Agers may purchase Maharishi's trademarked products, his full package deal is not an example of the New Age, however he might play on popular Aquarian sensibilities. Maharishi has created a trademarked method which he claims reaches Absolute Being—one that is the very antithesis of New Age Religion as it is most commonly understood. Maharishi requires all individual experience to be interpreted through the Advaitin belief system he provides. Thus, despite declaring his insights to be "perennial," "primordial," timeless truth accessible to each person, for Maharishi the perennial truth is fundamentally Vedic. Through his insistence on Vedic visions—painstakingly linking every major Advaitin interpretation to modern science by sophisticated if strained analogies—Maharishi aligns his system closely to the nineteenth-century Romantic dependence on cosmologies, again rejecting New Age reflections of a specific truth, and Elite Hinduism's privileging of individual experience.

To sustain the purity of his teaching, Maharishi has not contested traditional guru credentials. Rather, in the United States, Maharishi has asserted his own imaginative state of law, and fought over who has the right to use and interpret the Advaitin *products* and *services* he provides. He asserts that they are scientific "techniques" he has discovered, yet elsewhere he has suggested they are indeed invocations to deities, preserving distinct insider/outsider frames.

In shaping his movement in this way, Maharishi succeeds in drawing on New Age sensibilities without giving in to its least attractive and nonremunerative features: loss of authority for the guru, decentralizing Hindu thought, promiscuous spiritual eclecticism, and bliss-hopping. Thousands of New Agers fly all over the spiritual garden, picking up Zen techniques here, Hindu mantras there; they drop in on a self-actualization session of a new Master here, alight on a Wiccan empowerment ritual over there, and gobble up the latest pop psychology bestseller. Eventually, the eclectic New Ager exudes her own sweet bliss—streaming rivulets of nectar, drawn from the pollen of countless, seemingly unrelated, but ultimately interconnected blossoms. But Maharishi sees a danger in all this: it is but saccharine "mood-making."[46] The vision from such rampant eclecticism is a fractured image of Self, not a holistic microcosm. Thus, although echoing the perennialism and universalism of Hindu Renaissance Vedantic forbears, Maharishi clamps down on cross-pollination, insisting on brand loyalty to produce a trademarked Transcendental consciousness firmly rooted in the exported soil of Mother India.

The Transcendental Meditation Movement in America has meandered. First appearing as a plastic export Hinduism, it quickly segued into an Import, a nondevotional form of meditation marketed as a "scientific technique," only to morph again into a full-fledged incarnation of a multinational, capitalist Vedantic Export Religion. Playing on themes of universal Vedic wisdom and the primacy of personal experience first introduced to the West during the Hindu Renaissance, Maharishi appropriates the idiom of Western intellectualism and situates his movement as science and even "natural law," whereas to Indians, he boldly affirms his movement to be "Vedic Science."

Contrary to other contemporary gurus such as Sai Baba, whom Norris Palmer shows moved from the particulars of Hindu/Indian religion to a more universalist stance, TM has zigzagged back and forth depending on the audience's receptivity. Maharishi's strategy, while appealing to some, is at the root of many practitioners' dissatisfaction with the new and improved TM Movement, for although there are philosophical warrants to support such skillful application of teaching to meet the needs and circumstances of the adherent, such an approach is fundamentally at odds with a core American value: full and honest disclosure up front.[47] Many of those who bought into the program as a type of Import Hinduism felt deceived when ultimately faced with Maharishi's true end: exporting not just a mantric technique, but a religion, a lifestyle, a political ideology, all to buttress an alternative utopian world, indeed, Maharishi's own Global Country of World Peace, whose citizens are expected to accept not just his trademarked brand of TM, but his "Cosmic Constitution" rooted in a Natural Law he himself has adjudicated, and exchange their dollars or sterling for the divine currency.

This twenty-first-century Hindu leader only selectively bestows Vedantic wisdom to Westerners, and for a price at each step. Further, he picks and chooses which aspects of Western thought he wishes to appropriate as examples of what he deems to be in keeping with universal religion (*sanatana dharma*), consistently privileging the Indic over the Western. Maharishi has cleverly adapted strategies with a specific ultimate goal: to preserve the proud teachings of his guru, Brahmananda Saraswati. That great nineteenth-century *Shankaracharya* once exhorted his Indian devotees:

> Remember that you are the descendant of those *maharishis* who could do anything in *samsara.* Yet even though you descend from those who could create another world themselves at will,[48] you are now surrounded on all four sides by misery and lack of peace. If you have forgotten the treasure that is hidden in your own house, then you can only go begging from door to door.
>
> What a shame it would be were a tiger to join a herd of sheep, start bleating, "baa, baa,"[49] and then begin thinking he was actually happy. In the same way, what a great fall if a citizen of Bharat (India) forgets his own ancient spiritual and divine heritage, and starts thinking that happiness and contentment comes from obtaining worldly things such as superficial words, touch, form, taste, and smell.
>
> To become powerful, recall the examples of your forefathers. Enter the shelter of the omnipotent controller of creation. Develop your spiritual powers. Earn the authoritative power over the creative principle of the controller of creation. Only then can you become powerful in reality, and a firm, powerful force. Remain convinced that even today you can be a knower of past, present, and future, and you can make all the elements and powers of the universe favorable to you. Your birth took place in Bharata. Unlimited powers reside within you. Strive to manifest them and become powerful, with head held high.[50]

True to this mandate, Mahesh Varma has never forgotten his legacy as a descendent of the indomitable *maharishis*. In his fifth decade of teaching, drawing on the powers within himself, Maharishi Mahesh Yogi has succeeded in creating another world at his will, and he continues to exalt Bharat's ancient spiritual and divine heritage to all.

NOTES

1. The following terms used in this chapter are some of the many registered or common law trademarks and service marks licensed to Maharishi Vedic Education Development Corporation and used under its sublicense: ®Transcendental Meditation, TM, TM-Sidhi, Maharishi Ayur-Veda, Maharishi Ayurveda, Science of Creative Intelligence, Maharishi, Maharishi Sthapatya Veda, Maharishi Yoga, Maharishi Yagya, Maharishi Vedic Astrology, Maharishi Jyotish, Maharishi Gandharva Veda, Maharishi Vedic Vibration Technology, Maharishi University of Management, Maharishi Purusha, Purusha, Mother Divine, Maharishi Amrit Kalash, Vedic Science, Maharishi Vedic Science, Vastu Vidya, Maharishi Vastu.

2. Paul Heelas, *The New Age Movement: The Celebration of the Self and the Sacralization of Modernity*, 1st ed. (Oxford: Blackwell, 1996), 2.

3. Ibid., 2.

4. Ibid., 68.

5. See Jan Nattier, "Buddhism Comes to Main Street," *Wilson Quarterly* (1997): 72–80. I am grateful to my colleague Dana W. Sawyer for bringing this essay to my attention during the course of our shared research. He and I have spent years discussing the Transcendental Meditation Movement, and it is through his influence that I have turned to its study.

6. Ibid., 75.

7. Ibid., 76.

8. Ibid.

9. *Sidhi* is the specific spelling adopted by Maharishi for the Sanskrit "*siddhi*," designating his specific teachings and programs about the mode of "perfected powers."

10. An excellent record exists of Brahmananda Saraswati's teachings to the laity. Saraswati was a popular speaker and routinely attracted audiences numbering in the tens of thousands. The Jyotir Math staff began to sell thousands of daily copies of transcriptions, titled *Shri Shankaracharya Upadesh (The Teachings of Shri Shankaracharya)*. After his death, some scholars decided to collect some of his transcribed talks into a book, *Shri Shankaracharya Upadeshamrit* or "The Nectar of Shri Shankaracharya's Teachings." This information and all quotes from Brahmananda Saraswati are my original translations from this Hindi source prepared by Ramesvara Prasad Tiwari (Ilahabad: Sri Shankaracharya Sevak Samitim), iii.

11. Tiwari, *Shri Shankaracharya Upadeshamrit*, iii.

12. Personal interview with Jerome Jarvis, August 21, 1998. An almost verbatim variant is attributed to Maharishi in Elsa Dredgemark, *The Way to Maharishi's Himalayas*, 257.

13. Teaching 74, Tiwari, *Shri Shankaracharya Upadeshamrit*, 133. *Vaishyas* are of the "ordinary" merchant/middle class. Oil sellers and liquor merchants are considered less prestigious groups.

14. Viz., *Brahmavidya. Brahman* is the term for the ultimate ground of being, Godhead.

15. Teaching 74, Tiwari, *Shri Shankaracharya Upadeshamrit*, 132–33.

16. Women are also excluded from the title. Teaching 74, Tiwari, *Shri Shankaracharya Upadeshamrit*, 132–33.

17. Compare the published descriptions of meditation for laity attributed to Brahmananda Saraswati: "It is all well and good to perform worship, chanting, and meditation in the early morning each day, but at night before sleep one must without fail do ten to fifteen minutes of chanting one's chosen mantra and meditation on the chosen form of your favorite deity. From this spiritual program comes quick progress. In darkness, with eyes closed, one should sit and repeat one's mantra, after which you should meditate on your chosen deity mentally, still with eyes closed. One should not envision its whole body, but rather its feet or face, feeling that your chosen deity is looking at you with a compassionate and affectionate expression. The chosen one's seeing is itself effective. You should therefore not visualize your chosen deity with its eyes closed. Thus meditating in your heart on your chosen deity, who is looking at you with an

affectionate glance, you should repeat your chosen mantra. From this, fastness for the chosen deity will increase, and if the mind grabs fast onto the chosen one, then at the end, [the deity] will come without fail. On the strength of this [practice], you will cross the ocean of *samsara*." Teaching 48, Tiwari, *Shri Shankaracharya Upadeshamrit*, 84.

18. Bal Brahmachari Mahesh, "The Beacon Light of the Himalayas—The Dawn of the Happy New Era" (Kerala: Adhyatmic Vikas Mandal, 1955). This unpaginated pamphlet is the transcription of Mahesh's speeches in English to the crowds during the festival of October 23–26, 1955. Teaching 74, Tiwari, *Shri Shankaracharya Upadeshamrit*, 132–33.

19. Mahesh, "The Beacon Light of the Himalayas."

20. Ibid.

21. Ibid.

22. Helena and Roland Olson, *His Holiness Maharishi Mahesh Yogi: A Living Saint for the New Millennium*, 1st ed. (Samhita Productions, 1967). This warm account has seen two subsequent editions, the latest of which is published in a special commemorative edition by the couple's daughter, Theresa Olson, currently a faculty member at Maharishi University of Management.

23. Nancy Cooke de Herrera, *Beyond Gurus: A Woman of Many Worlds* (Rupa and Co, 1994).

24. See for example Olson, *His Holiness Maharishi Mahesh Yogi*, 102, recounting Maharishi's need at her home in 1959 for a "dark room where scientists can measure light rays from the glow on the face that comes after practicing the technique." He also purportedly debated scientists on whether his technique was mystical or scientific, leading him to arrange for an electrocardiogram to measure his heart activity. Olson, *His Holiness Maharishi Mahesh Yogi*, 142.

25. Jerry once commented to me offhandedly that he stopped counting how many initiations he had done after having taught TM to five thousand people. He then quickly said he did not intend to brag: Maharishi's message was simply so exciting that people literally lined up to accept initiation.

26. See, for example, Albert Goldman, *The Lives of John Lennon* (New York: William Marrow and Company, Inc.), 273, which recounts that the Beatles attended a lecture by Maharishi, "familiar to Londoners from posters in the underground advertising his book *The Science of Being and the Art of Living*." While the public falling out of several of the Beatles and Maharishi is often reported, little mention is made about the continued positive relationship Maharishi maintained with Paul McCartney and particularly George Harrison, who had played benefit concerts for the Natural Law Party in the 1990s.

27. Jerry Jarvis, personal communication.

28. Academic classes began first in Santa Barbara, California, before the movement purchased Parsons College in Iowa, which became Maharishi International University (MIU). In 1995, MIU officially became Maharishi University of Management.

29. Denise Denniston and Peter McWilliams, *The TM Book*, 19–20.

30. *Malnak v. Yogi*, Appeal from the United States Court for the District of New Jersey. (D.C. Civil Action No. 76-0341).

31. *Is TM a religion?* According to the *Malnak v. Yogi* case, "The teaching of SCI/TM and the Puja are religious in nature, no other inference is permissible or reasonable. . . ." This decision was subsequently upheld: MALNAK v. YOGI, Nos. 78-1568, 78-1882, UNITED STATES COURT OF APPEALS, THIRD CIRCUIT, 592 F.2d. 197, December 11, 1978, Argued, February 2, 1979, Decided. "We agree with the district court's finding that the SCI/TM course was religious in nature. Careful examination of the textbook, the expert testimony elicited, and the uncontested facts concerning the puja convince us that religious activity was involved. . . ."

32. Maharishi Mahesh Yogi, *"Chapters 1–6," Bhagavad-Gita: A New Translation and Commentary with Sanskrit Text* (London: Penguin and Arkana Press, 1990), 14.

33. The specific spelling of "*yagya*" was adopted by the Transcendental Meditation Movement for the word usually transliterated into English as "*yajna*," or sacrifice.

34. In Vedic mythology, Dhanvantari is the name of the physician to the gods themselves.

35. *Ageless Body, Timeless Mind: The Quantum Alternative to Growing Old* (New York: Harmony Books, 1993).

36. It is commonly known in Fairfield that public exposure of one's attendance at an event featuring Ammachi, for instance (a forbidden favorite), is sufficient cause to be ostracized from the Golden Dome meditation halls. Other privileges can also be revoked.

37. Letter dated July 30, 1993. Private collection.

38. Undated memorandum from Lenny Goldman to "All departments." Private collection.

39. For an excellent early essay on TM and the relation between the movement and its "consumers," see Hank Johnston's "The Marketed Social Movement: A Case Study of the Rapid Growth of TM," first published in the *Pacific Sociological Review* 23 (1980): 333–54, and later by the same name in James Richardson, ed., *Money and Power in the New Religions* (Lewiston, NY: Edwin Mellon Press, 1988), 163–83.

40. In the words of the Web site: "Negative consequences resulting from Transcendental Meditation and TM-Sidhi practices are described by Mahesh's TM Organization as 'unstressing' or 'stress release' and are therefore considered by them to be 'beneficial results.'" Available from World Wide Web: (http://www.unstress4less.org).

41. *His Holiness Maharishi Mahesh Yogi.* Available from World Wide Web: (http://www.global-country.org/maharishhi.html).

42. *Parliaments of World Peace to be Inaugurated on June 14, 2001.* Available from World Wide Web: (http://www.global-country.org/press/2001_06_12.html).

43. Ibid.

44. Ibid.

45. *Maharishi Inaugurates 2002 as the Year of His New Global Currency, the Raam, and Proclaims the Onset of a Harmonious, Peaceful World* [online]. Available from World Wide Web: (http://www.global-country.org/press/2002_01_12.html). The website adds helpfully, "One Raam is currently worth 11.0827 Euro."

46. "Mood-making" is a term used to describe wishful thinking by TM adherents not grounded in the direct experience of Transcendental Consciousness. Maharishi's system, founded on true knowledge, is considered the antidote to mood-making.

47. Maharishi wrote, "It has been the misfortune of every great teacher that, while he speaks from his level of consciousness, his followers can only receive his message on their level; and the gulf between the teaching and understanding grows wider with time." *Bhagavad-Gita*, 11.

48. The sage Vishvamitra's creation of an alternative heaven to establish the king Trishanku is one example from Hindu mythology of the awesome power of human seers. Maharishi's creation of his own alternate world, the Global Country of World Peace, has interesting parallels.

49. The onomatopoeic sound in Hindi is "bhen, bhen."

50. Teaching 27, Tiwari, *Shri Shankaracharya Upadeshamrit*, 45–47.

FOUR

KRISHNA AND CULTURE

What Happens When the Lord of Vrindavana Moves to New York City

TAMAL KRISHNA GOSWAMI

AND RAVI M. GUPTA

IMAGINE A SEVENTY-YEAR-OLD SCHOLAR journeying from India aboard a steamship bound for America. His personal effects consist of but a few sets of saffron renunciant's cloth, a pair of white rubber shoes, and forty rupees ("hardly a day's spending money," he would later remark after arriving in New York City). Though asking for alms is a privilege of his calling, he has no intention of begging. Before taking the vow of renunciation (*sannyasa*), he had family, a business, and hailed from a community of Bengali merchants who prospered during the British Raj. But rather than stowing the wares of his former profession, the elderly gentleman carries something far more valuable: three treasure chests filled with sets of his published translations of the *Bhagavata Purana*. Although these volumes are to be both the basis of his mission and the means of his survival, he nevertheless wonders how the West will receive them. Arriving at Boston Harbor on September 17, 1965, and observing the awesome display of material success played out on the American skyline, he composes the following lines:

> My dear Lord Krishna, You are so kind upon this useless soul, but I do not know why You have brought me here. Now You can do whatever You like with me. But I guess You have some business here, otherwise why would You bring me to this terrible place? Most of the population

here is covered by the material modes of ignorance and passion. Absorbed in material life, they think themselves very happy and satisfied, and therefore they have no taste for the transcendental message of Vasudeva [Krishna]. I do not know how they will be able to understand it.[1]

From the moment of his landing, his thoughts tinged with uncertainty, to the establishment of his first temples in the counterculture capitals of New York's Lower East Side and San Francisco's Haight, A. C. Bhaktivedanta Swami focused his mission: to transplant the sacred wisdom of India into the fertile soil of the West. His mission was time-bound, no less by his advanced age than by the growing secularism that had already begun to uproot his motherland's timeworn traditions. If his fledgling attempt succeeded in America, he would not only succeed in transplanting the transcendental message of Vasudeva all over the world, but rekindle the flagging spirit of his own countrymen.

In the decade that followed, Prabhupada—to use the term of respectful address later given to Bhaktivedanta Swami by his disciples—toured the globe continuously, delivering public lectures, initiating disciples, writing books, and managing the missionary activities of the International Society for Krishna Consciousness (ISKCON). He established more than one hundred temples dedicated to Krishna (now increased to over three hundred), including large international centers in Los Angeles, London, Bombay, Vrindavana, and Maya-pur (W. Bengal). Krishna devotees were soon seen in most major cities of the Western world, often singing the Hare Krishna mantra and dancing with jubilant ecstasy in processions down American streets. In 1970, the late George Harrison, long sympathetic to "Eastern" spirituality met devotees in London, helping them to produce, through the Apple label, an album that featured the "Hare Krishna" mantra. The mantra, said to be the most auspicious and effective spiritual help in this turbulent age of discord (*Kali Yuga*), is as follows: "Hare Krishna Hare Krishna, Krishna Krishna Hare Hare, Hare Rama Hare Rama, Rama Rama Hare Hare." The chanting of this mantra—often understood as extolling the limitless beauty of the Godhead—became both the premier spiritual practice of this community and its most identifiable marker. Indeed, Prabhupada's followers became known as *Hare Krishnas*, a title that they wholeheartedly adopted. These converts were enthusiastic, ambitious, and even occasionally aggressive as they sold copies of Prabhupada's *Bhagavata Purana* and *Bhagavad Gita* translations. They practiced an altogether foreign way of life, rising by 4:30 in the morning, wearing flowing saffron robes, and adhering to a diet of vegetarian food ritually offered first to Krishna. This latter practice reinforces the bond between devotees and God, establishing in quite concrete ways the broader Vaishnava truth that we are all fundamentally dependent on God (Vishnu); our food itself is a gift (*prasad*) flowing from divine abundance, graciously returned to the devotees as nourishment for the spirit as well as for the body. Prabhupada's success in transplanting Hindu practices in all their colorful details into a materially prosperous America is often considered a distinguishing feature of his movement.[2]

Yet the very notion of "transplantation" entails more than just the transport of an object from one locale to another. As any gardener can attest, success in transplanting depends as much on the conditions of the new environment as it does on having a healthy and vigorous specimen. The arrival of a plant in a new landscape means that the landscape will be changed, but it also requires the plant to adapt in response to its new environment. The plant's successful survival depends upon its ability to interact with, and adapt itself to, the differences in soil, water, light, and heat.

So also is the case with a cross-cultural transplant. For any institution whose interests are otherworldly, cultural negotiations can be problematic. In this essay, we will explore how A. C. Bhaktivedanta Swami Prabhupada and his followers wrestle with culture as they attempt to "market" their message of Krishna globally. Our interest is in their attitude toward cultural engagement in principle—that is, in the theological resources available to Krishna devotees for cross-cultural engagement. We are also interested in how those resources are utilized in real-life situations requiring cross-cultural encounter. The interface between Krishna and culture can be studied from a variety of disciplinary perspectives; one could, for example, locate the impetus for cultural adaptation in social, political, or economic circumstances. Our method will give primacy to the role of theology in shaping and delimiting the realm of cultural engagement. Theological studies of the Hare Krishna movement are far too few, especially considering the theologically focused nature of Prabhupada's mission to the West.

But first we must ask two simple yet fundamental questions: What is culture? And who is Krishna? At a basic level, the term *culture* refers to the ideas, values, and rules that guide behavior within society. Most culture theorists agree that mental constructs such as beliefs and perceptions are essential to any definition of culture. Clifford Geertz, for example, describes culture as "the fabric of meaning in terms of which human beings interpret their experience and guide their action."[3] What is not so easily decided is whether human behavior and its products should also be included as constituents of culture. Anthropologist Marvin Harris argues strongly for a more inclusive definition of culture, one that "embraces all aspects of social life, including both thought and behavior."[4]

For our purposes, a strictly intellectual understanding of culture would impose too narrow a frame on the colorful collage arising from the interplay of Krishna and culture. In training his young recruits, Prabhupada was as concerned with inculcating them in the proper lifestyle and behavior of a Vaishnava (a devotee of Vishnu or Krishna), as he was with teaching theological truths. Indeed, his disciples' attention to the minutiae of purity laws, dietary rules, and dress codes was crucial to their subsequent acceptance by Hindu communities in India.[5] Doxology, praxis, and their institutional supports went hand in hand in Prabhupada's missionary strategy, all of which profoundly implicate and reinforce a Vaishnava worldview.

The theology of Chaitanya Vaishnavism—the school of devotional Vedanta to which Prabhupada belongs—also favors a broad understanding of culture. This understanding is embedded in the theology at a deep level, for it is inferable from the very nature of the tradition's understanding of the Supreme Deity. Chaitanya Vaishnavism, also known as Gaudiya Vaishnavism due to its Bengali origins, was founded in the fifteenth century by the saint and spiritual teacher Shri Chaitanya, who is considered by the tradition to be an incarnation of God. Chaitanya taught that the singing of Krishna's names is the easiest means of attaining spiritual perfection in this age, and that unmotivated divine love (*prema*) for Krishna is the highest human goal, beyond even liberation (*moksha*).

Although Chaitanya began his movement in Bengal and established his personal headquarters in Orissa, the spiritual center of Gaudiya Vaishnavism is Vrindavana, Krishna's childhood home.[6] For Chaitanya and his followers, God's preeminence does not lie in his majesty, opulence, or power, nor do these awesome attributes provide enough reason to love him. The Supreme Deity is above all the lord of sweetness—a blue-hued cowherd boy who charms his friends and family with his beauty, tender words, and the sound of his flute. According to Chaitanya, this boy Krishna is the basis of the impersonal Brahman described by the *Upanishads*, the luminous Self of the *Yoga Sutra*, the creator of the universe, and the origin of innumerable divinities. Yet he is concerned with only one task—to enjoy relationships of love with his devotees. Every individual has a unique and personal relationship with Krishna—as a servant, friend, parent, or lover. The exemplars of sacred service are the residents of Vrindavana, whose love for Krishna springs not from regard for his majesty, but from spontaneous and adoring attachment. The topmost of these devotees is Radha, Krishna's beloved consort and active potency, who is viewed as utterly inseparable from him.

Krishna possesses infinite energies or potencies, by which he creates, controls, and enjoys all that exists. The energies of God are grouped into three principal categories in a manner unique to this school.[7] The spiritual energy (*chit* or *svarupa shakti*) is Krishna's own internal potency responsible for his abode, associates, and his own form; the material energy (*maya shakti*) is his external energy active in the material world; and the living entity (*jiva shakti*) is his marginal energy located on the borderline between the other two. According to Chaitanya Vaishnavism, Krishna and his energies are inconceivably one and different at the same time, a relationship known technically as *achintyabhedabheda*. Krishna's energies are pervaded by him, coexistent with him, dependent upon him, and controlled by him. They are the source of all the variety and splendor found in both the phenomenal and spiritual worlds, and they are inseparably associated with the Lord. That is, there is no time or place where Krishna exists without his abode, devotees, or attendant paraphernalia.[8] Moreover, the energies of God are dynamic and eventful; they make the spiritual world a realm of activity, relationships, and freshness.

The objective of Chaitanya spirituality is to reestablish a personal relationship with Krishna and recover a primordial, natural service to him. This becomes possible by the careful execution of daily devotional practice (*sadhana*) according to the rules and regulations laid down in scripture. Five types of practice are considered most important for developing this devotional sensibility: associating with devotees, chanting Krishna's name, studying the *Bhagavata Purana*, living in Vrindavana, and worshipping the Deity in the temple.[9] The devotee who faithfully performs these activities gradually awakens his or her dormant love for Krishna and reenters the divine realm of Krishna's pastimes.

Thus, to be consistent with Gaudiya theology, the realm of cultural engagement must be extended in fact beyond temporal existence. Unlike the nondual understanding of Advaita Vedanta, when Gaudiyas speak of liberation they refer to a state of existence that is as culturally specific as any found here in this world. Krishna's land Vrindavana, the cows, the cowherd folk, their dress, foods, language, activities, and so on, all of which are described in texts such as the *Bhagavata Purana*, are considered to be replicas of a transcendent realm existing beyond the mundane world in a space made sacred by a Krishna-centered culture. The importance of this view is seen in quite practical terms: Rural parts of India, especially in Bengal and Braj, are regarded as sacred vestiges of this original spiritual culture.

It is not too difficult, then, to see the challenges that might arise when the message of Krishna is extended globally. For a tradition in which cultural particulars cannot be brushed aside as superficial accretions, the interface between Krishna and other cultures is likely to be an enduring problem. Borrowing from H. Richard Niebuhr's expansion of a similar problematic—that of Christ and culture—we may discover three possible responses to this challenge for Vaishnavas: Krishna *against* culture, Krishna *of* culture, and a third that both distinguishes and affirms the two.

In charting the course of Krishna's move West, we find that Prabhupada and his followers oscillate between these alternatives—sometimes emphasizing opposition to culture, sometimes agreement with it, sometimes both. Apart from the immediate demands of management and missionary strategy, their flexibility has a theological basis. In fact, it has its basis in the same theory of energies that gave rise to the cultural specificity of Chaitanya Vaishnavism. The external energy, *maya*, covers the natural luminosity of the living entities, causing them to forget their relationship with Krishna. This leads to perennial bondage in the cycle of birth and death. Thus, the living entities are admonished not to become entangled in *maya's* illusions, which include humanly created cultural constructs. This gives rise to the rubric, *Krishna against culture*. On the other hand, cultural constructions, fueled by the fire of devotion, conduce to Krishna consciousness becoming eminently useful for sacred service; in this case, the tension is removed, giving rise to the rubric *Krishna of culture*.

This permission, or rather, prescription, to use the phenomenal world in Krishna's service bestows value on human creativity and endeavor, and tempers the world-negating aspects of Vedanta philosophy. This modus operandi is known as *yukta vairagya*, renunciation through proper utilization, or giving up the world by returning it to its proper status as related with God. Prabhupada's guru, Bhaktisiddhanta Sarasvati, who regularly employed modern conveniences to facilitate his mission, championed *yukta vairagya*. He traveled in cars and trains, wore sewn clothing, and sent disciples overseas—activities that were considered taboo for one in the renounced order. In 1935, Bhaktisiddhanta Sarasvati asked Prabhupada (then known as Abhay Charan De) to write books in English and travel to the West, and thus Prabhupada inherited the openness to cultural adaptation that was his guru's trademark.

Prabhupada sometimes compared his task to that of Hanuman, the monkey-hero of the *Ramayana*, whose mission was to reunite Rama with his wife Sita Devi.[10] Just as the terrible Ravana had kidnapped Sita (considered a form of Lakshmi, Goddess of wealth) for his own pleasure, modern civilization was employing wealth that rightfully belonged to God for its own hedonistic aims. The Krishna consciousness movement could reunite Sita and Rama through *yukta vairagya*, by using money, technology, and convenience in Krishna's service.

At other times Prabhupada's approach to cultural encounter was less reconciliatory. In a 1976 address to an international gathering at the birthplace of Chaitanya, in his society's world headquarters in Mayapur, West Bengal, Prabhupada polarized the audience with what he believed to be irreconcilable forces. "[W]e are trying to conquer over the demonic culture with this Vedic culture. . . . If you want to make the human society happy, give them this culture of Krishna consciousness."[11] Prabhupada's "demonic-culture" rhetoric, polarized against his strategy of subcontinental enculturation, must be seen in the context of a century of Hindu reverse-missionary discourse. Thomas Hopkins notes that unlike many exporters of India's spirituality, who made no effort to transport specific cultural markers, Bhaktivedanta Swami was "very, very concerned that the tradition be presented in its fullness, as it became more and more clear that the authentic tradition was irreplaceable, that the cultural tradition out of which Krishna consciousness came was essential to the purpose and practice of Krishna consciousness, and that any attempt to translate it into purely Western cultural terms might only serve to convolute it."[12] Yet in fact, we see more clearly in hindsight what has occurred: Krishna consciousness, beyond its ethnically Indian trappings, has turned out to be crossculturally hybrid.

A visit to any Hare Krishna temple plainly reveals this. Although ISKCON devotees conduct most of their daily liturgy and ritual in Sanskrit or Bengali, English is still the language of choice for interpersonal communication, even within temples in India. In part, this may simply be due to the convenience of using English as a common language in a region where several languages are spoken. But English's privileged status also has to do with Prabhupada's choice of the language for most of his books, public lectures, conversations, and letters. Indeed, disciples who traveled with Prabhupada in India recall that at times he would prefer to deliver a lecture in English for their benefit, even when some in the audience could not understand.[13] Prabhupada saw English as the emerging standard for international communication, and he was ready to adopt it for the purpose of mission.

Another locus of cultural blending in ISKCON is the weekly "Sunday Feast" service, an evening festival that is the main congregational event at many temples. The Sunday Feast began as a "Love Feast" in New York's Lower East Side, but was soon carried to all parts of the ISKCON world and adopted with suitable modifications for local culture. Although Prabhupada taught his disciples how to cook traditional Indian festive food for these events, the menu today varies considerably, depending on geographical location, the talents of the chef, and the preferences of the congregation. Many ISKCON temples are well known for their unique (and delicious) mix of East-West cooking styles and flavors.

To some extent, the cultural blending found within ISKCON is a consequence of the changing demographics of its membership. When Prabhupada arrived in New York in 1965, he "caught the powerful rising tide of what was called the counterculture, which included within its spectrum of concerns a fascination with India and an exceptional openness to exotic, consciousness-expanding spirituality."[14] Prabhupada's first recruits were unlikely leaders of a new institution—paupers, drug addicts, and disillusioned hippies—but Prabhupada cared for them like a father. Since that time, ISKCON has drawn followers from a broader social and ethnic base. The Indian community, in particular, has emerged as a significant presence in temple congregations around the world, providing them with financial stability and a sense of cultural authenticity. This diaspora community brings to the movement its own cultural concerns, as it strives to strike a balance between participation in mainstream society and preservation of cultural identity.

While Hopkins had not foreseen the hybridization of the Hare Krishna movement, he is right to assert that from the start Prabhupada intended little compromise with his host's culture. As he told a well-wishing god brother, he was not going to the West to learn how to use a knife and fork, nor change his dress style, nor alter his beliefs or practices.[15] "My only credit is that I have not changed anything," was a favorite remark, not an uncommon trope in South Asian traditions aiming to conserve a primordial tradition.[16] His transparency, he explained, was like that of a postman, a via media for the message delivered untampered. But as Marilyn Waldman has eloquently argued, expressions of fidelity, continuity, and solidarity with the past are not necessarily indications of stasis.[17] Rediscovery of the old for the purpose of envisioning a new, more ideal order can be a modality of change as much or more intense than radical discontinuity. For tradition, as one Gaudiya scholar defines it, "is a dynamic ongoing process of connecting and reconnecting present with past as it nurtures faithful practitioners in their pursuit of an enriched devotional future."[18] While upholding tradition, Prabhupada saw himself as a revolutionary fighting an age of decadent culture (*Kali Yuga*) by promoting an alternative and soteriologically significant culture. His was a movement of reform and renewal whose appeal lay in helping others uncover their primal consciousness, Krishna consciousness—a movement forward through return, by going "back to Godhead" (the title of ISKCON's bimonthly journal). Indeed, "back to Godhead" intimates this sacred return, a "retrieval" of personal consciousness that has salvific effects here and now.

At the same time, Prabhupada's "traditionalism" could not have been successful had he not made significant accommodations to his host's culture by moving in ways that were radically discontinuous with Gaudiya Vaishnava tradition. We mention two of the most significant here, each obvious instances of Krishna of culture. The first is the role of the guru vis-à-vis the Governing Body Commission or GBC, ISKCON's ultimate management authority. Prabhupada introduced the GBC as an overarching, democratic organizational structure—an institutional safety net of checks and balances—under which the gurus must function. While this can alleviate some of the dangers of what may happen when someone becomes the sole immediate presence of the Divine Will, it has been viewed by some as an institutional intrusion into the spiritual line. The concept of guru on the traditional Indian model is of "an inspired, charismatic, spiritual autocrat, an absolute and autonomously decisive authority, around whom an institution takes shape as the natural extension and embodiment of his charisma."[19] But Prabhupada was acutely aware of the dangers of premature spiritual leadership, and the frailties of human leaders. Thus, he told Tamal Krishna Goswami in 1977 with regard to ISKCON management, "No one of you alone but all of you together." Prabhupada had witnessed his own guru's institution, the Gaudiya Math, break apart into several factions, each led by its own *acharya*, although they had been asked by Bhaktisiddhanta Sarasvati to form a GBC after his demise. Prabhupada attributed the schism to his god brothers' failure to abide by their guru's order.

Fearing the same fate for his own institution, Prabhupada established the Governing Body Commission as early as 1970, four years after incorporating ISKCON. He intended the body to function like the board of directors of a modern corporation. (Incidentally, the name "Governing Body Commission" was the title of the board of directors of the Indian Railways during the British Raj.) At the GBC's first annual meeting in Mayapur, Prabhupada guided the proceedings, "showing how the GBC should strictly follow parliamentary procedure (as set forth in Robert's *Rules of Order*), how proposals should be put forward, discussed, and voted upon . . ."[20] Prabhupada envisioned a management structure that would be strong enough to carry the movement forward without him, and yet simple enough to allow members to remain focused on otherworldly pursuits. In 1972, Prabhupada requested Karandhara Dasa, GBC representative for Western USA, to write on his behalf to all ISKCON temple presidents:

> The formula for ISKCON organization is very simple and can be understood by everyone. The world is divided into twelve zones. For each zone there is one zonal secretary appointed by Shrila Prabhupada. The zonal secretary's duty is to see that the spiritual principles are being upheld in all the temples of the zone. . . . So far the practical management is concerned, that is required, but not that we should become too much absorbed in fancy organization. Our business is spiritual life, so whatever organization needs to be done, the [temple] presidents may handle and take advice and assistance from their GBC representative.[21]

Still, Prabhupada's insistence on creating a governing body was more than just an attempt to ensure his movement's institutional stability. It was also an acknowledgment of the cultural environment in which his institution was operating, and of the need to adapt to its prevailing attitudes toward leadership and authority.

In a letter dated October 13, 1969, prior to the GBC's establishment, Prabhupada wrote Tamal Krishna Goswami:

> I have seen the agenda of your presidents' meeting. This is nice. One thing should be followed, however, as your countrymen are more or less independent spirited and lovers of democracy. So everything should be done very carefully so that their sentiments may not be hurt. According to Sanskrit moral principles, everything has to be acted, taking consideration of the place, audience and time. As far as possible the centers should act freely, but conjointly. They must look forward to the common development.[22]

"Place, audience and time" were also important considerations for Prabhupada in deciding the place of women in his society. Unlike his predecessors, Prabhupada gave women a vital role in his mission. He established women's ashrams, gave women the *Gayatri Mantra* initiation, made them priests in his temples, and counted among them many of his best preachers. In addition to the many ways women contributed, Prabhupada credited his movement's success to their magnetic presence amidst the male members, nearly all of whom, he reasoned, would not have otherwise stayed. Still, orthodox Hindu circles objected to the change in traditional gender roles, and again Prabhupada defended himself by explaining the requirements of the new cultural environment, with special reference to the needs of a missionary movement.

> In this connection, *desha-kala-patra* (the place, the time and the object) should be taken into consideration. Since the European and American boys and girls in our Krishna consciousness movement preach together, less intelligent men criticize that they are mingling without restriction. In Europe and America boys and girls mingle unrestrictedly and have equal rights; therefore it is not possible to completely separate the men from the women. However, we are thoroughly instructing both men and women how to preach, and actually they are preaching wonderfully. Of course, we very strictly prohibit illicit sex. Boys and girls who are not married are not allowed to sleep together or live together, and there are separate arrangements for boys and girls in every temple. *Grihasthas* [householders] live outside the temple, for in the temple we do not allow even husband and wife to live together. The results of this are wonderful. Both men and women are preaching the gospel of Lord Chaitanya Mahaprabhu and Lord Krishna with redoubled strength.[23]

Both management structure and gender roles have been centers of contention in ISKCON since Prabhupada's demise. Much of the tension has revolved around determining the proper application of spiritual principles such as equality, purity, and obedience to divine authority, in the face of varying cultural expectations arising from the mundane contingencies of a global institution. ISKCON has struggled to emulate its founder's balance between fidelity and flexibility, principle and practicality.[24]

Even so, devotees have found themselves at home amid the blend and, sometimes, clash of cultures that is ISKCON. Prabhupada's claim that he was not spreading a religion but a culture is borne out by his followers' conversions.[25] More than individual transformations, their conversions are a reorientation toward culture if not a relocation in culture. It is also a swapping of cultures, or more accurately, a sharing of cultures. This symbiotic, two-way traffic of "old" and "new," of India and the West, makes purchase on the notion of exotic otherness. Klaus Klostermaier describes it paradoxically as "revolutionary conservatism,"[26] and A. L. Herman less appreciatively as "fundamentalist Krishnas."[27]

Few movements that are as Hindu in appearance as ISKCON claim not to be Hindu. Prabhupada manages this by the theological finesse mentioned earlier: claiming the culture of India, Bengal, or Braj, in all its detail to be the historical replica of a transhistorical reality—Krishna's eternal abode. The term

Hinduism, indicating a kind of faith tied to the vicissitudes of an individual or a nation's history, cannot be synonymous with Krishna consciousness or *sanatana dharma*, the constitutional condition of the eternal living entity. By emphasizing the universal, that is, transcultural values present within "Hinduism" while at the same resisting many of its associations, Prabhupada attempts to expose as false the identification with what he saw as a human construct—Hinduism—while affiliating himself with whatever he believed was of lasting value within it.[28] This "acceptance-in-rejection" allows him, for example, to place value in the Hindu social system, especially in the ministerial role of Brahmins, and at the same time reject the notion that such classification is based upon hereditary caste. Prabhupada gave the *Gayatri Mantra* initiation to his Western followers on the conviction that the universal value of good character—embodied in a Brahmin—cannot be limited by its historically narrow application in Hinduism. While devaluation of caste identity has been a characteristic of Gaudiya Vaishnavism since its beginnings,[29] Prabhupada forced the theoretical debate about the possibility of foreign Brahmins into an actual, public concern, by bringing his Western followers to India.[30] As it turns out, in this instance historical Hinduism has moved to realign itself with the transhistorical, for many Indians now see devotees as "legitimate religious specialists,"[31] accepting them in the role of priests, gurus, and pundits.[32]

If, as Prabhupada claimed, his mission was one of cultural conquest, the disquieting metaphor of "warfare" as a modality of mission strikes a sensitive nerve now more than ever before. Perhaps we would all breathe easier if those waging war today would trade their weapons of mass destruction for mantras and books. Nevertheless, we hesitate to speculate how many pedestrians have enjoyed "battling" aggressive Krishna devotees hawking their books at airports and parking lots across America. Devotees are often advised, not so subtly, "Why don't you go back to chanting on the streets?" What needs to be addressed is Prabhupada's motive, as the commander and chief of ISKCON's mission, for pushing book sales relentlessly. Economic reasons aside, Prabhupada inherited from his predecessors the conviction that printing and publishing was the key to the success of the mission. Written specifically for Western audiences, these translations reveal the text, not in isolation, but in the context of the devotional community and its rich history of commentaries and culture. They bridge the enormous gap that separates an audience entirely unfamiliar with Indian culture. Once the cultural context is clear, the theology becomes intelligible.

Prabhupada's writing goes beyond the exegesis and word-for-word gloss that is typical of the Sanskrit commentarial style, for he continually strives to relate the characters and plot of the text to the cultural knowledge bank of his audience. One of innumerable examples can be cited from the first book of the *Bhagavata Purana* (1.13.41), wherein Prabhupada writes, "Beginning from

Brahmaji, the leader of this universe, down to the insignificant ant, all are abiding by the order of the Supreme Lord. . . . Brahma, Shiva, Indra, Chandra, Maharaja Yudhishthira or, in modern history, Napoleon, Akbar, Alexander, Gandhi, Subhash and Nehru all are servants of the Lord, and they are placed in and removed from their respective positions by the supreme will of the Lord. None of them is independent."[33] Here Prabhupada establishes God's independent and unique nature by ruling out the closest contenders for his position amongst the classical pantheon. He then moves, however, from the world of scripture to (relatively) recent history, naming the "world-conquerors" of our own time and culture. This encourages the reader to see herself and her world as part of the same cosmic order that is described in scripture.

The dialectic between Krishna and culture has resonated with diverse audiences. Krishna against culture made sense to the 1960s and '70s counterculture from which most of Prabhupada's early followers came, galvanizing their disaffection with establishment society—its politics, economy, and social structures. The same strategy has struck a harmonious chord within the burgeoning Hindu diaspora who fearfully watch as their and their children's cultural ties to India falter before an unhalting march of globalization and secularity. The ecologically minded, searching for environmental solutions, have found Prabhupada's back-to-basics, rural-life formula appealing. Those reared on *Star Trek* and its spin-offs may have recognized Prabhupada as a fellow traveler when he reads them through the *Bhagavata Purana's* cosmographic imagery, never mind that it flies in the face of mainstream science. Within the Hard Core rock music scene, Straight Edge bands and their admirers turn their backs on hedonism, religiously observing ISKCON's four prohibitions (abstinence from gambling, intoxication, illicit sex, and nonvegetarian foods). Karma, reincarnation, yoga, shaved heads and many other ISKCON beliefs and practices are now widely accepted. In all these culturally alternative models, what begins as Krishna *against* culture becomes Krishna *of* culture.

We have tried in this brief exercise to locate what proves to be Prabhupada's (and by extension ISKCON's) unstable attitude toward Krishna and culture. If the thread of the argument seems never to settle on any one of the three alternatives—Krishna and culture's opposition, agreement, or both—this is because Prabhupada himself remains ever attentive to the principle of utility—a Vaishnava version of "skillful means." At times he demonizes culture, draws the line and warns against crossing it. Then again, he positions Krishna squarely on culture's side. But which culture is he speaking of or against? Modern Western culture and technology are recommended as often as the ancient ways of India; nor does he see them as necessarily opposed. Our conclusion is that he intentionally blurs the divide between Krishna and culture. Indeed, in a tradition that privileges the playful side of God, the shifting play of Krishna and his infinite energies permits the cross-cultural pollination so essential to the success of Prabhupada's mission.

NOTES

Tamal Krishna Goswami died in a car accident in India on March 12, 2002. The editors are grateful that Ravi M. Gupta agreed to complete his mentor and senior colleague's essay, significantly amplifying T. K.'s original submission, but retaining the essay's spirit.

1. Satsvarupa dasa Goswami, Shrila Prabhupada-Lilamrita, Vol. 2, 6 vols. (Los Angeles: Bhaktivedanta Book Trust, 1982–1983), 281. Prabhupada composed this prayer in Bengali verse.

2. See, for example, Thomas J. Hopkins, "Interview with Thomas J. Hopkins," in Stephen J. Gelberg, ed., Hare Krishna, Hare Krishna: Five Distinguished Scholars on the Krishna Movement in the West (New York: Grove Press, 1983).

3. Clifford Geertz, The Interpretation of Cultures (New York: Basic Books, 1973), 144–45.

4. Marvin Harris, Theories of Culture in Postmodern Times (Walnut Creek, CA: Alta Mira Press, 1998), 19.

5. This was especially the case in Vrindavana, Krishna's birthplace, where Prabhupada cautioned his disciples, "In the holy dharma, if one of my disciples drinks from a jug incorrectly and he contaminates that jug, everyone will notice it. Don't be criticized for uncleanliness, or I will be criticized. It is the duty of the disciple to follow these etiquette habits very austerely. I am putting so much energy into this party in India because I want to train you how to live here." S. Goswami, Shrila Prabhupada-Lilamrita, vol. 5, 29–30.

6. Vrindavana is in present day Uttar Pradesh, about ninety miles southeast of Delhi.

7. This distinctive theory of shakti is based upon the Vishnu Purana 6.7.61; for its explanation, see Chaitanya-Caritamrita 2.6.154–61. See also Bhagavad Gita 7. 4–5.

8. One of the essential verses of the Bhagavata Purana (2.9.33) states that the Lord alone existed before the creation. In his commentary, Prabhupada explains that "the Lord alone" means the Lord with his people and paraphernalia. "The Vaikuntha planets [the abode of Krishna] are full of transcendental variegatedness, including the four-handed residents of those planets, with great opulence of wealth and prosperity, and there are even airplanes and other amenities required for high-grade personalities. Therefore the Personality of Godhead exists before the creation, and He exists with all transcendental variegatedness in the Vaikunthalokas. . . . The existence of the Personality of Godhead implies the existence of the Vaikunthalokas, as the existence of a king implies the existence of a kingdom." Prabhupada, Shrimad Bhagavatam, vol. 2 (Los Angeles: Bhaktivedanta Book Trust, 1993), 540–41.

9. See Chaitanya-Caritamrita, "Madhya-Lila" (22.129).

10. See, for example, Prabhupada's commentary on Shrimad Bhagavatam 5.14.24 (vol. 6, 497–98), and Prabhupada, "Lecture in London," (London: 1973) vol. 1, 334.

11. Collected Lectures on Shrimad Bhagavatam, vol. 11 (Los Angeles: Bhaktivedanta Book Trust, 1993), 383.

12. Hopkins, "Interview with Thomas J. Hopkins," 108.

13. See Satsvarupa dasa Goswami, *Prabhupada-Lilamrita,* vol. 1, chap. 9, and volume 5, chap. 37.

14. Robert S. Ellwood, "ISKCON and the Spirituality of the 1960s," in David G. Bromley and Larry D. Shinn, eds., *Krishna Consciousness in the West* (Lewisburg: Bucknell University Press, 1989).

15. Goswami, *Shrila Prabhupada-Lilamrita,* 38.

16. See Francis X. Clooney, S. J., *Seeing Through Texts: Doing Theology Among the Srivaisnavas of South India* (Albany: State University of New York Press, 1996), 253–54. Speaking to the teaching tradition of Shrivaishnavism, Clooney writes that after the fourteenth or fifteenth century, "it became the *ideal* that very little in the way of new insight should ever occur, particularly if it proceeds by a new style or from new presuppositions. Even today, it seems to remain the highest praise of a Shrivaisnava speaker to observe 'He was magnificent, he said nothing new.'"

17. Marilyn Waldman, "Tradition As a Modality of Change: Islamic Examples," *History of Religions* 25 (1986): 318–40.

18. Kenneth Valpey, "A Tremendous Connection: Reflections on Tamal Krishna Goswami's Final Visit to Bhaktivedanta Manor," *Journal of Vaishnava Studies* 11, no. 2 (2003): 157.

19. Ravindra Svarupa Das, "Cleaning House and Cleaning Hearts: Reform and Renewal in ISKCON, Part Two," *ISKCON Communications Journal* 4 (1994): 25.

20. Svarupa Das, "Cleaning House and Cleaning Hearts," 25.

21. Shrila Prabhupada, *Letters from Shrila Prabhupada,* vol. 5 (Culver City: The Vaisnava Institute, 1987), 1966–67.

22. Ibid., 1054.

23. *Shri Chaitanya-Charitamrita,* vol. 1 (Los Angeles: Bhaktivedanta Book Trust, 1996), 685. For more on women in the movement, see Yamuna Devi Dasi, "Women in ISKCON: Presentations to the GBC," *ISKCON Communications Journal* 8, no. 1 (2000).

24. For a bibliography and historical overview of the struggles over authority, education, gender, and theology in the years following Prabhupada's departure, see Tamal Krishna Goswami, "Heresies of Authority and Continuity in the Hare Krishna Movement," *Journal of Vaishnava Studies* 8, no. 1 (1999) and Ravindra Svarupa Dasa, "Cleaning House and Cleaning Hearts." The *ISKCON Communications Journal* is a good source for current discussion on these matters.

25. See, for example, Tamal Krishna Goswami, "Being Hindu in North America: The Experience of a Western Convert," in C. Lamb and D. Bryant, eds., *Religious Conversion: Contemporary Practices and Controversies* (London: Cassell, 1999).

26. "Will India's Past Be America's Future? Reflections on the Caitanya Movement and Its Potentials," *Journal of Asian and African Studies* 15, nos. 1–2 (1980).

27. *A Brief Introduction to Hinduism: Religion, Philosophy, and Ways of Liberation* (Boulder: Westview Press, 1991), 137.

28. For a comprehensive survey of Prabhupada's use of the terms "Hindu" and "Hinduism," see Jan Brzezinski, "What was Srila Prabhupada's Position: The Hare Krsna Movement and Hinduism," *ISKCON Communications Journal* 6, no. 2 (1998).

29. Joseph O'Connell says about pre-nineteenth-century Gaudiya Vaishnavism, "[T]he Vaishnavas in Bengal did not place their religious commitment in the solidarity of the Hindu people, nor in the sacred ideals, if there were such, common to Hindus. Their religious faith was in Krishna, a mode of faith that in principle a non-Hindu could share." See O'Connell, "The Word 'Hindu' in Gaudiya Vaisnava Texts," *Journal of the American Oriental Society* 93, no. 3 (1973): 342.

30. Prabhupada brought his first group of "dancing white elephants" (as he affectionately called his Western disciples) to India in 1970.

31. Charles R. Brooks, "Understanding ISKCON," *ISKCON Communications Journal* 3, no. 2 (1995): 79.

32. This, of course, is not true everywhere; ISKCON devotees (often even those born in India) are not allowed entrance into the Jagannatha temple in Puri, Orissa. For an account of ISKCON's place among Hindus in India, see Charles R. Brooks, *Hare Krishnas in India* (Princeton: Princeton University Press, 1989).

33. Prabhupada, *Shrimad Bhagavatam,* vol. 1, 759.

FIVE

BABA'S WORLD

A Global Guru and His Movement

NORRIS W. PALMER

AMONG DEVOTEES of Bhagavan Shri Satya Sai Baba, a central—perhaps *the* central—belief is that he is God or, more accurately, God-man.[1] He is not simply guru or mahaguru, but the Divine Being *in toto* and an *avatar* of that being as well.[2] The title of one documentary-style devotional video states it simply and unmistakably in the present tense: *God Lives in India*. For the many millions of his followers in India and around the world—many of whom are indeed quite sophisticated—his divinity is self-evident through the miraculous nature of his life and works.[3] By contrast, his critics have alleged that Satya Sai Baba and his followers constitute a scandalous cult, chockful of abuse and deception.

In whatever fashion one understands Satya Sai Baba—God or fraud—he provides an intriguing example of the phenomenon many refer to as *maha-gurus*; that is, gurus with a global reach. The influence of his movement is indeed global and extends in some very surprising ways. The phrase "Love All, Serve All," stitched on the back of countless Hard Rock Café baseball caps, is one of Baba's central slogans. Hard Rock Café co-founder Isaac Tigrett is said to be a highly devoted follower, having given a $20 million donation to help fund one of Baba's hospitals in India.[4] Pop star Michael Jackson is also "reputed to be a follower." Other prominent persons, though not necessarily devotees, are said to have found him worth at least one visit: Fergie (the former Duchess of York), the late John Lennon, the king of Nepal, and some of the most prominent politicians of India (including presidents and prime ministers).[5] "Sai Baba's acolytes include the cream of India's elite. Former Prime

Minister A. B. Vajpayee is a devotee, as is former Prime Minister P.V. Narasimha Rao. A 1993 *Times of India* article counts among the guru's followers 'governors, chief ministers, assorted politicians, business tycoons, newspaper magnates, jurists, sportsmen, academics, and yes, even scientists.'"[6]

In this chapter, I will interpret Bhagavan Shri Satya Sai Baba and his global movement in the manner that most followers do, through the lives of other devotees. I do so for many reasons. First, while a relative few persons have become devotees as a direct result of a personal meeting with Baba (such meetings with him are called "interviews" and are highly cherished), by far most devotees have become so without ever having met him. They are introduced to his life and teachings through other devotees. In many ways, the movement is propagated only to the extent that devotees mediate his presence for others. A second reason for this approach is that it is, after all, only by virtue of his sizable, international following that he is designated "mahaguru" in the first place. There are, by internal count, some 1,200 organized "Sai Centers" in 137-plus countries.[7] In a very real sense, without the intense devotion of this global following, Bhagavan Shri Satya Sai Baba would be of little interest to us, especially in the context of this volume. A third reason to study the accounts of devotees is that most of what is known about him comes from believers. Very little information about him is available from outside that circle and even the foundations underpinning much of that are suspect. In one sense, the observer can *only* know him through the eyes of followers. To this, a fourth (and very practical) reason is added. Much of my research into Baba and his movement is ethnographic, focusing on the ways in which followers' identities are shaped by their devotion. It was after my initial meeting with devotees at the Sai Center in Stockton, California, that I first developed more than a passing, bookish interest in Baba and his movement. The intensity of devotion and quality of people there captivated me and led me to probe more deeply the scope and nature of this movement and what it means to be a devotee of Baba. The material in this essay draws on fieldwork conducted over several years, including participant observation in weekly devotional gatherings and Study Circles, monthly service projects, attendance at significant events in the lives of devotees, and a series of interviews with individual members.[8]

The purpose of this chapter, then, is to help the reader understand the world of Bhagavan Shri Satya Sai Baba and examine various aspects of it in the context of its being a global phenomenon. I begin the study with an examination of "The Nature of Bhagavan" in which I first trace a biography of this mahaguru and then examine aspects of his presumed divinity, closing with a look at the central messages of his teachings. In the second section of the chapter, our focus shifts to the experience of devotees as I provide a glimpse of "Life in Baba's World." Here, I begin by revealing the enchanted world in which devotees live, and I sketch the organizational structure of the movement within which they relate to Baba and one another. In the third section, I share my observations of devotional practices that sustain their faith, and briefly recount the assertions of Baba's critics and how his apologists respond. I conclude by focusing intensely on the self-perception of the devotee and his or her relationship with Satya Sai Baba, revealing that paramount in this godman's religious faith, service to others becomes another vehicle by which devotees of Baba may construct their identity.

THE NATURE OF BHAGAVAN

A LIFE OF BABA

Trying to recount Satya Sai Baba's actual life story and thus situate him firmly within history resists all attempts—hagiographic adulation has never been more complete. All, or nearly all, biographic details have been entirely reinscribed by the faithful. Lawrence Babb once remarked that "the humanly real Satya Sai Baba is not of greatest interest in any case . . . the most interesting Satya Sai Baba, and in a sense the most real too, is the one who is worshipped by his devotees."[9] Given the impenetrability of Baba's actual life history, the following synopsis captures what most of his followers say about him.[10]

Satya Sai Baba, born Satyanarayana Raju, entered this world in the village of Puttaparthi (now in the state of Andhra Pradesh) on November 23, 1926. Legends of Baba's incarnation tell that his birth was accompanied by a variety of great miracles. Musical instruments hanging on the wall of the family home are said to have announced his impending birth by spontaneously bursting into joyous song. Another story, perhaps more indicative of the lore surrounding Baba's birth, recounts that a cobra was mysteriously found under the bedding in the cradle on which the newborn lay—a clear allusion to the serpent bed of Vishnu. Though Baba would not explicitly reveal aspects of his true nature until 1940, signs of it were evident in his childhood and youth, and were retrospectively valorized: He was said to be "unusually intelligent and an instinctive vegetarian," "sympathetic toward the poor and destitute," and "able to materialize food for himself."[11] Though intellectually gifted, he was apparently not a stellar student. Rather than focus on school lessons, he directed his interests and energies in directions more suitable for a budding guru. He was, by all accounts, greatly interested in and apparently skilled in singing and composing devotional songs (bhajans), acting out Hindu mythology, and playfully materializing items for his friends.

While such intense devotion to spiritual endeavors did gain the notice of the more perceptive people around him, it was only following a series of seizures and a miraculous recovery in 1940, at the age of thirteen, that he first claimed to be more than just spiritually precocious. At that time he disclosed his identity as "Sai Baba," the reincarnation of the Maharashtrian Muslim saint, Shirdi Sai Baba, who had died in 1918 and left a sizable following of devotees. The seizures were reportedly caused by the bite of a "big black scorpion [or snake] . . . [a]lthough no scorpion or snake was discovered."[12] While some skeptics have interpreted the lack of a scorpion or snake to mean that the seizures were faked, devotees have underscored this same absence and interpreted it as a sign of divine agency.[13] A long-time member of Baba's inner circle and semiofficial court biographer, N. Kasturi, notes that many in the community, including members of Satyanarayana's own family, did not initially believe him to be the reincarnated Shirdi Sai Baba. In truth, one "officer who was an ardent worshipper of the Muslim recluse" and "was reputed to be well-versed in the lore of Sai Baba of Shirdi," upon examining Satyanarayana "pronounced it as a clear case of mental derangement and advised them to remove Satya to an institution."[14]

This lack of enthusiastic affirmation for the self-proclaimed heir of Shirdi Sai Baba apparently did not greatly bother the developing guru. Such a flat response is later interpreted as an early instance of what would become a consistent theme in response to those who disbelieve: If some human beings do not recognize his true nature, it is pitiable and due to their ignorance, blindness, or faithlessness, for even the forces of nature know and venerate him. Kasturi writes:

> Later, on one Thursday, someone challenged Satya, asking Him, "If you are Sai Baba, show us some proof now!" . . . Baba replied, "Yes, I shall." Then everyone came nearer. "Place in My hands those jasmine flowers," He commanded. It was done. With a quick gesture he threw them on the floor and said, "Look." They saw that the flowers had formed, while falling, the Telugu letters, "S A I B A B A."[15]

The implication, of course, is that the cosmic forces are not simply bending favorably in response to the exertion of his will but rather that the cosmos itself is a continuous and spontaneous declaration of his true nature, available for all who have eyes to see.

Following the 1940 disclosure of his reincarnation, Satya Sai Baba undertook some signature practices of Shirdi Sai Baba's, most notably the materialization and distribution of *vibhuthi*, a sacred ash that followers taste and/or apply to their throats and foreheads (in Shaivite fashion). As with Shirdi Sai Baba's following, *vibhuthi* has become a central symbol among the devotees of Satya Sai Baba who see his granting of it as a great spiritual boon and sign of blessing and protection.

As reports of Baba's miracles circulated and his reputation grew, large crowds began to gather around him seeking miraculous signs both in his cures and in the wide variety of objects he materialized. His main ashram, Prasanthi Nilayam ("Abode of Eternal Peace") at Puttaparthi, was initially built in 1950, and later expanded to accommodate an ever-increasing number of followers. Then, in 1963, a second "disclosure" came when Baba was struck with a seizure similar to those he had experienced in 1940. Hovering between coma and consciousness, he finally revealed that the illness was not his own but rather that of one of his devotees. After announcing that he had taken the illness upon himself in order to save this devotee's life, he then proceeded to effect an instantaneous and complete cure by sprinkling himself with water— a form of cure modeled on a story of Shiva. Satya Sai Baba then revealed another secret: He was not merely the reincarnation of Shirdi Sai Baba, he was the very incarnation of both Shiva and Shakti (Shiva's consort). He also recounted a story in which Shiva had declared "that they [Shiva and Shakti] would take human form . . . thrice: Shiva alone as Shirdi Sai Baba, Shiva and Shakti together at Puttaparthi as Satya Sai Baba, and Shakti alone as Prema Sai, later."[16]

With the 1963 revelation, the fullness of Satya Sai Baba's nature came to be known. He is not only the reincarnation of Shirdi Sai Baba, but an *avatar* of Shiva as well, and, as *avatar*, indeed Shiva himself. While the iconography of Satya Sai Baba most often depicts him as Lord Shiva, he is also seen in the form of many other Hindu gods, notably Vishnu. But the scope and universality of his claim extends far beyond the heavenly court of Hinduism: "In calling upon Baba, no particular Name is essential—Rama, Krishna, Jesus, Allah, Sai, be it any. All Names and Forms being His and His alone."[17] Transcending the boundaries and categories of religious ideologies, he is the deity of every religion. Satya Sai Baba is not only understood to be *a* divine presence; he is *the* Divine Presence.

Though Baba ultimately transcends the bounds of time and space, he is also incarnate within them; that is, he is the God-man, the infinite deity who also preaches a contextual message. As the God of all, he is impartial to all. As incarnate deity, however, his message heavily favors a Hindu outlook based largely on Vedantic paradigms. While each of his three incarnations (Shirdi Sai, Satya Sai, and Prema Sai) constitute what he and his devotees call the "Sai Age," this present life—that of Satya Sai Baba—is devoted to reestablishing Vedic and Shastric religion, and is divided into four phases:

> For the first sixteen years he engaged in playful pranks (*balalilas*), and during the second sixteen years he displayed miracles (*mahimas*). The third sixteen-year period is reserved for teaching (*upadesh*) and further miracles, and the remainder of his life will be devoted to the intensive teaching of spiritual discipline (*sadhana*) to restricted groups. He will die at the age of ninety-six, but his body will stay young until then.[18]

With roughly twenty years remaining for this incarnation, Satya Sai Baba spends most of the year at his main *ashram* in Puttaparthi and devotes himself chiefly to giving *darshan* (blessings of auspicious sights), providing "Divine Discourses" on matters of spiritual concern, and looking after the various public service projects established in his name.

Devotees readily say that if one looks closely into Baba's life and works with an open heart and an open mind, then only one conclusion is possible: Baba is divine, that is, omniscient, omnipresent, omnipotent, and, most importantly, all-loving. I turn now to examine Baba's divine characteristics in the context of a globalizing movement.

BABA KNOWS BEST

Like the 1950s American television series, *Father Knows Best*, devotees believe that Baba, the loving patrician, indeed knows best. He knows everything about each one of us, including what we each need. And, while Swami knows the needs of each, he does not, however, indiscriminately grant the desires of each. To do so would not only be potentially disastrous for the devotee, but would be both an abdication of his responsibility for that devotee as well as a breach of the trust given to him by that devotee. Were Baba to grant every wish, the unquestioned superiority of his discernment would soon be in jeopardy. In a sense, evidence of his divinity rests on his denial of requests. In the eyes of his devotees, apparent capriciousness on Baba's part is all the more confirmation of his divinity. The particular needs, concerns, problems, and so forth, of each devotee will be considered on an individual basis but only within the framework of a picture so grand in scale that its dimensions escape us entirely; we are not capable of taking it all in.

If Baba's understanding of a situation *seems* severely limited or clouded or flatly wrong (as it has at times seemed to be), that is not actually the case. Such instances are simply examples of *lila* (God's play), opportunities that he playfully provides to test the depth of his followers' faith in him. If his actions *seem* to contradict either his teachings or what is in a devotee's best interests, then we simply do not see the whole picture. Indeed, whenever Baba appears either wrong or malevolent, we are the ones with the limited understanding. Embarking on the journey to one's true, divine self—to Self-Realization— begins by acknowledging Swami's omniscience and trusting in his benevolence. Somewhat paradoxically, then, taking responsibility for one's own life begins with handing over the reins to Swami. "When you become more surrendered and detached, you begin to notice . . . [e]verything has its purpose, and it is no longer necessary to understand the reason. You become less selfish, because you realize you are just one of the actors on His stage."[19] As one devotee put it, "Let go, let Baba."

OMNIPRESENCE IN REAL TIME

That Satya Sai Baba is said to be omnipresent is not an astonishing claim for those who accept the statements of his divinity. Baba has, after all, often preached on the truth of advaita, the ultimate non-duality of reality, and to think that Baba is merely *present* to everything that has existed, does now or will exist, is something of an understatement, since he *is* everything. Baba demonstrates his omnipresence most famously through "the 'extracorporeal journey' which he undertakes"[20] to benefit his devotees; it is claimed that Baba periodically leaves his body and travels to the site of a devotee in distress to offer assistance. Baba says, "Wherever I am, whatever I may be doing when the distressed devotee calls, I have to go and give him succor."[21] In addition to Baba's saving devotees from certain calamity, he "often 'leaves' the body, goes to a devotee's side during the last moments of his earthly career, and gives Darshan, the joy of seeing Him in person."[22]

Extracorporeal journeys—or at least the belief in their possibility—greatly extend the range of Baba's influence by increasing his apparent availability to devotees around the world. Baba is capable of personally attending to each member of a global constituency, answering devotees' calls on their first ring, making it unnecessary to visit the ashram, and ensuring that the steadily increasing size of the movement is no hindrance to personal attention.

While this omnipresence makes possible a worldwide audience, it simultaneously risks the decentralization of authority were his presence to remain manifest in intermediaries. For this reason, "Satya Sai Baba is on the record as adamantly condemning instances in which he is said to have possessed devotees (see Kasturi 1975b, 191–92). Satya Sai Baba does not have human mediums, or at least not if he can put a stop to it."[23] In sum, while Baba's omnipresence assures global coverage, his status as the only true, fully realized incarnation of the divine assures that his will be a schism-free movement.

OMNIPOTENCY ON YOUR BEHALF

To devotees, Baba is not only omniscient and omnipresent, but omnipotent as well. In practical terms, this is demonstrated in a variety of ways: He effects countless miracles (cures, materializations, even resurrections), engenders unrivaled service in society (providing free schools, hospitals, water projects, etc.), and continuously reproduces his divine love in the hearts of each of his followers. And while this productivity, *his* efficaciousness in the things of this world, is significant, that's only the portion of his activity visible to us who are limited beings with truncated horizons. He is also said to keep the universe spinning and the flowers blooming; but then what sort of God would he be if these were not also a part of his portfolio? With his powers knowing no limits, devotees see his hand in everything that occurs. In the end, nothing happens unless he has willed it or allowed it to be so.

THE LOVE OF BABA

That Baba is omniscient, omnipresent, and omnipotent would mean very little to devotees were he not also completely benevolent. Kasturi quotes Baba as saying, "I never . . . do a deed without beneficial consequence."[24] Baba has only our best interests at heart. It is this tenet that explains, more than anything else, how it is that the movement continues to expand its ranks in spite of a rising chorus of very alarming accusations about its leader. Trust in Baba's complete benevolence and superior discernment (his omniscience) means that any deed committed by him, no matter how egregious it may appear on the surface of things, is understood to be in one's best interests.

To discuss Swami in terms of his all-pervasive knowing, being, power, and benevolence, while instructive at points, misses something of the poetry of "belonging" to Baba. Yes, he is all of those things, so say his devotees. But, he is also a compassionate God who delights in receiving the adoration of his followers and in returning his blessing upon them in a variety of ways. One central means of grace is through his divine teachings, to which I turn.

LESSONS AT BABA'S LOTUS FEET: BHARAT AND BEYOND

Devotees of Baba seldom claim that his spiritual teachings provide anything radically new; the Eternal Truth has little need of being updated. What they do claim is that his teachings are at once both the fullest possible and most accessible expression of Hinduism while simultaneously being the best distillation of the universal wisdom found in all of the world's major religions. Comments by devotees are revealing in this regard: "Swami takes the most difficult part of the Vedas and makes it easy." "Swami has taken the essence of all religions and put it into the five pillars of human values."

The praiseworthy, if hardly unique, five pillars of human values—truth (*satya*), nonviolence (*ahimsa*), divine love (*prema*), devotional service (*seva*), and right action (*dharma*)—outline the central values of his message. These five values provide the moral foundation of the movement and serve as categories of thought by which devotees sort Swami's voluminous, and often disorderly, body of teachings. In general, this larger body of teachings consists of transcriptions of his Divine Discourses, which are extemporaneous musings, spoken in the Telugu language. These Discourses range over many topics but generally are an amalgam of Hindu (especially Vedantic) ingredients mixed together with idiosyncratic interpretations of material from other religions, seemingly joined together to suit the particular needs of his message on any given day. These two sources of material—Hindu and other—are indicative of the two audiences he seeks to reach: his core following of (primarily Indian) Hindus and a growing number of "overseas" (a.k.a. "Western") devotees.

In the process of addressing these two audiences, the teachings of Satya Sai Baba often seem to pull in contradictory directions; the first toward reenergizing a sense of priority for Indian culture with emphasis on Hindu identity, and the second toward appreciating the universal truths found in all major religions. While these two directions seem incompatible to some, Baba and his devotees see their integration on a higher plane of reality. Baba's earlier teachings were focused more centrally and explicitly through the lens of Hindu thought. More recent expressions have sought to include a wider spectrum of religious perspectives. As the movement expands its global presence and seeks to incorporate increasingly diverse members, it appears that successfully integrating these two directions has become both more important and occasionally more difficult. Let us briefly examine these two bearings.

Bharat

While one may mistakenly gather that Satya Sai Baba is sharing a message of universal acceptance, he is, in essence, calling for a return to Vedic religion. With the heart of his audience historically being Hindu, he seldom finds it necessary to mention that the overwhelming majority of stories, images, and lessons he uses in his teaching are drawn from Hindu texts and traditions. These devotees are well versed in the traditions, knowing their source without it being explicitly stated. When Baba does discuss the origin and character of his material, however, he refers to it as "Indian" rather than "Hindu." But for Baba, to say "Indian" is to say "Hindu"—the two are coterminous realities. In effect, one is truly Indian only to the degree that one embraces the Hindu truth, forever at the core of Indian culture.

> Embodiments of Love: The fundamental principle in the Indian culture is this prayer that everybody in the world should be happy and peaceful. Let no one lead a life of misery and sadness, has been the main principle of the Aryan culture. This Bharat is a sacred land which has been the source of all the spiritual wealth and has shared with the rest of the countries of the world the ethical and moral values. Bharatiyas, nowadays, have forgotten this eternal truth contained in Indian culture and are losing their innate peace by spending their time in this fleeting world which is ephemeral.[25]

In this respect, Baba's sentiments are primordialist. He conflates being Hindu with being Indian and calls for the reassertion of a properly robust Indian—that is, Hindu—identity.

Bharat is a land of plenty. Bharat is a naturally well-endowed country. It is
the primary source of all morality, spirituality and worldly wisdom. . . . To
regard such a sacred land as a poor country is madness. We are not a destitute nation. It is a richly endowed country. If this had not been a
wealthy country, why did the Mughals, the Europeans and others invade
this country? . . . Everything originated from Bharat. Hence, having taken
birth in Bharat, strive to promote the glory of Bharat. Every devotee
should take a pledge to protect and promote the greatness of Bharat.[26]

This strand of Baba's teachings centers on reappropriating and reenergizing
Indian/Hindu culture and traditions to such a degree that Hindu nationalists
often count him as one of their own. They also count on him to energize sympathetic voters and deliver them to the polls. A strong proponent of "Indian"
superiority, Satya Sai Baba's influence has become dominant in state and
regional politics and of real significance in national contests as well. Prime
Minister Atal Bihari Vajpayee was among his devotees who, having embraced
him, in turn, found support among his followers.

In a number of discourses he has declared, "'Yanna bharathe, thanna
bharatha' is an old saying. What is not Indian is not knowledge; all knowledge
is the domain of the Indian intellect."[27] It is this understanding that India is the
source of all spiritual truth that makes possible his inclusion of other religious
outlooks, which are merely variations of Hindu themes and, as such, are both
congruent with Hinduism and appropriately incorporated within it.

Beyond Bharat

While Baba's teachings are firmly rooted in the texts and traditions of Hinduism, his audience and his message increasingly extend far beyond Bharat. In
an effort to reach this expanding congregation, he increasingly professes a kind
of universalism that would seem to embrace all religions equally. "Let the different faiths exist, let them flourish, and let the glory of God be sung in all the
languages and in a variety of tunes. That should be the Ideal. Respect the differences between the faiths and recognize them as valid as long as they do not
extinguish the flame of unity."[28] As I was told many times by devotees, "You
can be a Christian and follow Baba's teachings. You can be a Muslim and
follow Baba's teachings. It doesn't matter; he only wants you to be a better
Christian, a better Muslim." This movement is not, we are told, intended to be
a new religion. Rather, this is a spiritual movement: "[M]embers of Satya Sai
Centers are united by a common bond—love of God—and a common goal—
spiritual growth. . . . The membership includes people from all walks of life,
and the Center programs are compatible with all the major religions."[29]

This sort of apparent universalism, often famously characterized as "Hindu
tolerance," is also found in one of the logos of the Satya Sai Organization,

which includes symbols of five of the world's religions. Following is the brief description provided on one of the organization's web sites regarding how each of the five symbols is understood in light of Baba's message.

> (1) The Hindu Om: Listen to the primeval *Pranava* (Om) resounding in your heart as well as in the heart of the Universe. (2) The Buddhist wheel: Remember the wheel of cause and consequence, of deed and destiny, and the wheel of *dharma* [righteous action or duty] that rights them all. (3) The Zoroastrian fire symbol: Offer all bitterness in the sacred fire and emerge grand, great, and godly. (4) Islamic crescent and star: Be like the star, which never wavers from the crescent but is fixed in steady faith. (5) Christian cross: Cut the "I" feeling clean across and let your ego die on the cross, to endow on you Eternity.[30]

That the "Hindu Om" is included as one among the other symbols would seem to indicate its place alongside of—rather than above—the others. And, Baba's discourses do, in fact, borrow liberally from other religious voices (often without attribution), most notably Buddhist, Christian, and Muslim, though Taoist and Confucian thought appear as well.

If one were familiar only with his statements underscoring this inclusive nature of the movement, then one could easily believe it to be so. However, as Indian culture is the source of all that exists, it becomes clear that while Baba professes a universality of religious truth, what he offers is a form of acceptance that subsumes difference and particularity into the folds of an ever-absorbent Hindu tradition, a trait found in other groups privileging Advaita Vedanta.[31]

Furthermore, it should be noted that when Baba *seems* to have included, borrowed, or adapted a teaching from another tradition, it is not understood to be the case that he has actually cribbed from that tradition. Rather, as the source of all that exists, he is simply re-presenting in one context something that he previously taught in another.

Religious truth is universal only to the extent that Hinduism is the universal (if unacknowledged) religion. As Bharat "was once the guru of Humanity" and "the preceptor of all nations," all spiritual wisdom may be traced back to Bharat.[32] That Baba is the One God makes it substantially easier for him to promote the unity of religions. Conscious that many potential followers—folks from a variety of religious backgrounds or none—may be put off by joining another religion, the movement is increasingly being referred to as "spiritual" rather than "religious." If one is not turning one's back on the "religion" of one's family, then it is much easier for persons from all religious backgrounds to follow Satya Sai Baba. If all names are ultimately referents for the One True God, then it matters little by which name that God is addressed—Baba will respond.

As the movement has developed into a global phenomenon, it has become increasingly vague about its religious location, and this trend will likely continue. The particulars of differing religious traditions, which feed the movement, have been increasingly stripped away in favor of common elements. As evidenced by the description of the organization's logo, the religious symbols of different traditions are no longer signs pointing in different directions, but rather signs pointing out that all roads lead to the One God who, at present, lives in India.

HIS MOVEMENT: LIFE IN BABA'S WORLD

The claim that Baba is God overdetermines all other aspects of a devotee's life. From worldview to daily practices, Baba is front and center. In this next section, I thus shift my gaze away from Baba and his teachings to peering closely at his world, that is, the world of his devotees. I first look at their worldview, observe the structure of the movement, scrutinize their devotional practices, and briefly give voice to his apologists.

LIVING IN THE MAGIC KINGDOM

That the world experienced by Baba's devotees is enchanted is undeniable. Such was clear to me from my first evening with members of the Sai Center and it is, perhaps, this feature of Baba's devotees that I had the hardest time understanding, or believing. Whenever one member or another would make a comment about Baba's magical deeds, cosmic presence, or miracles, comments that would underscore this view of an enchanted reality, I would wait for someone else in the room to share a furtive wink or nod with me or as if to say, "That's the official line, but you and I know better." I have not yet received that wink or nod. Perhaps the reason I have been looking for that signal is that, for the most part, Baba's devotees, whether in Stockton, in India, or around the world, are not ignorant country bumpkins prone to being easily misled by chicanery and mere sleight of hand. Satya Sai Baba is, or so Lawrence Babb observes, "the premiere deity-saint of India's English-speaking and generally high-caste middle and upper-middle classes" and there is a "cosmopolitan sophistication of his main constituency."[33] This social location of his constituents would seem to stand in stark contrast to the magical worldview that both emanates from Baba and envelops his devotees. For these devotees, however, modernity does not automatically snuff out the magical. Given what elsewhere would appear to be a tension between the modern and the magical, how might we understand their integration within Baba's world?

This "reenchantment of the world"[34] among Baba's followers is perhaps best understood as the reclaiming of an epistemological outlook all but foreclosed by prevailing sensibilities. In one sense, this reenchantment appears to be a naïve throwback; in another, a radical critique of one dominant worldview— a strike against hegemonic forces that have seemingly and inappropriately cleaved all activity by the divine from our experience of the world. Though our actions in this world are important, Baba's are infinitely more so. This magical worldview not only makes possible the inclusion of divine activity but also makes it a central aspect. We need not, after all, make sense of the chaos of the world around us if things cohere at a higher level of reality. With the assurance of Baba's control comes a sense of sure footing in an otherwise rapidly shifting world where little or no solid ground exists; the dizzying and disorienting conditions often associated with rapid globalization make Baba's enchanted world an attractive alternative to those most directly impacted by globalization.

ENTERING A WORLD OF DEVOTION

While studying with one of the priests at the Shiva-Vishnu Temple in Livermore, California, I was introduced to the Patels, a pleasant Indian couple in their mid-seventies, who led me into the world of Bhagavan Shri Satya Sai Baba and the global movement surrounding him (the International Satya Sai Baba Organization), as manifest in its local form at the Stockton Sai Center.

Meeting with God, or Fridays at the Sai Center

On Friday evenings, members and guests of the Stockton Sai Center gather at an upper-middle-class home for devotional singing, study, and fellowship. The evening begins as members pass through the three-car garage and, leaving their shoes, enter the home to greet a small, framed portrait of Baba, which is illuminated in the softly lit hallway by a single votive candle. The temple (*mandir*) in which we gather is just down the hall to the right and is bathed in warm light. An elaborate, permanent altar has been constructed in this large room and at its center is a nearly life-sized, gold-framed color photograph of Bhagavan Shri Satya Sai Baba, bushy afro and all, seated on a maroon, upholstered throne. To the right of Baba's image sits an actual throne in the same design and color but apparently empty. Just below the throne is a pair of silver sandals, festooned with golden flowers, resting on a maroon pillow. To the left of Baba's image is another life-sized image, this one of Shirdi Sai Baba, his previous incarnation. Incense wafts over one-foot-plus tall statues of Krishna and Ganesha at Satya Sai Baba's feet as prerecorded *tabla* (drum) music floats in the air. It is quiet, save the lightly playing music, and the mood is one of reverence. Members are segregated by gender (women on the left, men on the right) and some sit in contemplation or prayer while others thumb through either the devotional program booklet or the hymnbook *(bhajanavali)*. Several of the women arrange the food others have brought as an offering *(prasad)* to place at Baba's feet.

Bhajans

When the clock on the wall to our right sweeps its hands to the appointed hour, the center's president turns slightly and nods to his fourteen-year-old son, who reaches over to a switch on the wall and turns off the piped-in music. At precisely 7:30 p.m. the first breaths of a hand-pumped harmonium, picked up by the expensive amplifiers and voiced through the loudspeakers, will focus the attention of the twenty to forty persons who have gathered and lead us into the evening's program. We begin with intoning the mantra *om* three times and move directly into the recitation of the 108 Names of Bhaga-van Shri Satya Sai Baba. We then continue with more chanting of prayers and invocations and, generally, during this time a few latecomers situate and pre-pare themselves for the period of lively singing, which will last about forty minutes. A small, dry-erase whiteboard near the clock lists the ten names of those who will lead the singing for the evening. The names alternate, male and female. Two microphones on foot-tall stands, one on each side, will be passed among the singers. The vast majority of the songs focus directly on praising Baba as the incarnation of one or another of the Hindu deities, and are in San-skrit, though at least one will be sung in English per Swami's mandate that the local language or dialect be included. Whether in English or Sanskrit, each leader—accompanied by harmonium, *tabla*, and various female members with finger cymbals and tambourines—will sing a single line, wait for devotees to sing that line, and then proceed to the next. As each song is sung through twice in this weaving of single and communal voices, it can take quite a bit of time to work through the ten songs. Those song leaders who find their names in the second half of the list are generally cognizant of the time remaining and will adjust their songs accordingly. As the songs draw to a close, the mood shifts again, this time from spirited singing back to reflective chanting. The *Sarva Dharma Prayer* celebrating the truths of all religions is then chanted. For the first time in fifty minutes, all those assembled rise from the floor. One of the women then performs *arati*, the waving of the *ghee*-fueled lamp, first to the deities represented in the *mandir* (Shirdi Sai Baba, Satya Sai Baba, Ganesha, and Krishna) and then to the devotees. As we sing, we gesture from where we are standing as if to touch the flame and transfer its blessing to our foreheads. When the song ends, we kneel and bow toward Baba, touching our foreheads to the ground, before resuming our cross-legged positions. A Meditation Prayer, sung softly and slowly, sets the tone for a two to five minute silent sit-ting/meditation which is then followed by two petitionary prayers for peace—The Universal Prayer (*Loka Samastha Sukhino Bhavanthu,* "May all the beings in all the worlds be happy!'")—and truth—the *Asathoma* (*Asatho Maa Sad Gamaya*, "From untruth lead me to the Truth").

At this point, having offered praise in prayer, song, and meditation, devotees will receive *vibhuthi,* the sacred ash that Baba materializes for the benefit of his devotees. We sing,

> Paramam Pavithram Baba Vibhuthim
> Paramam Vichithram Leela Vibhuthim
> Paramaartha Ishtaartha Moksha Pradhaanam
> Baba Vibhuthim Idamaashrayaami
> Sacred, Holy and Supreme is Baba's Vibhuthi
> Pouring Forth in Endless Stream—This Play of Vibhuthi
> So Auspicious is Its Might, It Grants Liberation
> Baba's Vibhuthi—Its Power Protects Me

As two youths, each bearing a small urn containing the sacred ash, respectively wind their ways through the seated men and women, we continue singing the *Vibhuthi* Song until every devotee has had opportunity to pinch a small bit of the sacred ash and apply it to his or her throat, tongue, and/or forehead.

The *Gayatri Mantra*, recited three times, followed by chanting *om* three times, ushers in the "thought for the day," which is a brief reading from Shri Satya Sai Baba's teachings narrated by a Sai Spiritual Education Student. Following this, any announcements are made and a brief moment of silence ensues. Devotees rise slowly and form a short queue in front of the empty throne. There, each devotee bows, prays, or prostrates him- or herself as they so choose. Some touch the silver sandals and picture of Baba's feet, while others will simply look at one or the other. In whatever manner each devotee has drawn her or his worship to a close, each will back away in silence from the shrine without turning his or her back to it.

Study Circle

With virtually no break following the *bhajans,* we reassemble in the *mandir* in a large semicircle facing the three shrines. The center's president generally sits at its midpoint, dividing the men and women and, once the photocopied materials have been passed around, we begin by reciting, in unison, the "Prayer for Study Circle" (with a Peace Invocation).

The material we then study falls into one of two categories: Either it is one of Swami's "Divine Discourses" (extemporaneous "conversations" that have been transcribed) or a devotional piece written by a devotee and distributed by one of the various Sai organizations—usually, though not always, the publishing house at Prasanthi Nilayam. The method of study consists of one or another member reading a section aloud (several paragraphs to several pages), and the study leader stopping the proceedings to ask what Swami is "teaching us here." If no one immediately volunteers, the study leader asks a particular member for his or her opinion and folks generally add their agreement, disagreement, or nuance of understanding. Whether reading a Divine Discourse or a devotional piece, members of the Stockton Sai Center first seek to interpret what the author has said, then place it in the context of their previous knowledge of Swami and his teachings, and finally apply it to their lives.

Prasad

Following the conclusion of Study Circle at 9:30 p.m., devotees repair to the kitchen and living room for informal fellowship centered around the taking of *prasad*. *Prasad* is the sanctified portion of the food that has been offered to the deity and, duly blessed or graced by that deity, is subsequently made available to devotees. During this time of fellowship, devotees often chat about upcoming events, news of the day, or catch up with one another. Whether the conversation consists of lighthearted teasing and jocularity, as it most often does, or somber reflection, the *prasad* is always approached with reverence. With respect to the role of *prasad*, "[t]he basic pattern is one in which devotees establish hierarchical intimacy with a deity by taking the deity's leavings as *prasad*."[35] While the devotee's identity is certainly elevated by means of this association with the deity, it is not on a par with the deity. A hierarchical relationship continues in place, though the devotee's status has certainly improved. Members of Sai Centers not only enjoy the fellowship of one another in the partaking of *prasad,* they participate in the being of Baba by doing so.

As the evening winds down around 10:00 p.m., members bid one another "sai ram" and, collecting their shoes, depart into the night air, once again refreshed and renewed by their rendezvous with God. This scene is repeated not only every Friday night at the Sai Center in Stockton, but at various times throughout the week at the 191 Sai Centers in the United States and 1,200 centers around the globe.

ASHRAM LIFE

The largest and most important ashram is Prasanthi Nilayam at Puttaparthi, about 125 kilometers north-by-northeast of Bangalore. Baba spends most of the year here, generally from mid-June through the end of March. April is often spent at Kodai Kanal, the hill station south of Bangalore which serves as another ashram, with May and June being reserved for time at another ashram at Brindavan (in Whitefield, a suburb of Bangalore).

Prasanthi Nilayam—reputed to be the largest Hindu ashram of any denomination or sect in the world—encompasses Baba's personal residence, the fifteen thousand-seat *mandir* in which he provides *darshan*, and the simple housing arrangements, which can accommodate up to ten thousand devotees, but which are only available when Baba is in town. The central offices for both the International Shri Satya Sai Baba Organization and the Shri Satya Sai Central Trust are located here. Numerous facilities associated with the social welfare programs of the movement have been developed, including the Shri Satya Sai Institute of Higher Medical Sciences and the three hundred-bed Super Speciality Hospital, where services have been rendered free of charge since it opened in 1991; the Shri Satya Sai Airport, inaugurated in 1990, it remains quiet except during festivals and celebrations; the Chaitanya Museum based on the life and works of Satya Sai Baba, founded in 2000 as a "Spiritual Museum" of human spiritual evolution; the Shri Satya Sai Hill View Stadium, which hosts annual athletic competitions on Baba's birthday; and a number of educational institutions. With numerous other organizations' facilities located in and around its environs, Puttaparthi is clearly a company village; the local economy is heavily dependent on ashram life, just as the resident community is deeply impacted by it.

The ashram is a holy institution and the thousands who come to congregate on its grounds are asked to observe strict codes of moral conduct. These guidelines include dress codes ("modest, clean, and sober clothing is required at all times"), strictures on socializing with the opposite sex, and regulations that remind devotees that "smoking, gambling, consumption of alcoholic beverages or non-vegetarian food (including eggs), and drugs are strictly forbidden in the *ashram*."[36] The goal of these guidelines is, of course, not to unduly burden devotees, but rather to assure that devotees, to whatever degree possible, are able to focus on developing their *sadhana* (spiritual discipline).

The Focus of the Day

When Swami is in residence at Prasanthi Nilayam, the day revolves around the ritual of morning and afternoon *darshan*, for despite many other spiritual activities, the most important reason why everyone is present on the compound is to catch a glimpse of Baba to receive his divine blessing. Devotees (reported to be as many as twenty to thirty thousand for special celebrations) will wait in queues for much of the day in hopes of being chosen to sit closer to the front of the *mandir* where Swami is more likely to make eye contact, distribute *vibhuthi,* accept their letters, listen to their prayers, or possibly provide words of hope or healing. Though any interchange with Swami, however brief, is deeply cherished, the most highly regarded interactions are the "interviews" that Baba conducts in his private chambers.

Specifics of these interviews are the source of many of the stories that circulate within and around the movement. Stories of healing, materialization, and clairvoyance abound. So, too, the most scandalous transgressions associated

with Satya Sai Baba and his movement are said to have occurred during interviews. While supporters claim that he has cured cancer and materialized price-
less diamond rings for devotees during interviews, some ex-devotees have
accused him of also molesting boys and young men during this time. These
accusations aside, a private audience with Baba continues to be highly prized
by devotees and is considered *the* high point of not only one's visit to the
ashram but also of one's entire life.

After interviews have been completed, Swami returns to the *mandir* where
he is seated on an elaborate throne in order to soak up the prayers of his devotees while *bhajans* are being sung. Following *bhajans* and *arati*, he will often sit
on the veranda of the *mandir* and consult with staff on matters of business. A
second round of *darshan* is normally provided in the late afternoon, around
three o'clock, again followed by *bhajans* and *arati*.

The experience of ashram life functions in important ways in the lives of
all devotees, furnishing an important and inspirational example of how humans
are to dwell together, ever mindful of being in the presence of God. The peace
and harmony of the ashram provides a beacon of hope, a constant reminder to
devotees around the world that if they are willing to "let go and let Baba,"
they, too, will dwell in this peace. The impact of ashram life is due also, in part,
to the sheer magnitude of the institution, especially at Puttaparthi, with beds
for ten thousand and a *mandir* with space for fifteen thousand; if its scale
impresses outsiders, it inspires devotees, who view the massive crowds gathering around Bhagavan as proof of his nature.

TWO ARMS OF GLOBAL COORDINATION:
THE STRUCTURE OF THE MOVEMENT

The two entities generally perceived as being central to much of the movement's coordination are the Shri Satya Sai Central Trust (SSSCT) and the International Satya Sai Baba Organization (ISSBO). I'll briefly examine them here.

The Shri Satya Sai Central Trust

The Shri Satya Sai Central Trust was established as a nonprofit charitable trust
in 1972 by Baba to serve better the needs of society. The Trust is one of the
controlling legal entities of the movement and, in many ways, its locus of
power. It is believed to control the purse strings of the various other organizations and, with a treasury estimated to be somewhere between $1.5 and $2 bil-
lion, its sole trustee—Shri Satya Sai Baba—wields significant power. The Trust
concerns itself mainly with benevolent projects within India and is said to have
established an impressive record in providing education, health care, relief to
the most destitute, and, more recently, potable water to hundreds of thousands,

all without cost to those receiving the benefits. The many institutions in and around Prasanthi Nilayam, mentioned in an earlier section, are representative examples of the interests of the Trust, and projects of a similar nature dot the landscape of southern India.

The International Satya Sai Baba Organization

Apart from the energies of Baba himself, the ISSBO is primarily responsible for propagating Baba's spiritual teachings and for maintaining the infrastructure necessary for a global movement. Located at Prasanthi Nilayam, it coordinates the network of roughly 1,200 Sai Centers worldwide. These centers, active in at least 137 countries, are in many respects the front line when it comes to the Shri Satya Sai Baba movement, especially in terms of its expansion. It is here that devotees meet in the company of kindred souls to pursue their spiritual paths and it is here that Baba's local presence is most often experienced. In many respects, the vitality of the movement is dependent on what happens in the local centers.

Centers are administratively grouped under one of the regions of the country (or continent) in which they are located, and each region has its own officers and activities. In the United States, for example, there are ten regions and 191 active centers coordinated by the Satya Sai Baba Council of America, which was founded in 1975. Only six of the fifty states lack a center, while California is home to the most of any state, with forty centers. Coordinators from fifteen international regions make up the Central Council of the ISSBO, which is directed by Satya Sai Baba and accredits both administrative bodies within regions as well as the local centers.

The energies of the ISSBO—and hence of regional bodies and local centers—are focused primarily along three lines, which are organized around three religious goals: Devotion, Education, and Selfless Service. Centers organize their activities under these three areas with each wing led by a coordinator. The purpose of centers and their activities is both to provide devotees with a place for spiritual growth and to be a blessing in their community.

While all of the centers are required to follow the regulations and guidelines provided by the ISSBO, each individual center will develop its own specific emphases, depending on its particular mix of spiritual aspirants and local cultural influences. At present, considerable energies are being poured into finding ways to make the local centers ever more sensitive to their diverse cultural settings while at the same time maintaining appropriate coherence with the cultural paradigms on which the movement was founded: "The program is adaptable to all countries and diverse cultures, yet its essence remains the same."[37]

In preparation for the 7th World Conference of the International Satya Sai Baba Organization, held at Prasanthi Nilayam in November 2000, the

American Council met in June of that year to discuss and summarize the concerns by devotees of the U.S. Sai Centers. Among other items, that report suggested that the best way to improve the U.S. Sai Centers is to make them more culturally relevant, particularly in regard to devotional practices: "Many people wanted more English devotional songs and fewer Sanskrit *bhajans*. They wanted less ritual (e.g., *arati*, Sanskrit prayers, prostration). And yet, many western devotees thrive on the eastern ways of doing things and would rather not switch styles."[38] In the same report, United States regional leaders were asked to consider the question, "How can the Sai Organization promote Unity in Diversity?" The responses were divided according to the three wings of the organization: education, devotion, and service. Some suggestions were: "separating spirituality from religion, culture, and nationality" and "providing literature demonstrating the unity of all religions—i.e., emphasizing the one-ness of the essential truths of the world's religions."[39]

In the end, centers must preserve a careful balance between being sensitive to the cultural influences around them, on the one hand, while maintaining proper devotion to Baba, on the other hand. In some centers this requirement for balance has meant following Swami's mandate that at every *satsang* at which overseas devotees are present, at least one *bhajan* must be sung in the native tongue of that devotee, and that the spiritual significance of Sai Programs is to be explained in newcomer orientation workshops to ward off the possible appearance of cultism.

It is on this last note—to avoid the appearance of cultism—that I now turn to look briefly at accusations critics have made about Baba and how devotees have answered on his behalf.

OF GODS, FRAUDS, AND LILA: BABA, HIS CRITICS, AND ANSWERING FOR GOD'S MISTAKES

In his "Divine Discourse" delivered on Christmas Day, 2000, Baba himself addressed the presence of conflict, saying, "Some people out of their mean-mindedness are trying to tarnish the image of Sai Baba," and he also refered to modern-day "Judases" who, "easily tempted by money . . . distort the truth, and make false propaganda."[40]

Shri Satya Sai Baba is not without his critics. While a number of detractors see him as little more than a harmless fraud, duping naïve masses by sleight of hand, others have leveled charges against him that are significantly more substantial—money laundering, fraudulent service projects, child molestation, and murder. The truth of these allegations is, much like determining a factual history of Baba's life, neither easily substantiated nor entirely of interest in the context of this study. If Web reports from ex-devotees/victims are credible, a number of legal cases are currently in the investigative stage, and may result in public hearings and/or trials in several countries. As observers also report, given the strong following Baba has among prominent local and national civic leaders in India, it is extremely unlikely that a case against Baba would be heard there or that he would be extradited to face charges elsewhere. And so, we are left with first- and secondhand reports made by disenchanted former devotees.

My paramount concern in this chapter is to discuss the effects of such accusations on devotees, not their veracity. How have devotees integrated these accusations within their worldview, and reconciled them with their understanding of Baba? How have their understandings shaped their identities and the global movement which they constitute? Which categories of understanding do they employ, and which do they avoid?

I have met very few devotees who will even admit the mere *possibility* that something could be awry with either Baba (he is, after all, God) or the Sai Organization in Prasanthi Nilayam, let alone entertain the possibility that something is horribly awry. Devotees of Shri Satya Sai Baba are fiercely loyal and will either discredit the accuser or fall back on one of several arguments, each of which appears to employ the Hindu concept of *lila,* or God's play. *Lila* is invoked both to explain the alleged or apparent misdeeds of Baba and to maintain his perfection in the face of what can only be understood as the critic's limited and naïve understanding of the real situation.

Clearly, the first line of defense is simple denial: "You got the facts wrong." Such devotees cite, in Baba's defense, that those making the claims are ex-devotees and, as such, have an axe to grind. Ex-devotees, they say, are disgruntled simply because Baba did not materialize for them the trinket that they felt they deserved. Similarly, some say that ex-devotees are vindictive because Baba did not favor them with an interview or a position in the inner circle and did not thereby bestow on them the status they felt they deserved. The status of ex-devotees is not reputable, his adherents assert, and in no way is it true that Baba was involved in any sort of sexual misconduct. As one online writer puts it, "Only a week ago, Swami was their all-in-all, and they would never tire of telling wonderful stories about Him. The next week, they're having their Baba rings appraised and saying they don't know what they ever saw in Him."[41] In other words, how can anyone believe such fickle people?

A second line of defense suggests that, while critics may indeed have some of the "facts" correct, they simply do not properly understand the context. Some of Baba's devotees do accept that Baba has had what appear—to the uninitiated—to be sexual encounters, but they deny that this is actually the case. In actuality, what some devotees have mistakenly understood to be sexual interaction is actually Baba's divine, tantric healing of a devotee's unhealthy sexual energy. Arguments supporting this view are often highly detailed and refer to "esoteric" knowledge not readily available to the common layperson. In short, Baba's actions are entirely benevolent and they are healing rather than abusive in nature.

A third argument set out in support of Baba is to admit that while, yes, perhaps some materializations are fraudulent and charges of sexual misconduct are true, the bottom line is: Who are we to pass judgments on God? We are too limited in our perceptions to understand divine actions and to attempt to do so is surely to distort the Truth, and grossly so. God's ways are beyond the feeble understanding of mere mortals. Does God ever really fit into our concepts? In fact, if we could comprehend everything that Baba does, then either we would be God, or Baba would not be God. One could argue that Baba's divinity is maintained, then, by the very fact that he transgresses our ideas of what is or should be holy. Following this logic, the greater the transgression, the more certain his divinity.

At present, the accusations against Baba have had little impact on the growth of his movement. As the movement continues to expand its global presence, however, it is an open question as to whether or not his alleged missteps will prove to be a significant hindrance. On at least one front, Baba has already recognized the potential for that sort of trouble—the Internet.

The ease of communication and accessibility of information associated with the Internet have, in many ways, increased the awareness of the allegations against Baba both within and without the circle of devotees. One evening as Study Circle was just getting under way, a woman mentioned some "troubling news" she had heard about Swami and wondered if anyone else had heard about it as well. She said that a lot of people from all over the world are saying things about Baba on the Internet and that it "doesn't look good for Baba." "Some of them," she continued, "used to be great devotees." No one in the community admitted to having read anything like that on-line. Several members mentioned that lots of people are jealous of Baba and that he is always being criticized. The center's president reported that "Baba has said that he has nothing to do with the Internet and neither should we." Although agreeing with this statement, another gentleman added, "Still, there's a lot of good material about Baba there [on-line]. There're even official Baba Web sites, so I don't think Baba wants us to ignore it completely."

Apparently, local devotees aren't the only ones confused about the role of the Internet in Baba's world. In his October 15, 1999, Dasara Sandesh, Sai Baba speaks about the role of the Internet in spreading "false propaganda" and he asserts that he "has nothing to do with [the] Internet." Moreover, "All the trials and tribulations faced in this world are due to the so-called development in science and technology. It is not technology but it is 'tricknology.' Do not become a slave to such technology. . . . Swami has nothing to do with internet. Not only now, even in future also you should not indulge in such wrong activities."[42] Somewhat confusingly, this statement can be downloaded from an *official* Satya Sai Baba Web site, which is one of the primary modes of disseminating Baba's message to the world.

Swami's comments about the Internet indicate that he is aware of the vast potential it has for rapidly disseminating information, true or false. And, though he has stated that he has nothing to do with it, the amount of information about Sai Baba available on-line is staggering, and both the International Satya Sai Baba Organization and the Shri Satya Sai Central Trust have extensive Web sites. So, too, many regional associations have a significant presence on the Web. The global movement of Shri Satya Sai Baba is now mediated not only by Baba's presence at Prasanthi Nilayam or by the 1,200 Sai Centers around the globe, but by the flow of information on-line as well. The free flow of information via the Internet provides an indication of the degree to which geopolitical borders are meaningless. Yet potential action resulting from this flow of information is contingent on geopolitical borders. Many prominent persons in India are devotees of Satya Sai Baba and he is also instrumental to many politicians in securing votes. Baba is accordingly largely left alone by the government and, therefore, relatively free from prosecution for any alleged offense related over the Internet, which has the twin effects of leaving his detractors angry about lack of due process and his proponents angry about unsubstantiated libel without recourse.

THOUGHTS IN CLOSING

That "God lives in India" is not a conclusion for the many millions of devotees of Bhagavan Shri Satya Sai Baba; it is, rather, a starting point. The belief that Baba is God is ubiquitous among the faithful, and it orients every aspect of their lives, individually and collectively. While theirs is an enchanted world, his followers cannot simply be written off as naïve people; they come from all walks of life and are frequently intelligent, well-placed, and wonderfully gracious people dedicated to improving themselves and the world around them. They organize their identity in terms of their relation to Bhagavan Shri Satya Sai Baba and measure their success in life by the degree to which they live up to his teachings.

As the movement has grown beyond India, it has had to simultaneously reinterpret aspects of its Hindu roots and become increasingly global in perspective; that is, the scope of cultural dynamics it has had to consider has increased dramatically. It has done this in part by valorizing particular aspects of its Hindu foundations—universality and tolerance—in such a way that makes possible both a very strong call to revitalize Indian culture and religion as well as express appreciation for all religious truths. At the heart of Baba's theology, however, is the understanding that all religious truth is a subset of Hindu truth.

The controversies mentioned briefly in the last section of this chapter should serve simply to illustrate how identity is articulated when it is contested. They need and should not distract us from some of the larger truths associated with the movement. The impulse of devotees to improve the world, to offer selfless service to other human beings, is directly derived from Baba's teachings and is one of the primary aspects of devotion I witnessed among members in Stockton. While some have suggested that the amount of actual service rendered by Baba is much less than the amount publicized, from my observation, members of many Sai Centers are exemplary in terms of their service to the community. In a sense, service to others is service to Baba. Service to others, then, becomes another vehicle by which devotees of Baba may construct their religious identity.

In the end, we may say that devotees of Bhagavan Shri Satya Sai Baba overwhelmingly define their sense of self in terms of their relationship with Baba. Certainly, faith in Baba and in the goodness of his intentions ranks among the top aspects of devotees' self-understanding. In addition, willingness on the part of devotees to suspend their own judgments about themselves and about the apparent reality of this world, in favor of Baba's assessment, is central as well. His devotees are beings who find their completion by living *in* him, in Baba. Satya Sai Baba has successfully provided tens of millions of devotees with an invigorated epistemological outlook that allows them to experience an enchanted world, in which they never lose sight of the fact that although their human actions in this world are important, Baba's actions are infinitely more so, and to the extent that they can partake of his being, they clarify, purify, and provide meaning to their own being.

NOTES

1. In an effort to convey the world of Satya Sai Baba as it was conveyed to me by his devotees, I have retained the terms and conventions they regularly use. Many of the terms used by devotees are not gender neutral (e.g., "God-man"). A variety of terms (and spellings) interchangeably refer to Bhagavan Shri Satya Sai Baba: "Baba," "Swami," "Swamiji," and "Bhagavan." Unless otherwise noted, these and other terms refer to Bhagavan Shri Satya Sai Baba. Finally, I have not capitalized the pronouns "he," "his," or "him" when referring to Baba, but when quoting others, I have done so to give the full flavor of their devotional stance.

2. The very name that devotees use reveals a good deal about this twofold nature. He is Bhagavan (God/Lord) Shri (a term of respect) Satya (Truth) Sai Baba. Baba gives the following etymology of the name "Sai Baba." "*Sa* means 'Divine'; *ai* or *ayi* means 'mother' and *Baba* means 'father'. The name indicates the divine mother and father." *Satya Sai Speaks IX* (9 June 1974, 91).

3. Claims about the number of adherents vary widely, ranging somewhere between five and fifty million, with many suggesting a figure between ten and twenty million to be most accurate.

4. Michelle Goldberg, *Untouchable*. Available from World Wide Web: (http://www.salon.com).

5. Tony O' Clery, "Sai Baba's Influence," *David Icke E-Magizine* April 2000.

6. Goldberg, "Untouchable."

7. These are the numbers listed on the International Sai Baba Organization's Web site. Available from World Wide Web: (*http://www.sathyasai.org*/organize/content.htm# SaiOrg).

8. Unless otherwise cited, ethnographic material in this essay is drawn from my field notes.

9. Lawrence Babb, *Redemptive Encounters: Three Modern Styles in the Hindu Tradition* (Berkeley: University of California Press, 1986), 162.

10. My condensed account is taken primarily from two sources: (a) the inexhaustible supply of stories told to me by devotees and (b) the numerous books and documents produced by or in association with the Shri Satya Sai Baba Education Trust, especially N. Kasturi's *The Life of Sri Sathya Sai Baba: American Edition*, 2nd ed. (Bombay, Sri Sathya Sai: Sai Education Foundation, 1971). Kasturi's multipart work, *Satyam, Shivam, Sundaram,* is another excellent resource from an insider's perspective, and Lawrence Babb's *Redemptive Encounters* is an excellent scholarly source from outside the movement.

11. Babb, *Redemptive Encounters*, 162.

12. Kasturi, *The Life of Sri Sathya Sai Baba*, 37.

13. Some interpret the seizures as epileptic rather than divine.

14. Kasturi, *The Life of Sri Sathya Sai Baba*, 47.

15. Ibid., 48.

16. *Satya Sai Speaks III,* 5, 9. He has subsequently let it be known that Prema Sai will be born in Karnataka State.

17. Kasturi, *The Life of Sri Sathya Sai Baba*, 133.

18. Babb, *Redemptive Encounters*, 166.

19. Judy Warner Scher, page 62 in an undated issue of *Sanathana Sarathi,* the monthly magazine published at Prasanthi Nilayam. *Sanathana Sarathi* translates as "Eternal Charioteer" and refers to Krishna's incarnation and his role in guiding Arjuna through difficult times. Kasturi writes, "The word 'Sarathi' is an assurance from Baba that He will guide the seeker if only he takes the initial step of inviting Him to take over the reins of his life." Kasturi, *The Life of Sri Sathya Sai Baba*, 224.

20. Ibid., 219.

21. Ibid., 218.

22. Ibid., 221.

23. Babb, *Redemptive Encounters*, 180–81.

24. Kasturi, *The Life of Sri Sathya Sai Baba,* 196.

25. Sathya Sai Baba in his Divine Discourse of November 17, 1995.

26. *Aum Sri Sai Ram: Indian Culture and Tradition.* Available from World Wide Web: (http://www.srisathyasai.org.in).

27. *Aum Sri Sai Ram,* "Indian Culture and Tradition."

28. *The Logo of the Satha Sai Organizations."* Available from World Wide Web: (http://www.sathyasai.org/logo/logo.htm).

29. Ibid.

30. Ibid.

31. Harold Coward, "Can Religions Live Together in Today's World? Intolerance and Tolerance in Religious Pluralism," in *Pluralism, Tolerance, and Dialogue: Six Studies,* ed. M. Darrol Bryant (Waterloo, Ontario: University of Waterloo Press, 1989).

32. Aum Sri Sai Ram, "Indian Culture and Tradition."

33. Babb, *Redemptive Encounters,* 160 and 178. See also C. J. Fuller, *The Camphor Flame: Popular Hinduism and Society in India* (New Delhi: Penguin Books India, 1992), 177–81.

34. For a helpful discussion of Baba's followers, see Babb's chapter by this title, 176 ff.

35. Babb, *Redemptive Encounters,* 210.

36. Available from World Wide Web: (http://www.sathyasai.org/ashrams/prasanthi/guidelines.html).

37. Sri Sathya Sai Baba of America, *Philosophy of SSEHV,* 2003. Available from World Wide Web: (http://www.ssehvusa.org/phil.html).

38. *Pre-World Conferences, USA Report.* Available from World Wide Web: (http://www.sathyasai.org/organize/content.htm).

39. *Pre-World Conferences, USA Report.*

40. *Christmas Sandesh.* Available from World Wide Web: (http://www.sathyasai.org/discour/2000/d001225.html).

41. Anonymous Devotee, *The Most Precious Substance in the Universe.* Available from World Wide Web: (http://www.saibaba-aclearview.com).

42. Available from World Wide Web: (http://www.geocities.com/Athens/Olympus/9158/d15101999.html).

SIX

PASSAGE TO AMERICA

Ammachi on American Soil

SELVA J. RAJ

FOR NEARLY THREE DECADES, a tiny dark-skinned Indian holy woman has comforted, blessed, and—many believe—healed millions of devotees of all ages, races, religions, and walks of life, simply by her gentle, loving spiritual embraces. Mata Amritanandamayi, the Mother of Immortal Bliss—affectionately called Amma or Ammachi (Mother)—has emerged as one of the most prominent female spiritual leaders in the world, commanding a large following of devotees both in her native country and beyond. Likened to Mother Teresa by some and revered as a great mystic by many, this woman from rural south India is regarded by her devotees as the embodiment of the Divine Mother. In recognition of her contributions to the global religious community, Ammachi was invited to address the World Parliament of Religions in Chicago in 1993 at which she was named "President of Hinduism."[1] In October 2002 she was awarded the Gandhi-King Award for Non-Violence at the United Nations General Assembly Hall in Geneva, Switzerland, in recognition of her lifelong work in furthering the principles of nonviolence.[2]

In this essay, I examine the career, charisma, and authority of Ammachi, noting in particular how in her hands tradition is at once defied, redefined, and transcended. Based on field research at two of her congregations in the United States (San Ramon, California, and Chicago, Illinois), I reflect on the careful, selective application of traditional strategies and creative innovations introduced by Ammachi and her American devotees to help facilitate the acculturation of Ammachi's movement in the United States.

DEVOTIONAL ACCOUNTS OF THE CAREER
AND CHARISMA OF AMMACHI

Ammachi's meteoric rise to spiritual fame since the early 1990s has spawned
several accounts of her spiritual career, new contributions to the genre of
hagiographical literature that commonly mushrooms when a spiritual leader
gains fame and recognition.[3] In hagiographic texts, historical facts are lavishly
embellished to render the story and text appealing to devotees and to provide
a theological frame for followers to understand their object of devotion. To
date, no objective historical account of Ammachi's life is available to the critical
reader. Among the various devotional biographies, the oldest account was
penned by one of Ammachi's senior disciples, Swami Amritaswarupananda, and
in many respects it remains the most useful, for it is still recognized by
Ammachi organizations as her authoritative biography. In one sense, Amritaswarupananda's biography functions as the *ur* hagiography by one of
Ammachi's most esteemed followers. In a second sense, his work serves as an
informed and reliable barometer to gauge the Ammachi Movement's understanding of itself and their guru, the Divine Mother. Accordingly, I provide the
reader here with a deeper insight into how Ammachi is understood by drawing and commenting on this important disciple's account of her career and
charisma.

In 1978, a young man named Balu, who had been born in a wealthy
family of Kerala, India, committed his life to following Ammachi's spiritual
teachings and became one of her first disciples. Now known as Swami Amritaswarupananda Puri, he drew on his long discipleship with the Divine
Mother to trace the religious career of Ammachi from a humble and impover-
ished childhood of abuse and ill treatment by her family to the greatest heights
of God-realization and spirituality. Swami Amritaswarupananda Puri continues
to offer many books and speeches, giving voice to the true meaning of
Ammachi, the Divine Mother.

Sudhamani—as Ammachi was known before her apotheosis—was born
on September 27, 1953, as the fourth child to Sugunanandan and Damayanti
in a poor, low-caste family in the rural fishing village of Parayakadavu in
Kerala, south India. Amritaswarupananda described in detail the miraculous
events surrounding Ammachi's birth. "During her fourth pregnancy," he writes,
"Damayanti [Ammachi's mother] began having strange visions. Sometimes she
had wonderful dreams of Lord Krishna; at others she beheld the divine play of
Lord Siva and Devi, the Divine Mother. One night Damayanti dreamt that a
mysterious figure came to entrust her with an idol of Shri Krishna which was
cast in pure gold."[4] He recounts how after Damayanti had had a dream that
she had given birth to Krishna, the next morning she gave birth effortlessly to
a girl strangely reminiscent of the famously blue deity:

The parents were puzzled by the babe's dark blue complexion and the fact that the child lay in *padmasana* [the lotus posture of *hatha yoga*] holding her fingers in *chinmudra* [a posture symbolizing oneness of the individual self with the Supreme Self] with the tip of her thumb and forefinger touching to form a circle. They feared that this dark blue shade might be the symptom of some strange disease and that the peculiar posture might be due to abnormal bone structure or dislocation.[5]

Despite some minor variations in detail, most hagiographical accounts of Ammachi's early life follow Amritaswarupananda's lead: All underscore her similarities to deities at birth, assert that she was a gifted child, and claim that she was barely six months old when she began speaking in her native tongue, and by the age of two, was singing devotional songs to the god Krishna. At the age of six, she purportedly composed devotional songs filled with intense longing for union with Krishna. According to Swami Amritaswarupananda's account, even at an early age Sudhamani exhibited certain mystical and super-human traits including compassion for the destitute. In her late teens, she developed such an intense devotion to and longing for Krishna that she often was overwhelmed. "Sometimes she would enter the bathroom for a shower," he writes, "but would be discovered there hours later, oblivious to the surroundings."[7] Sometimes she danced in spiritual ecstasy and at other times she wept bitterly at the separation from her beloved Krishna. "From childhood I had an intense love of the divine name," Ammachi is quoted. "I would repeat the Lord's name incessantly with every breath, and a constant flow of divine thoughts was kept up in my mind."[7]

Also common in Hindu hagiography are accounts of adversity that the saint must overcome. Some villagers called Sudhamani "the crazy girl" because she worked and sang in longing worship, often slipping into profound God-intoxicated states.[8] Similarly, Sudhamani's parents and relatives interpreted these spiritual excursions as symptoms of temporary mental disorder or depression, and they made several attempts to get her married, which, according to Amritaswarupananda, she strongly resisted. "Sudhamani angrily warned her parents," he writes, "If you succeed in giving me in marriage, I will kill the man."[9] Fortunately, as is also common in Hindu hagiographies of spiritual women who wish to remain unmarried, divine intervention occurred; in Ammachi's case, an astrologer admonished her parents to abandon further attempts to arrange for her marriage. Even the lives of Hindu saints is some-times at stake: It is a truism in Ammachi circles that one of her own brothers tried to kill her in an effort to avert the social embarrassment occasioned by her decidedly abnormal behavior.

In September 1975, Sudhamani's spiritual career took a dramatic turn. Amritaswarupananda reported that one day, as she was returning home after tending the cattle, she heard recitations from the *Shrimad Bhagavatam* (a Hindu devotional text) emanating from a neighbor's house, which caused her to go into spiritual rapture. She entered the home and stood amidst the devotees. Her external appearance and mood changed dramatically, resulting in her manifestation of *Krishna Bhava*, that is, the "mood of Krishna," physically "transforming her features and movements into those of Shri Krishna himself."[10]

It was that experience that led her to realize her identification with Krishna. Later recalling her oneness with Krishna, Sudhamani said: "One day I strongly felt the urge to be absorbed in the Supreme Being. . . . Then I heard a voice from within saying, 'Thousands and thousands of people in the world are steeped in misery. I have much for you to do, you are one with Me . . .' I was able to know everything concerning everyone . . . I was fully conscious that I, myself, was Krishna, not only during that particular moment of manifestation but at all other times as well."[11]

Although her hagiographies brim with miraculous stories that serve to legitimate her close relationship with certain deities and affirm that she holds special powers of manifestation, initially Ammachi rejected demands for miracles as proof of her divine manifestation. "My intention" says Ammachi, "is not to show miracles. My goal is to inspire people with the desire for liberation through realization of their Eternal Self. Miracles are illusory. They are not the essence of spirituality."[12] However, a month later she reportedly convinced skeptics by changing water into a holy milk mixture,[13] and subsequently, many other miracles have been attributed to her, including the widely circulated story of healing a leper.[14] The miracles have attracted many followers to Ammachi and support for her many philanthropic service programs.

Approximately six months later, another great shift in her spiritual career occurred when Sudhamani had an intense vision and experience of oneness with the Divine Mother: "One day at the end of the *sadhana* [spiritual practice], I felt that a large canine tooth was coming out of my mouth. Simultaneously, I heard a terrific humming sound. I perceived the form of Devi with large canine teeth, a long protruding tongue, thick black curly hair, reddish bulging eyes and dark blue in color. I thought, 'Quick! Escape! Devi is coming to kill me!' I was about to run away. Suddenly I realized that I myself am Devi."[15] According to her biographer, in the months following this event, Ammachi began manifesting both *Krishna Bhava* as well as *Devi Bhava*, the mood of the Divine Mother. Today she assumes only the mood of the Divine Mother, which has become her spiritual trademark. The advent of *Devi Bhava* also "marked the beginning of Ammachi's broader spiritual mission" as she began to attract more and more Western disciples.[16]

On *Devi Bhava* nights, Ammachi is believed to reveal her identity as the Divine Mother, reflected in certain visible physical changes in her person. In her characteristic third-person style of expression, Ammachi tells a group of disciples: "If you were to really see Amma as She is, it would overwhelm you—

you couldn't possibly bear it. Because of this, Amma always covers Herself with a thick layer of *Maya* (illusion). But during *Devi Bhava*, Mother removes one or two of Her veils, revealing a little more of what She really is."[17]

With the shift in divine mood also came a shift in Ammachi's personality. Amritaswarupananda writes: "During Her *Devi Sadhana*, She was generally aloof and uncommunicative. All the time was devoted to prayer and meditation on the form of the Divine Mother. If Her parents or brother abused Her physically or verbally, She kept silent. Now She became more daring, even Her facial expression changed. Her nature became fearless and unyielding when it came to dealing with Her parents and brother."[18]

This greater inner strength and resolve stood her in good stead as Ammachi's spiritual fame began to spread. Devotees described moving stories about her miraculous powers that include clairvoyance, bilocation, levitation, dramatic healing of various physical illnesses and psychological disorders, answering devotees' special needs, stimulating conception for the barren, and absorbing devotees' negative karma.

Throughout these various spiritual phases, Sudhamani strove for God-realization without the mediation of a teacher or guru. She recalls: "I never had a guru, nor was I ever initiated by anyone and given a particular mantra. The mantra I used to chant was 'Amma, Amma.'"[19] But her disciples revere this uninitiated mystic as the perfect spiritual master (*sat guru*) who has the power to "directly induce God-realization."[20] In 1979, one year after Balu—now known as Swami Amritaswarupananda—committed his life to following Ammachi, as her first disciple, two Westerners joined him—Neal Rosner, an American who is now known as Swami Paramatmananda, and Gayatri, an Australian lady now known as Amritprana, who is Amma's devoted personal attendant and companion. A small thatched hut constructed near Ammachi's house served as the initial ashram.[21] Soon the inner circle of devotees grew as other young men and women joined the ashram. A formal ashram named "Amritpuri" was instituted in May 1981, near Kollam, Kerala. Since then, the number of male and female celibate aspirants (*brahmacharis* and *brahmacharinis*)—both Indian and others—has increased steadily. Currently, there are more than three hundred permanent residents at the Amritpuri ashram, fifteen of whom are fully initiated *sannyasis* and *sannyasinis* who have taken full vows of renunciation, and several hundred short-term visitors, the vast majority of whom are in their twenties and thirties. Those male and female renunciants who have received full initiation (*sannyasa*) have the title "Puri" added to their names to indicate their monastic lineage to the Puri Math.[22]

Although the movement has grown tremendously over the past two decades, Ammachi functions as not only the guiding spiritual force of the movement but also the central administrative authority. In addition to a hectic schedule of daily spiritual activities, she is said to make all the important decisions concerning her ever-growing network of charitable, educational, medical, and religious institutions.[23] Both temporal and spiritual powers are thus de jure consolidated in and around Ammachi, but the day-to-day administration of these institutions is delegated to her immediate circle of trusted monastic and lay disciples. For example, the newly founded high-tech Amrita Institute of Medical Sciences (AIMS) in Cochin—a premier medical center and hospital in Kerala—is administered by one of her most trusted American lay disciples who has moved his residence to Cochin. Thus, within the movement, religious leadership, power, and authority are hierarchically structured such that spiritual power resides solely in Ammachi, whereas the temporal power flowing from her efforts is de facto distributed at Ammachi's personal choice to her band of trusted disciples.

AMMACHI IN THE UNITED STATES

Ammachi first visited the United States in May 1987 at the invitation of her American disciples. Since 1987, Ammachi's spiritual appeal in America has grown so immensely that her U.S. tour has become an annual feature, and in 1989, she established her first U.S. ashram in San Ramon, California. Located on a hill donated by an American devotee, the Mata Amritanandamayi Center or simply MA Center, has grown into a full-fledged ashram housing several permanent and some temporary male and female celibate aspirants. While the MA Center serves as the U.S. headquarters for the Ammachi movement, local chapters have been established in Seattle, Los Angeles, Dallas, Chicago, New York, Phoenix, Santa Fe, Boston, and Washington, D.C. Efforts are being made to institute local chapters in other major U.S. cities.[24]

My introduction to Mata Amritanandamayi's ashram in San Ramon occurred on June 14, 1999. Arriving at the ashram around 7 p.m., I noted a long line of diverse devotees gathered near the temple door: small children, teenagers, young adults, older men and women, all of various ethnicities, but predominantly Caucasian and non-Indian. While some were clearly first-time visitors like me, most seemed to be regular devotees, evidenced by their dress, speech, and the obvious familiarity and ease with which they moved around the ashram and temple. Many were dressed in the traditional Indian attire (*saris, salwar kamiz,* and *kurta*), and some had nametags with such Indian or Hindu names as "Shridhar" or "Lavanya" inscribed on them. A good number were also wearing a string of beads sacred to Hindu god Siva and traditionally worn by Indian ascetics (*rudraksha mala*) or other necklaces and bracelets of Indian provenance. Eyes cast down in prayerful meditation, several hundred devotees stood at the entrance of the temple, chanting the mantra "Praise to the Blissful One," or "Om Amriteshwariye Namaha." Suddenly, our chanting grew louder and more intense as a cream-colored Lexus sedan arrived. A tiny, dark-skinned Indian woman clad in a simple white cotton sari emerged, smiling radiantly at the visibly expectant and excited crowd. She walked briskly into the temple as devotees respectfully knelt, prostrated, or bowed their heads in the palpably charged atmosphere.

Ammachi stood on a decorated floor mat. A female Indian disciple dressed in a white *sari* performed *pada puja,* or worship to the lotus feet (*pada*) of Her Holiness Shri Mata Amritanandamayi. She sprinkled a few drops of water on Ammachi's feet, gently wiped them away, applied sandal paste, and placed three rose flowers and petals on her feet as two saffron-robed Indian monks of the order—simply referred by Ammachi's American devotees as Swamijis—recited the following Sanskritic *shlokas* (verses) in praise of the guru and her feet:

> I prostrate to the Universal Teacher, Who is Satchitananda [Pure Being-Knowledge-Absolute Bliss], Who is beyond all differences, Who is eternal, all-full, attributeless, formless and ever-centered in the Self; Whatever merit is acquired by one, through pilgrimages and from bathing in the Sacred Waters extending to the seven seas, cannot be equal to even one thousandth part of the merit derived from partaking the water with which the Guru's feet are washed.[25]

A lay devotee offered the ritual waving of a lamp (*arati*) before Ammachi while another garlanded Ammachi, who in turn blessed them by sprinkling a few rose petals. After the worship of her feet, she walked briskly through the main aisle of the temple, touching and blessing devotees on either side of the aisle, and finally ascended to take her seat on an elevated platform. A young Indian female renunciant delivered a brief discourse on Ammachi's spiritual message, interspersed with several moving anecdotes and testimonials of her special spiritual powers and unconditional love for all. Next came ninety minutes of ecstatic and soulful devotional singing (*bhajan*) led by Ammachi and her band of gifted Indian musicians. Temple lights were switched off to provide the proper setting for a ten-minute meditation on the Divine Mother embodied in Ammachi. The senior male disciple who led the congregation in the meditation exercise invited the devotees to surrender themselves at the feet of Ammachi, the Divine Mother. After the ritual waving of the lamp in front of Ammachi concluded the evening rites, devotees took their place for the spiritual embrace session, called Ammachi *darshan*. Ammachi hugged each one in turn, uttering tender and loving words in the devotee's ear, and gave each admirer a Hershey's kiss, a few rose petals, and a tiny packet of sacred ash.

Ammachi's American devotees come from all walks of life, ages, religions, and races. In San Ramon, I interviewed more than three dozen devotees, many with distinguished careers as industrialists, businessmen, university professors, social workers, and medical professionals. According to an informal estimate provided by an *ashram* official at San Ramon, Caucasians are by far the single largest ethnic group among Ammachi's American devotees. A large number of these Caucasian devotees are former—and in many cases, current—members of the Transcendental Meditation (TM) movement. Some are disillusioned Christian feminists who see in Ammachi a validation for the feminization of the Divine. Immigrant Asian Indians, African Americans, and others of Asian descent account for the rest. Many of these American devotees regard Ammachi as a New Age guru, and are drawn to her personal spiritual charisma and her message of unconditional love for all. Still others are, as one devotee put it, "*avatar* tourists" in pursuit of espying authentic Eastern gurus. Although Ammachi attracts male devotees, women occupy the vast majority of leadership roles and functions, acting as song leaders, receptionists, temple ushers, bookstore administrators, leaders of the local chapters (*satsang*), preachers, interpreters, media representatives, *darshan*-hosts, cashiers, and directors of food services.

In 1999 there were forty-five residents at the Mata Amritanandamayi Center in San Ramon. According to Swami Paramatmananda, the center's current spiritual leader, the MA Center has "a floating population that goes anywhere from forty-five to sixty."[26] The aspirants follow a daily schedule of reciting Ammachi's 101 names, the 1001 names of the Divine Mother, meditation, and selfless service (*seva*). Though attached to the ashram, these aspirants pursue regular secular careers in the outside world.

In Ammachi's U.S. congregations, there seems to be a conscious effort among her Anglo devotees to look and act in accord with Indian cultural norms; some have even adopted Indian spiritual names. When in her physical presence, many of her Anglo devotees wear white Indian clothing in imitation of Ammachi's habit of wearing white *saris* (for example, white *salwar kamiz*, *saris*, and *kurta*) as well as an assortment of Indian accoutrements such as jewelry, beads, forehead marks (*tilak*), bracelets, and shawls. Most Indian women wear bright colored silk *saris*, but such a deliberate shift in dress or behavioral code is conspicuously absent among their Indian male counterparts, who wear regular Western clothes. The spontaneous comment by one of my students who accompanied me to Ammachi's *darshan* in Ann Arbor in November 1999 captures this dynamic of cultural adoption. She remarked: "The Anglos seem more Indian than the Indians and the Indians seem more Anglo and less Indian." My student's casual remark highlights an important variable that differentiates the attitudes of Ammachi's Western and Indian devotees. Western disciples seem more attracted to the asceticism of Ammachi's spirituality, and embody their religiosity by adopting the plain white clothing and cultural markers of commitment. By contrast, Indians seem more drawn to the devotional tradition that Ammachi embodies, and they are not motivated to change their behavior or dress.

Another notable feature of Ammachi's American Western devotees is their dual personal and religious identity. Many maintain a legal Western name to use in secular and professional contexts, and adopt an Indian spiritual name such as "Ramya" or "Krishna" to use within the movement, and especially in Ammachi's physical presence. Furthermore, while professing personal affection, faith, and loyalty to Ammachi and her spiritual message, many nevertheless maintain formal ties and affiliation with their respective religious traditions. Both in San Ramon and Chicago, I met Catholic, Protestant, and Jewish devotees of Ammachi who claimed to be Christians and Jews of good standing in their respective parishes and congregations. This applies also to those devotees who maintain loyalty to two gurus. The case of Trina is instructive. She is a follower of both Sai Baba—the famous Indian male guru—and Ammachi. Together, they represent for her the father and mother images of the Divine. A dental surgeon from Iowa, who has been associated with the TM movement since the early eighties, told me in confidence that he has adopted Ammachi as his personal guru (*ishta guru*) in addition to his TM guru, Maharishi Mahesh Yogi.[27]

Currently, most of Ammachi's U.S. congregations are administered by lay volunteers and disciples. Except for San Ramon and Santa Fe, where there are established ashrams under the spiritual leadership of a fully initiated renunciant, most local chapters do not have a resident renunciant monk or nun (*sannyasi* or *sannyasini*) to serve as spiritual guide. Uninitiated lay local leaders conduct monthly prayer gatherings, devotional singing (*bhajans*), and rituals in devotees' homes. These lay leaders claim to have received a personal calling from Ammachi to organize the monthly gatherings and rituals. Some describe their voluntary ritual roles as expressions of gratitude, and others comment that these ritual activities act as an effective way to maintain a personal relationship with Ammachi. One American devotee wrote, "I always felt like I was feeding and dressing Mother whenever I did *puja* [worship], and I felt blessed while doing this. Every time I took care of the altar, cleaning and tidying it up, I felt Mother's presence . . . the *puja* articles were like a living entity. They were alive, and it was as though they were living, breathing parts of the Mother. Now I have the same feeling about the San Ramon *ashram*. I can feel the whole place breathe as a unit, alive with Her."[28]

EMBODIED GURU, EMBODIED GODDESS

Although Ammachi was never initiated by a guru, her devotees revere her as the *sat guru*, the true or perfect spiritual master. The guru *puja* offered to Ammachi each time she enters the temple confirms the devotees' belief in her guru status. She describes herself as a compassionate guru for her devotees. She exhorts her disciples to cultivate attachment to the *sat guru* as both the means and end of the spiritual quest. When asked whether attachment to the master's external form is necessary to realize the ultimate goal of god-realization, Ammachi responds:

Children, first of all remember that attachment to the Master is an attachment to God. Your problem is that you try to differentiate between God
and the true Master. Attachment to a true Master's physical form intensi-
fies your longing to realize the Supreme. It is like living with God. He
makes your spiritual journey much easier. Such a Master is both the
means and the end. But at the same time there must be conscious effort
to see the Master in all creation. . . . You cannot experience the state of
God-consciousness through your mere senses or through the scriptures
you have learned. To experience it, you need to develop a new eye, the
inner, third eye. . . . The inner eye, or the eye of true knowledge, can only
be opened by a real Master. . . . Being attached to the external form of a
Satguru is like having a direct contact with the Supreme Truth.[29]

Ammachi's self-understanding as a *sat guru* is reflected in her teaching roles.
She offers formal discourses in her native language of Malayalam, which are
translated by a native interpreter. She leads daily devotional singing, teaches
meditation, and conducts regular retreats for her disciples.

Along with her role and identity as *sat guru* is her self-recognized and self-
professed identity as the embodied goddess (*devi*)—the form much revered by
the devotees. Ammachi's goddess identity is revealed in her weekly *Devi Bhava*
when she assumes the mood or form of the Divine Mother for the benefit and
at the request of her devotees. She permits devotees to offer religious worship
to her for their spiritual edification.

Ammachi has dual, conflated roles and identities as simultaneously guru
and goddess. While many of her devotees privilege her identity as the Divine
Mother, others prefer to stress her essential nature as the perfect human guru
who inspires and facilitates their god-realization. Sivaraman, an immigrant
Indian lay leader of Ammachi's Chicago congregation, echoes the sentiments
of a large number of devotees that recognize her guruhood to be uniquely
devotional: "Amma is the guru for my entire family. She is our *ishta guru*
[chosen guru]. In the past I have had several male gurus. But Amma stands
unique as a guru. Whereas I only had an intellectual and rational relationship
with the male gurus, I feel a certain inner and deeper resonance with Amma, a
sort of meeting of the hearts."[30]

EMBODIED RITUAL: DIVINE HUGS
AND HERSHEY'S KISSES

In the Hindu tradition, the central ritual moment in worship is the exchange
of sight—*darshan*—between god and the devotee. But disciples of Ammachi
are not content with mere sight of her; *darshan* is reconfigured to include

tactile embrace. *Darshan* of Ammachi becomes a warm, motherly, spiritual hug. This type of *darshan* is one of the intriguing trademark features of Ammachi's movement and her spirituality.

In the course of my field research, I witnessed hundreds of devotees—many of whom traveled from afar—wait for several hours for just a few precious seconds of personal *darshan* with Ammachi. They come with varying concerns, ranging from the completely mundane to the ascetic, and Ammachi greets each on his or her level or need. In the final moments of *Devi Bhava darshan*, for instance, Ammachi performs nuptial rites for a select number of couples, most of whom are Caucasian devotees dressed in traditional Indian wedding attire.

I, too, went for personal *darshan* with Ammachi, both out of curiosity and also to gain a participatory experience and understanding of the ritual and its impact on the devotees. But just like her devotees, I received much more than I had anticipated, and interestingly, at the precise level of my concern. When I went for my second *darshan* during a morning session, a trusted Ammachi devotee whom I had interviewed earlier that day introduced me to Ammachi directly, telling her about my scholarly interest in her teachings and movement. After hugging me closely, she turned to Swami Amritaswarupananda who was standing beside her and instructed him to assist me in obtaining necessary literature from the bookstore. Later, as Ammachi was leaving the temple after the morning session, she specifically sought me out in the crowded congregation gathered outside the temple and personally wished me success in my research. She met my specific concern: to learn more about her and her movement so that I could report about each in a scholarly context.

Before devotees are ushered into the presence of Ammachi, they must have proper instructions on *darshan* etiquette, or "*darshan dharma.*" Then, they are invited into her presence as she sits on a colorfully decorated throne, flanked by a male *sannyasi* who translates devotees' special requests or questions, and a female attendant who ministers to Ammachi's personal needs. Throughout *darshan*, the atmosphere and ambience undulates: intense, prayerful, relaxed, and festive at the same time. Devotional *bhajans* in Hindi and Malayalam led by a group of singers provides the spiritual and musical backdrop. Throughout, a scattered few browse in the adjacent bookstore perusing various Ammachi souvenirs and wares. Various groups take turns in leading the devotional singing throughout the *darshan* service. On *Devi Bhava* nights, Caucasian children dressed in colorful Indian costumes perform Indian classical dances. As Ammachi receives into her lap the continuous stream of devotees one by one, responses differ. Some sit in prayerful meditation as if inhaling the power and energy exuding from her person; others become spiritually intoxicated and dance in ecstasy. Still others observe the *darshan* proceedings in a state of awe and wonderment. After the *darshan*, many consume the Hershey's

Kiss—the sacred leftover or *prasad*—whereas others take it home to keep as a sacred relic.[31]

Whereas on normal days Ammachi gives hugs to more than one thousand devotees, this number is doubled on the weekly *Devi Bhava* nights, when Ammachi wears a bright *sari* and a silver crown to reveal the majestic glory and tender love of the Divine Mother. In India, *Devi Bhava* nights attract over ten thousand *darshan* seekers. The duration of the *darshan* is contingent upon the location, the number of individuals seeking *darshan*, and Ammachi's own physical health. Currently, an individual *darshan* in America usually lasts for about a minute or two while in India because of the large numbers of *darshan* seekers it lasts for about ten to fifteen seconds. To maintain crowd control in India, *darshan* seekers are given numbered tickets and grouped into lots of 250, and then called up when it is their lot's turn. Although American *darshan* seekers have more time by comparison, during her first two visits to the U.S., Ammachi used to spend a lot more time with her devotees during *darshan* than is currently the case. "Sometimes, a person could spend up to ten minutes in Mother's lap," recalls Amritaswarupananda, "especially when Mother spontaneously burst into song during *darshan*. Mother would then slip into a state of rapture, and the person . . . could stay in Her lap until the song came to an end."[32] The transition from the spontaneous and extended *darshans* to the current carefully controlled and structured *darshan* context reflects the gradual routinization and institutionalization of the charismatic aspects and practices occurring within her growing movement.

During *Devi Bhava*, scores of devotees receive personal initiation and a mantra from Ammachi who usually imparts mantras drawn from the Hindu ritual and meditative tradition.[33] The following personal account from devotee Janet Turner highlights the basic procedures for receiving the mantra:

> On *Devi Bhava* nights in America, they hand out a leaflet in the *darshan* line explaining that receiving the mantra is a serious commitment not to be taken lightly. If after reading the pamphlet, you are serious about receiving a mantra, you stand in a line to Ammachi's right side, a line much shorter than the *darshan* line. Then, you receive a brief pre-mantra counseling by a long-time devotee of Ammachi who reiterates the seriousness of receiving a mantra and asks you to decide what kind of mantra you'd like, if it's a Krishna mantra, a Devi mantra, a Jesus mantra or a Buddha mantra. You could also ask for a mantra that is not deity-specific. I was told that when it's my turn Ammachi will say the mantra in my ear and repeat it. . . . When I got to the front of the line, it was very late, maybe one or two o'clock in the morning. . . . She turned to me and smiled. . . . Somebody behind her told her what kind of mantra I wanted. She leaned over and pulled my head to her mouth. And she said my mantra twice and the hand that was pulling my head to her mouth was

full of flower petals. I don't know how to describe but it was very special. Being in her presence, I felt an instant relief.[34]

In the Hindu ascetic and monastic tradition, receiving a mantra is a long and painstaking process involving many years of intense discipline on the part of the spiritual aspirant. The spiritual master imparts a secret mantra when he is satisfied with the disciple's spiritual progress, sealing a sacred bond between a guru and an aspirant. Ammachi's mantras, by contrast, are comparatively much easier to attain for the average, often untrained, layperson. In so doing, Ammachi seems to assert that "the brahminical regulations and restrictions governing the giving and receiving of mantras are not as important as the actual practice of the mantra."[35] She is both defying and defining *brahminical* or priestly positions on the mantra.

According to her devotees, she is known to give the mantra appropriate to the devotee's particular religious sensibility and spiritual state.[36] On *Devi Bhava* nights, a number of Ammachi's Christian devotees receive the "Christ mantra" or "Mary mantra," because, her devotees explain, her goal is not to convert people but to strengthen their spirituality in the tradition they are rooted.[37]

The "Christ mantra" phenomenon sheds important light on both Ammachi and her Western devotees. It reveals Ammachi's inclusive religious philosophy and her movement's acculturative strategies necessary for the vitality of a transnational and transcontinental movement such as hers. Like other Indian gurus who have preceded her in the West, Ammachi, although firmly grounded in the Hindu religious and ritual tradition, freely mixes Hindu ritual idioms with Western, Christian categories to make her message culturally palatable.[38] Not surprisingly, some of her Christian followers in the West regard Ammachi as a female Christ. An incident during Ammachi's first U.S. tour illustrates this attitude. "An elderly Afro-American man," writes Amritaswarupananda, "suddenly got up and spontaneously started singing and dancing, 'we have seen Christ! In Mother, and in Her divine love and compassion, we have seen Christ, the Lord! In Mother, and in Her self-sacrifice, we have seen Jesus Christ, the Saviour!' He looked divinely intoxicated, and his joy was so contagious that the rest of the devotees joined in by clapping their hands and responding to the song."[39] Speaking of Ammachi *darshan* in a similar vein, another Western devotee wrote, "[F]or our sake, Mother is being daily crucified on a chair."[40]

Ammachi's willingness to impart Christ mantras also provides clues to her views on other religions and their truth claims. Ammachi locates herself in the classical Hindu universalist position advocated by such modern Hindu reformers as Ramakrishna and Vivekananda. Cornell quotes Ammachi's views: "We are like chocolates wrapped in different colored wrappers. When the wrappers are removed, all the chocolate is the same. If we light a green and blue candle, the flames will be the same color. The nectar of different flowers is all the same to the honeybee. And though the shapes of ice may differ, it is all just water. So too everyone in this world is the one Atman [Soul]. We are all God's children."[41] In her address to the United Nations in August 2000, Ammachi declared:

> There is one Truth that shines through all of creation. Rivers and moun-
> tains, plants and animals, the sun, the moon and the stars, you and I—all
> are expressions of this one Reality. It is by assimilating this truth in our
> lives, and thus gaining a deeper understanding, that we can discover the
> inherent beauty in this diversity. When we work together as a global
> family, not merely belonging to a particular race, religion or nation, peace
> and happiness will once again prevail on this earth which is drenched
> with the tears of division and conflict.[42]

It is doubtful that most of her American devotees fully comprehend the extent and significance of the ancient Hindu assumptions that undergird the *Devi Bhava*. Some describe it as a time when Ammachi merely dresses in fine clothes and jewelry, while others regard it, in the words of one devotee, as "a disco night."[43] "Americans don't really get the *Devi Bhava*," says one American devotee. "I remember that I was uncomfortable with *Devi Bhava*. . . . I didn't understand that until I came to India. So, imagine when typical Americans who do not understand anything about Devi as a goddess witness this event. . . . Being a Protestant Christian, I didn't have any understanding of the dressing of the deity."[44] By contrast, Hindu devotees, who are familiar with such ritual traditions, and who are religiously conversant with the notion of a god-incarnate person or *avatar* embodied in contemporary figures such as Satya Sai Baba, seem intuitively to understand and relate to Ammachi; they seem to demonstrate greater reverence and devotion than the sense of awe and thrill that typify the reaction of her Western devotees.

TOWARD A HERMENEUTIC OF AMMACHI DARSHAN: TRADITION DEFIED AND TRANSCENDED

In the Ammachi movement, *darshan* is the most intimate, direct, and personal mode of interaction between the spiritual master and her devotees. Given that Ammachi does not deliver many formal spiritual discourses in the United States as she has limited fluency in the English language, *darshan* also functions as her principal spiritual discourse to her American devotees. Amritaswaru-pananda explains to the devotees the spiritual significance Ammachi attaches to hugs and kisses. In a passage attributed to Ammachi—who today invariably refers to herself in third person—he writes: "Amma's hugs and kisses should not be considered ordinary. When Amma embraces or kisses someone, it is a process of purification and inner healing. Amma is transmitting a part of Her pure vital energy into Her children. It also allows them to experience true, unconditional love. When Amma holds someone it can help to awaken the dormant spiritual energy within them, which will eventually take them to the ultimate goal of Self-realization."[45]

Devotees tell moving stories about their *darshan* experience and their direct, intuitive dialogue with her. When asked how they communicate with Ammachi since she does not speak English, devotees repeatedly told me that they communicate in the language of the heart as a child communicates with its mother. "We don't have to say anything as she knows all our thoughts even before we speak."[46] The remarks of a staunch follower of the TM movement exemplifies the attitude of many a Western devotee to Ammachi *darshan*: "She gives you one look and you remember it; it's like carved into your nervous system forever. During *darshan*, you just see her smiling inside your soul, and looking out. . . . She leaves a permanent impression on a level that's way beyond language or thought . . . from her perspective, she is you. She's just trying to wake you up to realize that you are Her [the divine]... during *darshan*, she awakes the divine in you with a smile and a hug."[47] Mary Hatfield— an Ammachi devotee from Hawaii—highlights the personal relationship initiated or sustained by the *darshan* experience: "Mother is so personable and endearing that each of us feels that we have a personal relationship with her. Maybe that is the reason it is easy to sustain faith in her without the institutional fellowship found in many of the larger religions."[48]

Apart from effecting a certain meta-communion between Ammachi and her devotees, *darshan* also provides a meta-discourse on the departures, innovations, and reforms she has subtly introduced into an ancient Hindu ritual tradition. Ammachi's creative innovation of Hindu ritual praxis is best understood by revisiting the traditional understanding of *darshan* in the Hindu devotional tradition.

Darshan literally means "seeing." Translated sometimes as the "auspicious sight" of the divine, in popular Hindu devotional scheme, *darshan* is the auspicious seeing of the deity indwelling in an icon or image whereby the devotee seeks to establish contact with the deity. The act of standing in the presence of the deity and beholding the image with one's own eyes, seeing the divine and being seen by the divine, is a central act of Hindu worship.[49] Though it involves the body, *darshan* is primarily a mental, spiritual, and mystical contact. Direct bodily contact with the deity is both ritually inauspicious and forbidden for the average devotee. Even the priest whose ritual functions necessitate regular physical contact with the image is governed by strict prescriptions and observances to offset the inherent dangers of such contact.

Physicality is the hallmark of Ammachi *darshans*. Given her status as the embodied Divine Mother and perfect spiritual master (*sat guru*), *darshan* is no doubt the appropriate mode of interaction. But in form and function, Ammachi *darshan* radically differs from the traditional pattern insofar as it entails close and intense bodily contact in the form of touching, hugging, and kissing. Beyond the ritual and religious contexts, touching and kissing a person of another gender, especially strangers, is a taboo in Hindu social relations. This is all the more so when it involves touching and kissing a religious teacher or guru. But Ammachi embraces, hugs, strokes, and kisses her devotees with total disregard to their gender, moral condition, and physical purity. Thus, her *darshan* defies not only traditional Hindu norms concerning purity, pollution, and bodily contact between the devotee and the embodied divine, but also societal norms and rules governing gender relations. In this sense, *darshan* can be "read" as Ammachi's public discourse of defiance. Her style of *darshan* defies and transcends traditional caste boundaries and the purity-impurity distinctions that undergird most of Hindu social and religious life. One wonders whether her low caste status gives her the freedom and predisposition to transgress with some ease orthodox religious and social norms.

Unschooled in Hindu ideas about ritual purity, devotional exercises, and caste considerations, most of her American devotees—raised in a culture that regards hugging as a normal human expression—seem oblivious of the radical departures Ammachi is initiating within the Hindu tradition, and perceive the *darshan* essentially as a novel psycho-spiritual experience. Ammachi's penchant for physical contact evokes a reciprocal response from her American devotees who seek to prolong, memorialize, concretize, and perpetuate their *darshan* experience and physical contact with Ammachi with the help of an assortment of Ammachi mementos that will be discussed in the next section.

During my field research in India in January–February 2003, I learned of an innovation in the Ammachi *darshan* tradition. Ammachi reportedly has been suffering for several years from a severe case of arthritis as a result of the countless hours she has spent each day over the past twenty years giving *darshan* to hundreds of thousands of devotees. Some say that she also suffers from a degenerative bone condition in her neck.[50] At the Amritpuri ashram in Kerala, Ammachi's primary residence, a swimming pool was installed, and the ashram introduced a novel *darshan* procedure described by devotees as "swimming pool *darshan*" and "water *darshan*," intended to minimize the impact of tactile contact on Ammachi's physical body. Devotees say that "water *darshan*" is a lot like regular *darshan*, except that Ammachi gives *darshan* to devotees while seated on a conveniently positioned chair within the swimming pool.[51]

Ammachi also departs from Hindu tradition through her empowerment of women's public ritual roles. Despite opposition from some Hindu scholars and pundits, recently Ammachi has been authorizing her female renunciants (*brahmacharinis*) to study the sacred texts, and she has also installed them as temple priestesses authorized to perform *puja* in temples. In November 1997, she appointed women as priestesses (*pujarinis*) in her temples at Kaimanam and Kodungallur in Kerala.[52] Devotees attribute Ammachi's daring innovation to her firm belief in the equality of men and women in the religious realm. "In the eyes of God," says Ammachi, "men and women are equal. How can one possibly justify saying that a woman, who is the creator of man, is inferior to man?"[53] Again, she is said to admonish her disciples, "[I]t is not enough to just preach liberty to women. It has to be practiced and demonstrated."[54]

Notwithstanding this daring empowerment of women's public ritual roles, Ammachi's views on women do retain some of Hinduism's conservatism. While women are portrayed as models of selfless service and given prominent roles and functions within her order, menstruating women are dissuaded from going for *darshan* with Ammachi. *Darshan* guidelines require women "to cover their shoulders and to wear dresses or skirts [and] not wear see-through dresses or tight dresses that reveal the shape of the body."[55] Moreover, despite Ammachi's express public statements about gender equality, as of today, the highest leadership roles within the movement are largely assigned to and exercised by male renunciants. Perhaps this conservatism illustrates the internal dialectic between tradition and change, between fidelity to core Hindu religious messages and the urge to reform Hindu praxis. The struggle for balance between preserving the essential Hindu character of the movement and widening its appeal to a non-Hindu audience continues.

TRANSPLANTING TRADITION

From its modest beginnings in the calm backwaters of the Indian state of Kerala, the spiritual movement Ammachi initiated has matured into a dynamic, worldwide phenomenon with a growing and impressive network of charitable institutions and transnational congregations in the West. Her annual tours to the United States and Europe attract thousands who endure great physical and financial hardship to be in her compassionate presence and company, in order, as one devotee put it, "to inhale her spiritual power." In the process of acculturation, the Ammachi movement, while preserving its core spiritual message and much of the Hindu ritual idiom, has adopted new secular and religious elements to render the movement accessible, attractive, and marketable to Ammachi's diverse ethnic and religious Western audience. For brevity's sake, I focus on just three specific instances of acculturation.

Ammachi does not charge a fee for *darshan* or giving mantras, relying only on freely given donations at the devotees' discretion. At the MA Center in San Ramon, *darshans* are conducted in the temple hall. In back of the temple hall is a large gift shop. As devotees wait for their individual *darshan*, which might take anywhere from one to three hours, devotees are repeatedly encouraged through public announcements to support Ammachi's numerous charitable institutions and to visit the bookstore-cum-gift shop located in the back of the temple hall. Multimedia presentations through high tech laptops and TV screens are prominently on display advertising Ammachi's spiritual discourses and her numerous charitable projects. A wide assortment of Ammachi souvenirs are on sale in the gift shop, including books, CDs, audio and video cassettes, Krishna and Christ bracelets, beads, Amma T-shirts, photos, *saris*, pictures, and Amma dolls.

In India, devotees of famous gurus often prefer to purchase some kind of image of their spiritual master to allow them continuous daily *darshan*. In an interesting twist of this tradition, the most popular among the Amma souvenirs, and much sought after by her Western female devotees, are the Amma dolls that cost anywhere from $45 to $195. Said to be made from the white *saris* and petticoats worn by Ammachi and containing a flower petal blessed by Ammachi during *Devi Bhava*, these dolls are believed to be charged with extra spiritual power. Devotees regard these dolls as containers of Amma's spiritual charisma and sacred presence. Their power becomes even more enhanced when blessed by Ammachi during individual *darshan*. During my field research, I witnessed numerous devotees carrying the Amma dolls to have them blessed by Ammachi. (When I presented a version of this chapter at the 2001 Annual Meeting of the American Academy of Religion in Denver, a Harvard graduate student stood up to announce that she, too, was the proud owner of an Amma doll blessed by Ammachi.)

Through Amma dolls and other souvenirs, devotees seek to prolong, memorialize, concretize, and perpetuate their *darshan* experience and physical contact with Ammachi. Many devotees asserted that the dolls are the primary, if not the sole, medium of communication with Ammachi long after she returns to India. For others, they serve as a source of solace and comfort particularly during crisis moments in their personal lives. "Whenever I'm confronted with a personal crisis," testified a forty-year-old Caucasian female devotee, "I speak to the Amma doll and receive spiritual counsel and comfort."[56] The Amma doll phenomenon represents the creative and innovative synthesis of Hindu appreciation for guru and divine icons and American popular culture and market economy. Cross-culturally, following the logic of Joachim Wach, the Amma dolls also represent the process of gradual objectification and concretization of a charismatic religious leader's personal spiritual charisma found in many religious sects and movements.[57] Tambiah discusses the process whereby the charismatic leader's spiritual powers are rendered concrete, tangible, portable, and available.[58] Seen from this perspective, the Amma dolls not only reflect the portable, indeed "exportable," quality of Ammachi's spiritual charisma but they also represent the institutionalized objectification, commercialization, and expansion of Ammachi's personal and official charisma. Interestingly, these images of the guru also serve to invert Ammachi's *Devi Darshan* practice: The devotee is invited to cuddle the passive guru/deity in a loving embrace that can last as long and as often as desired.

Another gift shop item popular among many Western devotees is an eight by eleven color lithograph. This montage of various Christian figures and scenes from the Gospel stories holds in its center a prominent picture of the dark-skinned Ammachi holding the Caucasian child Jesus in her arms, revealing Ammachi as an Indian face of the Virgin Mary. Illustrating Ammachi's central message of God's love and God's transcendence over name and form, and religious, cultural, gender, and national boundaries, this lithograph is also an inspired acculturative strategy employed by the movement to appeal to Ammachi's Western—predominantly Christian female—audience in search of manifestations of female sacred power and feminine divine imagery lacking in the patriarchal Christian tradition.

The advertising and sale of Amma souvenirs is skillfully administered and carefully monitored by a select group of Amma's Western disciples with professional training and skill in liberal capitalism and market economy. Joseph Smith, an MBA and a former marketing manager for a major corporation, coordinates the marketing and sale of Amma souvenirs. At the adjacent "Amma cafeteria" Indian snacks and sweets are sold to devotees. The atmosphere in the bookstore and cafeteria is reminiscent of the gift shops in a sports stadium or museum. When on tour to different U.S. cities, a makeshift gift shop is conveniently positioned at the entrance of the *darshan* hall for everyone to see. The careful display and marketing of Ammachi's spiritual charisma in the gift shop carry the common features of Western capitalist and free market enterprise, since the movement holds the trademark rights to her image and name. During my field research in San Ramon, a senior disciple of the movement, learning of my intention to publish an essay on Ammachi, insisted that I obtain copyright permission from the ashram. The various advertising and marketing techniques employed by the movement is one instance of acculturation to the social, cultural, and religious landscape of America.

The second example of acculturation to the American scene concerns the sites selected for Ammachi's *darshans* in the United States. With the exception of San Ramon, where religious programs are held in a traditional Hindu temple hall, during her U.S. tour Ammachi rarely conducts religious programs in the plethora of Hindu temples that have mushroomed rapidly in almost every major U.S. city. Instead, her *darshans* are held in secular spaces such as public auditoriums and hotels and nondenominational Christian churches. For example, during her numerous visits to Chicago over the past decade, only once did the local Hindu temple serve as the venue for her programs. In July 1999 Ammachi *darshans* in Chicago were held at the Ramada Inn in Lisle, Illinois, even though the Hindu temple in the neighboring suburb of Lemont has a large enough hall to accommodate the devotees; indeed, it is at least as large as the one used at the Ramada Inn. The selection of such secular spaces appears to be guided by a desire to appeal to her predominantly non-Hindu, Western Christian audience, and suggests that Ammachi consciously locates herself and her movement outside mainstream Hinduism.

The third instance of acculturation or adaptation is the "*Devi Puja*" ritual preceding the weekly *Devi Bhava*. Discourses by Ammachi and a meditation exercise on divine *shakti* provide the spiritual backdrop for the *Devi Puja* rituals. The seating for the *puja* is arranged in such a way that devotees sit in groups of four facing each other. Placed in front of the devotees are a brass lamp with oil and wick, four brass spoons each containing a piece of camphor, four small plastic cups containing water blessed by Ammachi, and a donation envelope. At the instruction of the master of ceremonies, devotees light the camphor and wave it in front of their chest. Devotees are then instructed to drink the holy water on site or take it home, mix it with large quantities of water, and share it with relatives. The holy water is said to contain Ammachi's divine presence and *shakti*. When the water ritual is concluded, devotees are requested to place a voluntary worship offering (*Puja Dakshina*) in the donation envelope and hand it to one of the attendants. The entire ritual sequence strongly resembles the Christian communion service. While drinking the water used for ritual purposes and consuming the food offered to deities are familiar ritual practices in the Hindu worship tradition, the controlled environment, the institutional context, and the congregational character of the rite strikingly parallel—if not entirely replicate or duplicate—the Christian communion service, and seem to reinforce ritual adaptations appealing to her Western Christian audience. The development of *Devi Puja* is another way Ammachi is acculturating her message and her ritual tradition to an audience familiar with the Christian communion service tradition.

In this chapter I have spelled out just three instances of deliberate acculturations. Given that the movement is in its infancy in the United States, it is safe to assume that in due course the movement will develop additional new and creative ways of acculturating its leader and her message to ensure the successful transplantation of Ammachi's movement in the new social, cultural, and religious landscape of America.

CONCLUSION

Ammachi's life and career reveal the classic traits and features associated with many charismatic Indian female spiritual figures: low-caste birth, life of poverty, abused childhood, unloved and misunderstood adolescence, resistance to domestic life and marriage, and rejection by her family. Through her vast network of transnational congregations and institutions catering to an ever widening global audience, Ammachi has emerged as a powerful *mahaguru*—perhaps the most influential Hindu female guru of recent history. Scholars such as Gold have classified *mahagurus* under two distinct, though not mutually exclusive types—gurus who are respected teachers and gurus who are, or those who claim to be either implicitly or explicitly, the embodied divine.[59] Ammachi's claims to guru-status are obvious. Recently, Ammachi has strongly emphasized the chanting and study of the *Tantra* text called "The Thousand Names of Lalita," the *Lalitasahasranama*. This is now available to devotees on an interactive CD, with special *stotras* (praise hymns) composed to Amma as Lalita, revealing the clear claim that Amma is the direct embodiment of the great South Indian deity, Lalitambika.

Ammachi not only represents the confluence of these two types or categories of holy figures, but she also embodies in her person, message, and rituals the confluence of two distinct streams that are hallmarks of her spiritual message and movement: tradition and change, fidelity to and defiance of tradition. Ammachi both supports and confounds the status quo through her simple message of unconditional love for all, as embodied and transmitted through her innovative *darshan* ritual, and her ability to acculturate her message and medium to an ever widening global audience that extends beyond Hindu, Indian frontiers.

Ammachi achieves this through the dual strategy of preservation/reformulation and radical departure/defiance of Hindu religious, ritual, and devotional traditions. The features that Ammachi has chosen to retain—some in their totality and others after minor reformulation and reconstruction—include the basic assumptions and teachings of Hindu philosophical, ascetic, and mystical traditions with particular emphasis on the Vedantic goal of self-realization, and, the neo-Vedantic approach to religious pluralism advocated by Ramakrishna and Vivekananda. She has retained and in some ways magnified the vital role of the guru in the disciple's self-realization process. She weaves into her movement strands of the Hindu devotional (*bhakti*) tradition and Hindu ritual idiom, that is, the characteristic worship patterns and religious language of Hinduism. Areas of radical defiance, departure, and innovation include valorizing and supporting women's public ritual roles and women's religious leadership and authority. Her behavior and unique style of *darshan* defy orthodox Hindu notions of purity, pollution, and caste distinctions. Perhaps most radical, she violates Hindu norms regarding physicality between guru and disciple, between divine and human.

In her defiant rejection of many Hindu norms and practices as well as in her radical innovations, Ammachi succeeds in revolutionizing the Hindu religious and ritual tradition in which she is deeply grounded, resulting in an outpouring of interest in her message and movement in the West. Ammachi calls for her disciples and devotees, in India and abroad, to transcend the historical accidents and cultural constraints of the Hindu religious tradition, and places within her devotees' grasp the core truth and central message of god-realization, achievable through unconditional love to all. In her embodied self as guru and goddess, as well as in her embodied ritual of *darshan*, Ammachi concretizes and mediates this divine message of unconditional love.

NOTES

A differently focused discussion of Ammachi and her movement appears in K. Pechilis, ed., *The Graceful Guru* (Oxford: Oxford University Press, 2004). I am thankful to Karen Pechilis, Cynthia Humes, and Thomas Forsthoefel for their valuable suggestions and comments that aided in revising this essay. Thanks are also due to Amanda Fiedler and Kevin Nothnagel for their research assistance, and to Albion College for the Hewlett-Mellon Grant that funded this field research. To protect their privacy, I have used pseudonyms for my informants.

1. Mata Amritanandamayi, *Keep Science at Peace with Nature*, June 1997, *Hinduism Today.* Available from World Wide Web: (http://www.hinduismtoday.com/1997/6/1997-6-07.html).

2. Ibid.

3. Swami Amritaswarupananda, *Ammachi: A Biography of Mata Amritanandamayi* (San Ramon, CA: Mata Amritanandamayi Center, 1994); Timothy Conway, *Women of Power and Grace* (Santa Barbara, CA: The Wake Up Press, 1994); Linda Johnson, *Daughters of the Goddess: The Women Saints of India* (St. Paul: Yes International Publishers, 1994); Savitri L. Bess, *The Path of the Mother* (New York: The Ballantine Publishing Group, 2000); Judith Cornell, *Amma: Healing the Heart of the World* (New York: Harper Collins, 2001).

4. Amritaswarupananda, *Ammachi: A Biography of Mata Amritanandamayi*, 13.

5. Ibid., 14-15.

6. Ibid., 78.

7. M. A. Center, *Amma's Early Years.* Available from World Wide Web: (http://www.ammachi.org/amma/early-years.html).

8. Ibid.

9. Amritaswarupananda, *Ammachi: A Biography of Mata Amritanandamayi*, 91.

10. Ibid., 85.

11. Ibid., 87.

12. Ibid., 86. In the early phase of her spiritual career, Ammachi generally spoke in the first person, but later in her career she began to use the third person when referring to herself.

13. Ibid., 86.

14. Ibid., 92–93, 228–30.

15. Ibid., 146.

16. Marty Gottler, ed., *Come Quickly, My Darling Children: Stories by Western Devotees of Mata Amritanandamayi* (Grass Valley, CA: Sierra Vista Publishing, 1996), 11.

17. Swami Amritaswarupananda, *Awaken Children!*, vol. IX (San Ramon, CA: Mata Amritanandamayi Center, 1998), 45.

18. Throughout this chapter, I have retained the writer or devotee's usage of capitalizing pronouns that refer to Ammachi. Amritaswarupananda, *Ammachi: A Biography of Mata Amritanandamayi*, 144–45.

19. Ibid., 114.

20. Conway, *Women of Power and Grace*, 258.

21. Ibid., 253.

22. Amritaswarupananda, *Awaken Children!*, vii–viii.

23. According to the organization's official Web site, the movement's current network of institutions includes a high tech medical center and hospital, hospice centers, medical outreach programs, eighteen educational institutions specializing in such diverse fields as engineering, business management, industrial training, computers, and Sanskrit, and a series of social development centers such as orphanages, homes for the elderly, and kitchens for the homeless. See M. A. Center, *Amma's Charities*. Available from World Wide Web: (http://www.ammachi.org/charities/index.html). In January 2003, the government of India conferred on Ammachi's educational institutions the "deemed-to-be university" status, an important step in accreditation. Available from World Wide Web: (*http://www.amritapuri.org/education/university.htm*).

24. As of this writing, Ammachi's followers provide constantly updated information on Ammachi *satsangs* in the United States on a Web site. M. A. Center, *United States Satsangs*. Available from World Wide Web: (http://www.ammachi.org/ashram-satsangs/satsang-united-states.html).

25. *Guru Gita*, vs. 157, 87, quoted in Swami Amritaswarupananda, *Awaken Children!*, vol. VI (San Ramon, CA: Mata Amritanandamayi Center, 1995), v.

26. Interview with Swami Paramatmananda in San Ramon on June 20, 1999.

27. Interview in Chicago on July 5, 1999.

28. Tina (Hari Sudha), "God Won't Put Away the Dishes," in M. Gottler, ed., *Come Quickly, My Darling Children*, 128.

29. Amritaswarupananda, *Awaken Children!*, 231–34.

30. Interview in Chicago on July 1, 1999.

31. I once noticed, for instance, an American female devotee wearing the blessed Hershey's Kiss as a pendant in her *rudraksha mala,* the necklace of beads sacred to god Siva.

32. Amritaswarupaananda, *Awaken Children!*, 22.

33. Reportedly, Ammachi does not do *Devi Bhava* when on tour in India although *Devi Bhava* is a regular feature during her tour in the United States.

34. Interview with Janet Turner in Madurai, India, on February 3, 2003.

35. Interview with Janet Turner in Madurai, India, on February 3, 2003.

36. Conway, *Women of Power and Grace*, 257.

37. See Cornell, *Amma: Healing the Heart of the World*, 139–40.

38. Daniel Gold, "Response to 'Mahagurus and their Movements in a Global Context' Panel," *Annual meeting of American Academy of Religion* (Denver: Unpublished, 2001).

39. Amritaswarupananda, *Awaken Children!*, 21.

40. Conway, *Women of Power and Grace*, 265.

41. Cornell, *Amma: Healing the Heart of the World*, 141–42.

42. M. A. Center, *Amma in the Media*. Available from World Wide Web: (http://www.ammachi.org/in-the-media/index.html).

43. Interview with Mary Hatfield in San Ramon, on June 18, 1999.

44. Interview with Janet Turner in Madurai, India, on February 3, 2003.

45. Amritaswarupananda, *Awaken Children!*, 4.

46. This is a statement that was affirmed by devotees after an intensive research stay in San Ramon, June 14–29, 1999.

47. Interview with Donald Semple in Chicago on July 5, 1999.

48. Interview with Mary Hatfield in San Ramon, on June 18, 1999.

49. Diana Eck, *Darshan: Seeing the Divine Image in India* (Chambersburg, PA: Anima Books, 1981), 3.

50. Conway, *Women of Power and Grace*, 265.

51. Although I have not personally witnessed this type of *darshan*, an American devotee who received the "swimming pool *darshan*" at Amritpuri ashram has confirmed this fact during an interview on February 5, 2003, in Madurai, Tamil Nadu.

52. Cited in Cornell, *Amma: Healing the Heart of the World*, 137.

53. Ibid., 139.

54. Ibid., 138.

55. M. A. Center, "An Introduction: Mata Amritanandamayi Devi," (1999) vol. 14. Ashram Brochure.

56. Interview with Amanda Schwartz in Chicago on July 5, 1999.

57. See Joachim Wach, *The Comparative Study of Religions* (New York: Columbia University Press, 1954).

58. See Stanley Tambiah, *The Buddhist Saints of the Forest and the Cult of the Amulets* (Cambridge: Cambridge University Press, 1984).

59. Gold, "Response to 'Mahagurus and their Movements in a Global Context' Panel."

SEVEN

THE PERFECTIBILITY OF PERFECTION

Siddha Yoga as a Global Movement

LOLA WILLIAMSON

IN THE EARLY 1950s in the tiny village of Ganeshpuri located in the Indian state of Maharashtra, a man, dressed in only a loincloth, receives visitors. People from cities and villages around the state and farther travel great distances and stand in line in the hot sun for hours to take sight (*darshan*) of this holy man (*sadhu*), Nityananda. They may or may not see his face, for often he lies on a bed with his back to his visitors. At other times he yells at them to go away. He usually does not speak, and may even throw pieces of fruit, or even stones, at his visitors. When he does speak, he mixes several Indian languages, and his message, consisting of just a few words, is often cryptic.

Jumping ahead twenty years to the early 1970s, a group of disciples are gathered in the courtyard of Shri Gurudev Ashram in Ganeshpuri.[1] It is the evening, and about forty or so disciples, a mixture of Indians and Westerners from various countries, listen to Swami Muktananda as he answers their questions. He speaks in Hindi as a professor translates his words into English. The questions, clearly revealing the concerns of the disciples, stream forth in rapid succession: "What are the qualities of a worthy disciple?" "Which is better for the attainment of peace: meditation or love for the guru?" "How can I overcome jealousy?"[2] Muktananda occasionally warns his disciples that they should not ask so many questions; instead they should focus on their own inner experience. Nevertheless, he patiently responds to their questions and concerns.

Jumping ahead another thirty years, on New Year's Day of 2002, Guru-mayi delivers a carefully planned speech in English to a large audience gath-ered before her. She sits on a chair on a raised platform in a large hall with plush carpet and elaborate chandeliers. She is delivering her message in what has come to be termed Shri Muktananda Ashram in the Catskill Mountains of New York, the international headquarters for Siddha Yoga ("Perfected Yoga"). To ensure that everyone in the hall can see her, Gurumayi's image is projected on large screens slightly above and to either side of her. Perhaps a thousand people sit in front of her, hanging on every word she says as she imparts her New Year's message, just as she has done every New Year's Day since 1992. This year is a bit different though. For the first time, people in other Siddha Yoga ashrams and centers in 164 locations around the world are also receiving her message on television screens via digital satellite or computer webcast, or aurally through a telephone audio interface. Technology has been used before to connect the "global community" of Siddha Yoga devotees, but this is the first time that followers of Siddha Yoga have received her New Year's message together as a world community, or "global *sangham*." The technological support represents and reinforces a communal conviction that Siddha Yoga, a modern development in Hinduism with nonetheless medieval roots, is a transnational community united across boundaries of space, time, and culture.

This is the Siddha Yoga lineage:[3] the enigmatic, mostly silent Nityananda (d. 1961), often referred to as *Bade Baba* (or "Big Baba"); the energetic, at times fiery Muktananda (1908–1982), also referred to as Baba; and the articulate and savvy Chidvilasananda (1955 to present), also referred to as Gurumayi. This lin-eage is understood within the context of the Siddha Yoga movement to be unilinear. This means that, although others may claim to be a part of a descending lineage from Nityananda or Muktananda, the Siddha Yoga move-ment does not recognize them as such.[4] Siddha Yoga itself legitimates and oversees the proper transmission of spiritual authority.

Little is known about the background of Nityananda, the first guru of the Siddha Yoga lineage. He lived as a child in South India, but later took up resi-dence in Ganeshpuri in the Tansa River Valley of Maharashtra not far from Bombay. Anecdotes circulate about his life, but it is difficult to separate histori-cal fact from hagiography. He is considered by his disciples and by Muktananda himself to have come into this world as a self-realized being rather than having attained the state through spiritual practices under the tutelage of a guru. According to Muktananda, Nityananda submitted himself as a youth to an accomplished *Brahmin* (member of the priestly caste) and *yogi* named Ishvara Iyer merely to fulfill a spiritual law.[5] There is also evidence that Nityananda spent time in his early life in the ashram of a Tantric guru, Swami Shivananda.[6] However, it is likely that Nityananda would not be known outside of India were it not for his disciple, Muktananda, who often spoke and wrote of him with great reverence.

The second guru of the lineage, Muktananda, began the process of global-ization through three world tours, leaving behind groups of disciples wherever he went. On his first world tour in 1970, he visited the United States, several European countries, Australia, and Singapore, as well as several major cities in India. His second world tour occurred from 1974 to 1976, and his third from 1978 to 1981. By the time of his death in 1982 he had established centers and ashrams for Siddha Yoga in major cities in the United States, Europe, and Aus-tralia. When Gurumayi succeeded Muktananda, she continued to expand the globalization of the movement, traveling to Mexico, Poland, and Japan, among other places. Books by Muktananda and Gurumayi have been translated into fifteen languages, including Chinese, Russian, and several Indian languages. Today there are eight hundred meditation centers and six ashrams for Siddha Yoga in more than fifty countries. The Northern American Region (the United States, Canada, and the Caribbean) has 214 centers for Siddha Yoga Meditation, with each center in the United States serving an average of thirty-five devotees. The average age of those attending is over forty.[7]

The Siddha Yoga movement is one of many guru-centered meditation movements in which elements of Hinduism have been taken out of their tradi-tionally South Asian context and integrated into other cultures. In the process of global expansion, alterations can often occur in the way spiritual knowledge is conveyed and received. Many changes have occurred in Siddha Yoga over the years due to cultural negotiation and other factors. For one, the simple fact of growth necessitates change. Modifications have also occurred because of the unique personalities of the two gurus who have headed Siddha Yoga since it has become established in different countries. Further, the same technologies that have influenced economic globalization have influenced cultural globalization, including spirituality. Finally, changes have occurred in Siddha Yoga because of unexpected events of succession, a subject I will address later.

Critical elements of this movement have remained the same, of course. The Siddha Yoga path has two foundational beliefs: (1) the grace of the guru, which is given in an initiation called *shaktipat,* in which the spiritual energy (*kundalini*) of the aspirant is awakened and then guided from within,[8] and (2) self-effort, which is the disciple's willingness to follow the spiritual discipline prescribed by the guru and to imbibe his or her teachings. Although both ele-ments remain essential, their form of expression has changed over the years, and it is their transformations that I will characterize here. I write with first-hand knowledge, for I received *shaktipat* from Baba Muktananda and have con-tinued to pursue the practices of Siddha Yoga as a disciple of Gurumayi. I do not claim that my observations of Siddha Yoga are "objective"—everyone sees and makes judgments based on a particular perspective. However, I intend to give a balanced view of what I have observed and studied.

The most obvious change is that Siddha Yoga has had two charismatic gurus who have made Siddha Yoga a world movement, each with a unique style of leadership. Since Muktananda's time as leader of the movement in the 1970s, I have witnessed a rapid growth (which peaked in the late 1980s to early 1990s) and, subsequently, a slow decline in the popularity of Siddha Yoga. The ashram that serves as the international headquarters of Siddha Yoga has expanded from one rather poorly maintained hotel to an estate of three elegant and elaborate hotels, able to house thousands of people attending summer retreats. By 2003, one of these hotels has undergone preparations for its sale due to lack of funds for its upkeep. The clothing styles of visitors to ashrams have changed, too, from hippie to upbeat New York fashion-style to the more relaxed but modest styles popular today. Even the food at ashrams has changed from simple Indian fare to elaborate feasts offered variously by Mexican, Japanese, or European devotees to "tofu pups" and peanut butter and jelly sandwiches (served to make the children feel at home). Social customs of Siddha Yoga change just as they do in the natural course of any modern society—particularly one that is made up of diverse populations from around the world.

On the other hand, some things haven't changed. People visit Siddha Yoga ashrams and practice Siddha Yoga in their homes and local centers to fulfill a longing to know God. Siddha Yoga practitioners chant and meditate. Practitioners share a desire to serve the guru and other devotees. Finally, in Siddha Yoga, there is enthusiasm about *shaktipat*.

SHAKTIPAT INITIATION: THE GRACE OF THE GURU

Shaktipat initiation is a defining foundation of the Siddha Yoga movement. This section will examine what *shaktipat* is, how the form in which it is given has changed over time, and how these changes coincide with and support a globalization of Siddha Yoga.

Medieval texts of Kashmir Shaivism, a sect of Hinduism, describe *shaktipat* as the "descent of grace," which awakens a type of spiritual energy called *kundalini*. Until it is awakened, *kundalini*, often depicted as a serpent, is understood to lie dormant in an energy center (*chakra*) located in the subtle body at base of the spine (*muladhara chakra*). When *shaktipat* occurs, this *kundalini* "uncoils" and rises up the spine to the other *chakras* until it eventually reaches the highest subtle energy center (*sahasrara*), known as the "thousand-petaled lotus." At this culmination, the aspirant attains liberation (*moksha*).[9] Siddha Yoga teaches that the safest and easiest way for this energy to be awakened is through the grace of a *shaktipat* guru.

Although references to *shaktipat* in scriptures are scanty and sometimes appear in veiled language, nevertheless it has been documented in textual sources since the sixth or seventh centuries as a very rare occurrence.[10] Kashmir Shaivite philosopher Abhinavagupta wrote about it more extensively.[11] When Muktananda first received *shaktipat*, he did not understand the full import of this initiation. In his autobiography, *Play of Consciousness,* Muktananda describes his experience of receiving *shaktipat* from Nityananda:

> He looked into my eyes. . . . A ray of light was coming from his pupils, and going right inside me. Its touch was searing, red hot, and its brilliance dazzled my eyes like a high-powered bulb. As this ray flowed from Bhagavan Nityananda's eyes into my own, the very hair on my body rose in wonder, awe, ecstasy and fear. I went on repeating his mantra Guru Om, watching the colors of this ray. It was an unbroken stream of divine radiance. Sometimes it was the color of molten gold, sometimes saffron, sometimes a deep blue, more lustrous than a shining star. I stood there, stunned, watching the brilliant rays passing into me.[12]

He became confused and sometimes frightened when he began to witness the *kundalini* working to purify his mind and body. Later, he found scriptural sources to support his experiences and began to align himself with the Kashmir Shaivite school, which is considered part of a broader categorization of medieval texts and practices called *Tantra.*

While both Muktananda and Gurumayi have drawn on Kashmiri Shaivite texts to support their teaching, they have also drawn on Vedantic and Yogic philosophical schools, Indian folklore, the great Indian epics, medieval poet-saints, the Sufi tradition, as well as mystical traditions from other world religions. Their eclecticism is unified by the philosophy and practice of *shaktipat.*

All three Siddha Yoga gurus are believed to be *shaktipat* gurus with the ability to awaken and guide the *kundalini* energy in their disciples. However, the way in which *shaktipat* is given in Siddha Yoga is not conventional. *Shaktipat* has traditionally been reserved for people who have prepared for it through years of spiritual practice under the guidance of a guru.[13] In its Tantric context, *shaktipat* was also given as part of a ritual.[14] In Siddha Yoga, the requirement that the aspirant must be qualified through preliminary practice and the use of elaborate rituals were abandoned. In Nityananda's time, and in the early days of Muktananda's time, *shaktipat* simply occurred—often by surprise. Following is a description from a person who witnessed his friend receiving *shaktipat* from Nityananda:

> Nityananda was standing there, and this other man was standing in front of him. . . . I saw a blue light coming [from Bade Baba's eyes], like the light that comes when you hold a flashlight in the darkness, a blue light going in and entering his forehead like this. It was going from Nityananda's eyes to this man's forehead, like a continuous light entering. The man shouted "Om" and then fell down. He was shaking on the ground like a bird. I saw all this. I wept like a child, because [I thought], "I have brought one man and he dies here."[15]

Shaktipat occurred in a similarly unexpected manner in Muktananda's ashram in Ganeshpuri. There was no ritual or program surrounding the initiation. Later, when he first traveled to the West, people often received *shaktipat* in informal gatherings or retreats with Muktananda. At times, even people who were not seeking it—a journalist reporting on Muktananda, for example—would receive *shaktipat*. In 1974, during Muktananda's second world tour, the bestowal of *shaktipat* was formalized by the creation of the "Intensive," in which hundreds of people were given *shaktipat* at the same time. The Intensive was a two-day retreat in which people practiced meditation, chanted, and listened as Muktananda spoke about *kundalini* awakening and the path of practice or *sadhana* that they were to follow.

The creation of the Intensive is a good example of the cross-fertilization of cultural idioms. Weekend programs during the mid-1970s such as est (Erhard Seminars Training) and other various human development movements were popular, and it is likely that they helped inspire this format. An ancient Tantric tradition of initiation was made to fit into a Western format of a weekend course, complete with a set fee. People who took an Intensive were guaranteed to have results at the end of the two days, which plays into the Western emphasis on instant gratification. For the most part, the desire for transformation was (and is) satisfied by taking an Intensive, and some people have experienced profound transformation in these weekend Intensives. However, such a Western consumerist notion of guaranteed results in exchange for money put down may be taking the American dream too far. *Shaktipat* depends not only on the will of the guru, but also on the receptiveness of the initiate, and thus cannot be guaranteed. I have talked to people who feel that they did not receive anything in an Intensive, and the explanation that they received a "subtle" form of *shaktipat* did not satisfy them.[16]

While some may not be satisfied in a weekend, changes initiated by Muktananda succeeded in aiding Siddha Yoga to become a global movement. By doing away with the requirement of spiritual qualification to receive *shaktipat*, Muktananda democratized initiation. Obviously, there would be no world Siddha Yoga movement based on *shaktipat* if it were only given to a qualified few. The later innovation of giving *shaktipat* in a "packaged format" gave the movement uniformity so that it could be transported easily from place to place. In fact, Muktananda even instructed others to give Intensives in his name, with the understanding that *shaktipat* would occur through his will.[17] Intensives could also be marketed to the public in a way that was not possible when *shaktipat* was given more informally. Finally, charging a fee made the process more tangible to a Western consumer-oriented culture.[18] Of course, charging a fee also had practical implications; it paid for many of the expenses of travel, facility rental, etc., making it possible to offer more Intensives.

When Gurumayi succeeded Muktananda, she adopted a similar format for the Intensive, but over time, she made less and less direct personal contact with the people taking Intensives. Muktananda, from the time he established Intensives until his death, and Gurumayi, in the early 1980s, typically walked around and touched each person during meditation sessions, usually on the forehead between the eyebrows, an area of the physical body that corresponds to a spiritual center called the *ajña chakra*. Persons might also be touched at the base of the spine. Both are gestures intended to awaken the *kundalini*. In the mid- to late-1980s Gurumayi stopped doing these active gestures and instead gave *shaktipat* by her will. In 1989, the first satellite broadcast Intensive occurred with people receiving *shaktipat* again through her will, not through her physical presence or touch. Even before this time people who had traveled to an ashram to be with Gurumayi were often not in the same room with her during an Intensive due to the large number of people in attendance. Video cameras carried the Intensive to "overflow rooms" when talks were being given. Prior to the development of audio and satellite hookups that allowed for a new kind of *shaktipat* transmission, people sometimes had to sit so close together during Intensives that the knees of disciples sitting on the floor were touching the backs of the people in front of them.

Today, global satellite Intensives are becoming more and more popular because people can participate from their local meditation center without having to undertake burdensome travel. Moreover, the ashram itself is usually more comfortable because it is less crowded. In short, the technological advances associated with the satellite Intensives signal a major change in the understanding of *shaktipat*. While Tantric texts explain that *shaktipat* can be given through look, touch, mantra, or will, that *shaktipat* might be transmitted globally to hundreds of different locations simultaneously is quite an innovation. This innovation changes the understanding of what a personal relationship between a guru and his or her disciples means, a topic that I will discuss later.

SADHANA: THE DISCIPLE'S SELF-EFFORT

Changes have also occurred over the years regarding what constitutes "the path of Siddha Yoga." Some of these changes are due to the different styles of Muktananda and Gurumayi, and some of them are due to the need to "globalize" Siddha Yoga so that the path is amenable to a broader range of people. It should be noted, however, that the majority of Siddha Yoga practitioners, although they may come from different cultures, often have more in common with each other than different groups of people from the same culture. Siddha Yoga seems to attract professional middle to upper-middle-class people, the majority of whom are in their midlife; however, among middle-aged disciples, many began practicing Siddha Yoga in their twenties.

When Muktananda was the guru, *sadhana* consisted of following a daily routine that he prescribed for his devotees. When people visited his ashrams, they followed this routine completely. When they left the ashram and returned to their daily lives, they were encouraged to maintain as much of the routine as was possible for their circumstances. Within the ashram, and also within retreats that were given as Baba traveled to different locations, the day began at 3:00 a.m. with meditation. There was also an early morning temple ceremony of chanting and waving lights before a statue of Nityananda, Muktananda's guru, or to Nityananda's picture, if the ceremony took place at different retreat sites. The rest of the day consisted of alternating periods of chanting and communal work, such as cooking or gardening. The schedule varied slightly over the years, and the texts that were chanted also varied. However, Muktananda always maintained strict discipline for himself until the day he died, and he expected similar discipline from ashram residents. When people left the ashram and returned to their homes, the two practices that most people followed were an early morning meditation and the chanting of the *Guru Gita*, a medieval text that expresses the qualities of an enlightened guru and the benefits of devotion to that guru.

While the ashram schedule remained the same for several years after Gurumayi became the guru, gradually changes were initiated that reflect a shift in the overall attitude of practitioners of Siddha Yoga. In Muktananda's time, as well as in the early days of Gurumayi's time as leader, there was a lot of emphasis on attaining enlightenment, and it was believed that performing lots of spiritual practices—particularly chanting, meditation, and service to the guru—was the way to that end. The emphasis has shifted from attaining quick enlightenment to enjoying the path and preserving it for future generations. This transition corresponds to a shift in the focus of many Siddha Yoga practitioners from self-absorption to more active social involvement with families and careers.

The differences in approach between Muktananda and Gurumayi approximate distinctions that Richard Gombrich has made to describe two kinds of religion: soteriological and communal.[19] Soteriological religions emphasize the practices and beliefs that are necessary for attaining salvation—and attaining it quickly. Communal religions emphasize practices and beliefs that ensure the continuity of social life. Muktananda's and Gurumayi's approaches are representative of soteriological and communal religions respectively. Enlightenment remains the goal of the Siddha Yoga mission today as it was when Muktananda first traveled to the West. However, the road to enlightenment is slower and gentler today in contrast to earlier times. In the last five years, there is a growing awareness within the movement of the need to preserve the teachings of Siddha Yoga for future generations. This awareness draws people's attention away from concern for their own spiritual enlightenment, to a certain extent, and toward more concern for the well-being of others.

Two areas in particular point to the difference in the two gurus' approaches: attitudes toward sexuality and toward the types of spiritual practices that each emphasized. Muktananda reiterated many times the value of celibacy for the practitioner (*sadhaka*). He advocated restraint, even for those married, to convert sexual energy into spiritual energy. Muktananda oversaw the initiation of sixty-five monks (*sannyasis*) between the years of 1972 and 1982. Muktananda's followers were well aware of the potential to become a *sannyasi*, or at least of informally maintaining a status of celibacy. In contrast, Gurumayi has not overseen the initiation of any *sannyasis*. In fact, she has openly encouraged single disciples to get married and married disciples to have children. In the mid-1980s, she initiated an annual singles' dance. This dance later became open to everyone, single or married, but the purpose of the occasion for single people remains the same: matchmaking. Perhaps Gurumayi knows that followers of Siddha Yoga—most of them accustomed to a modern and westernized lifestyle—are not able to embrace the rigors of renunciation.[20]

The distinction between their approaches should not be viewed as dichotomous. Muktananda never advocated that people in committed social relationships should leave their families. He taught, as Gurumayi after him, that both householders and renunciants could attain the goal of enlightenment. What occurred under Gurumayi's leadership, however, was a shift in emphasis. Much of her teaching is directed toward practical, everyday matters of living in the world. An example of this is the interest she has taken in families. She has initiated the development of resources for the spiritual education of children, including toys, books, songs, and special courses. During summer retreats at Shree Muktananda Ashram in New York, the children perform plays with an Indian spiritual theme, such as the life of a poet-saint. Gurumayi has also established special family retreats. Gatherings (*satsangs*) with Gurumayi may revolve around the topic of family issues. For example, during the summer retreat of 2000 at Shree Muktananda Ashram Gurumayi held daily *satsangs* for a period of a week for children and their caretakers in which she posed questions, sometimes to the children and sometimes to the adults, about how to nurture loving and supportive relationships within the family.

A second area that provides evidence of a change from a soteriological to a communal approach occurs in the spiritual practices that each guru has emphasized. Muktananda loved to lead long ecstatic chants, sometimes lasting throughout the night, or even for days at a time. He also emphasized the chanting of texts such as the *Bhagavad Gita*, the *Shiva Mahima*, and the *Rudram*. In Muktananda's time, people sometimes pushed themselves to the point of exhaustion to keep up with the strict discipline that he enforced in his ashrams. While chanting is still very much a part of Siddha Yoga life under Gurumayi's leadership, it is incorporated into *sadhana* in a more balanced way. Gurumayi stresses the importance of being gentle with oneself and listening to one's need for rest and relaxation. This change has occurred gradually. In the early days of her role as guru, she also held all-night chants and sometimes all-night *seva* or service sessions. But, over time, the discipline has changed so that being well rested in order to maintain one's health is encouraged. While the time for rising at ashrams is still very early (usually 4:00 a.m.), everyone is encouraged to be in bed by 9:00 p.m. The sense of urgency to attain enlightenment quickly, which was often apparent in Muktananda's time, is gone. Balancing chanting and meditation with other activities, including ample physical exercise and time for enjoying social activities or communing with nature, is now encouraged.

Although the Hindu-based practices of chanting Sanskrit texts and performing worship (*puja*) still occur in Siddha Yoga, Gurumayi's emphasis is discovering one's own inner wisdom through contemplating ordinary daily experiences within the context of scriptural texts or Gurumayi's or Muktananda's words. Technology aids this form of *sadhana* as monthly themes are posted on the Siddha Yoga Web site for devotees around the world to contemplate. Gurumayi has also established a tradition of giving a talk on New Year's Day that includes a statement to guide people's contemplation for the coming year. Contemplation is both individual and communal. Devotees of Gurumayi, whether living in Australia, Poland, India, or Africa, are contemplating the same theme as other devotees around the world. Study groups are often formed at ashrams and local centers to share insights on the monthly or yearly theme. These themes are meant to serve as guides to help people bring spiritual values into everyday life situations. The process of contemplation involves keeping a journal and sharing one's thoughts with other devotees. By emphasizing the contemplation of day-to-day life experiences, Gurumayi seems to be creating a *sadhana* that is more socially oriented than the *sadhana* that was practiced in Muktananda's time. Since contemplation does not depend on Hindu religious forms, it can be easily practiced by people from different cultural backgrounds. However, it should be noted again that the majority of Siddha Yoga students come from the same economic and educational class for whom the study of ideas through writing, reading, and conversation is quite often appealing.[21]

As Siddha Yoga globalizes, there has also been a change in the types of experiences deemed worthy of discussion and public presentation. Discussing experiences on the path has always been a part of Siddha Yoga. However, today there is a softening in the language used in making assertions about mystical experiences. *Kundalini* experiences are not talked about in public programs as they were in earlier days of the movement (although they still may be discussed in private conversations). There was a time when a person attending an introductory program in Siddha Yoga would be given a feast of experiences by an array of people who had received *shaktipat*. One might stand up and describe how in Gurumayi's presence a bolt of lightening had entered through the top of her head and she had suddenly merged into infinite space. A second might then describe how he had seen a cobra in meditation, merging with that cobra, finally finding himself hissing like a snake.[22] A third might describe suddenly having x-ray vision as the walls melted and she could see into the next room. While these experiences may still be discussed in private conversations, they are not talked about in public venues. If a person were to attend an introductory program today, he or she would be shown a video highlighting smiling faces of people in centers and ashrams and told about the peacefulness that meditation brings to one's life and about the charity work of the SYDA foundation. This type of presentation gives a softer and more acceptable public face to Siddha Yoga than the dramatic, even frightening, accounts of the awakened *kundalini*.

THE GURU-DISCIPLE RELATIONSHIP AND THE QUEST FOR PERFECTION

Both *shaktipat* and *sadhana* are based on a relationship between the guru and the disciple, and changes have occurred in the expression of this relationship as Siddha Yoga has become a global movement. As Hindu gurus establish ashrams and centers for meditation in Western countries, an Indian paradigm of authority structure often travels with them. This system has two aspects, both of which can be problematic when placed in a Western cultural framework that esteems egalitarianism and independent thinking. One aspect is seen in the religious realm, which understands spiritual perfection as the goal of life, and which views people who are believed to have attained that goal as equivalent to God. This concept can make Siddha Yoga's acceptance by a Western audience difficult. It is easier for a person raised with values of independent thinking and material and intellectual achievement to accept a meditation movement such as TM that promises better IQ scores or a reduction in stress levels than it is to accept one that emphasizes the spiritual perfectibility of human beings. Another aspect is seen in the traditionally hierarchical social structure of Indian society, which values obedience to those higher in the structure. Both of these traditions play an important role in ashrams and schools of gurus (*guru kulas*) in India, and often continue to play an important role in Hindu-based ashrams and meditation centers in Western countries.

The concept of an "enlightened" person has a long and rich history in the philosophy and practice of Hinduism as well as in the other Indian religions of Sikhism, Jainism, Buddhism, and Sufism. The descriptions of this state and the means for attaining it vary from one tradition to another, but the state itself—a heightened state of consciousness that transcends "ordinary" or habituated consciousness—is not questioned in the Indian tradition. The concept of such a state, however, has been inimical to much of Western thought, especially in the twentieth century. Moreover, the notion of an intrinsic and exalted state of consciousness finds little support in Western religious traditions, which instead emphasize the innate sinfulness of humanity. Many Christians, Jews, and Muslims, operating from a dualism of Creator and created, hold with considerable suspicion the notion that humans can attain a state of liberation here and now. Yet Muktananda held forth the promise of a liberating consciousness free of the identifications of mind and body. Indeed, he described the awareness of the enlightened guru as above the body and senses. For Muktananda, "the guru is entirely God."[23] Muktananda assured his followers that the state of perfection that he had attained would be theirs, too, after they followed the Siddha path. "The difference between you and the guru," he stated, "is that you are the seed and the Guru is the full-grown tree: you are beginning, and he is the end. Inherently, the only difference between you is that one step."[24]

The very name "Siddha Yoga" encapsulates the idea of the spiritual perfectibility of human beings, for a *siddha* is understood within this movement to mean one who has attained perfection and who can lead others to this same perfection. Even if the idea of human perfectibility is acceded to, the idea that this perfection can be transmitted to another human being is highly problematic for many Westerners. Those who leave the Siddha Yoga movement often do so because they no longer believe that the living guru or a former guru of this lineage is "perfect," or they do not believe that a guru has the ability to guide others to a state of perfection, both tenets of the Siddha Yoga movement. For example, a group of former Siddha Yoga devotees wrote, "We now know it is not in Gurumayi's or anyone else's power to grant enlightenment. Grace is in each of us to do that for ourselves, each in our own way."[25] This statement accords well with the Enlightenment "turn to the subject" that has so influenced the West since the seventeenth century. It contrasts sharply with Muktananda's assertion that "[a] Siddha student shouldn't forget that he cannot achieve spiritual perfection through his own efforts. . . . Modern ideas on freedom and self-expression are considered obstacles to Siddha students."[26] Certainly, the idea that grace is within each of us and we can and do attain an enlightened state through our own efforts and in our own way is more attractive to Western sensibilities than the idea that freedom and self-expression are obstacles to attaining an enlightened state.

How has Siddha Yoga dealt with this gap in cultural perspectives? To answer this question, we must first understand why Siddha Yoga students believe their guru is perfect and can lead them to that same state of perfection. Very simply, it is because followers of this path value their experience of *shaktipat* which gave them a taste of perfection. It is the power of this experience, more than any verbal assertions or outer display of power (*siddhi*), that drew people to Muktananda and that now draws people to Gurumayi. The following description of one person's experience of *shaktipat* is illustrative of how Siddha Yoga devotees' faith in people's inherent divinity is kindled.

> What happened next was like a bolt of lightening going up my spine. It literally threw me to the floor. A flood of blissful energy surged through every cell of my body until, at one point, I was aware that I was nothing

but totally peaceful, loving, joyful energy, scintillating in the form of a human body. I also "knew" with utmost certainty that this energy had created the universe, that it was divine, and that it was me.[27]

Experiences like this, which vary from person to person, but which in some way offer a feeling of connection to something larger than one's ordinary sense of limitation, provide an affiliation between devotees on the Siddha Yoga path. One could say that Muktananda and Gurumayi have "globalized" the belief in perfection, not by convincing people on an intellectual level, but by giving them an intimate experience of its potency. But where does this leave the outside observer? Could not the whole experience of supposed perfection, or glimpses of perfection—the state in which consciousness "penetrates" divine, infinite, transcendental reality—be fabricated? Could it not be the result of an infantile fantasy to return to a state where the ego does not have to assert its independence? And further, after people have these experiences, should not the way they live their lives reflect their experience of inner divinity, offering outward proof of their inner experiences?[28]

These are not just the questions of outsiders. Some followers of the Siddha Yoga path also began to ask similar questions following a succession scandal after Muktananda's death in 1982. In 1981, in anticipation of his death, Baba Muktananda named two devotees as his successors. First he chose Subhash, a young man of eighteen, giving him the name of his own guru: Nityananda. Many were surprised because not only did Nityananda seem very young for assuming this responsibility, but he also possessed an unassuming and casual manner. Six months later, Muktananda named this young man's sister, Malti, Subhash's senior by eight years, as his successor as well, giving her the name Chidvilasananda. People once again were surprised. Not only was she a woman, but she was a beautiful woman. She did not fit the idea of a wise old master that people associated with the word *guru*. Some people left the Siddha Yoga movement because they could not accept these young, somewhat westernized, English-speaking "kids" as their guru. In fact, younger devotees, who had been around Baba for many years, had grown up with Subhash and Malti. For some of them, it seemed impossible to accept a friend as a guru. There was also confusion about having two gurus. The teaching in Siddha Yoga, as in much of the Indian Hindu tradition, is that a person should dedicate him or herself to one guru.

The confusion about two gurus came to a head when Nityananda announced his resignation in 1985. He said in a public program that Muktananda had told him that he was only to serve as guru for three years, and then Gurumayi was to be the sole guru. Perhaps the affair would have ended there if Nityananda did not come back later to assert that he still was a guru. At this point several female swamis and other long-term residents of the ashram spoke openly of having sexual encounters with Nityananda.[29] At the same time, other swamis admitted to having broken their vows of celibacy with other partners and many of them left the ashram at this time or shortly after. Leadership of the SYDA Foundation revealed that Nityananda had been told to announce that he would be a guru for only three years in order to save face for himself and for the Siddha Yoga movement. Nityananda left the official Siddha Yoga movement and began to act as a guru in his own right. This was taken as an affront by the original Siddha Yoga community, and people were sent to harass Nityananda in public. Many felt, and still feel, that the entire situation was handled in a highly flawed manner by both parties.

The personal experiences Siddha Yoga devotees had with this path did not correlate with what they saw taking place in the organization's hierarchy. This caused them to deny that perfection, in any sense of the word, could exist. It may have been a combination of the events of the mid-eighties, as well as the need to lessen the gap between insider and outsider as Siddha Yoga grew as a world movement, that led to a softening of language about human perfectibility and an increased emphasis on pure, simple morality. Followers of the Siddha path, and even the gurus of the Siddha path, came to be viewed as fallible, in the sense that they could make mistakes in the human, relative world, even while maintaining a connection to their inner divine nature.

This change actually brought Westerners more in line with the traditional Hindu view of liberation (moksha). The Western conception of perfection has traditionally revolved around the idea that the human personality must become morally good. In Indian yogic philosophy, however, it is not the personality that attains salvation; rather, the personality—understood to always be involved in the vicissitudes of life dramas—is transcended. The Yoga Sutras, a key text in the yoga system of philosophy, describes this realization of the separateness of relative and transcendental levels as "isolation" or "transcendental aloneness" (kaivalya). The realm of morality lies in the relative realm of existence where perfection can never exist. However, as Hindu and Western conceptions of perfection mingle, as they have since Christian missionaries have influenced Indians and Hindu gurus have influenced the West, notions of spiritual perfection may be evolving.

The conflict raised questions about the authenticity of the gurus—not only of the two successors, but also of Baba Muktananda himself. Some who had bypassed earlier accusations against Muktananda now began to question his authority.[30] Could he have made a mistake when choosing Subhash as his successor? Other questions also arose and have been articulated by those who left the movement at this time or later. Many of these questions centered on the core concept of Siddha Yoga: that it is possible for a human being to attain perfection. Since the organization of Siddha Yoga was involved in these scandals and in their cover-up, questions about its role also arose. How does the authority of the organization intersect with the authority of the guru? How can leaders in this organization who have been practicing Siddha Yoga for many years make such bad decisions? It is likely that questions also arose for people who did not leave the movement, questions that may have been discussed in private conversations, or perhaps never articulated at all, remaining half-formed doubts within their minds. Questions about perfection and authority are worthy of consideration by anyone, and, indeed, they have tremendous importance for the seeker who dedicates his or her life to a guru. It is my opinion that these questions have not been dealt with adequately and openly within the Siddha Yoga community. The scandal of the 1980s could well serve this evolving idea of perfection if the Siddha Yoga organization were open to examining it fully.

While there has not been an open discussion about these issues, Gurumayi has guided her disciples' thinking about matters of spiritual perfection and authority in several ways. First, she has diverted attention away from attaining a future state of perfection and placed it on working in the present with one's individual tendencies that obscure the experience of peace and love. Second, she has diverted attention away from herself as an exemplar of perfection and placed it on her disciples' abilities to access their own inner wisdom in making practical and spiritual decisions. These changes have affected not only the way *sadhana* is conceived, but also the way the guru-disciple relationship is experienced. In the past, physical proximity to the guru was emphasized, for it was believed that the closer one could get to the guru, the better the chances were of having an electrifying experience. There was a time when Gurumayi could not walk around the ashram without people practically pushing others out of the way to get closer to her. Being seated close to Gurumayi as she gave talks or held Intensives was considered so important that people would line up for hours ahead of time. Devotees also used to feel that they should discuss—either in person or through writing letters—both major and minor decisions with Gurumayi. All of that clamoring after the guru's attention and personal direction has changed, in large part due to Gurumayi's insistence that her devotees learn to listen to the "inner guru," the perfection within themselves.

The traditionally hierarchical social structure of India has also been challenged as a result of the globalization of Siddha Yoga, and perhaps also as a result of the succession scandal of the mid-eighties. In traditional South Asian ashrams and guru *kulas* or schools, the guru's word is final. However, in "global" Siddha Yoga there is more and more interaction between the guru and the various evolving organizational structures. In the mid-1970s a legal structure called the SYDA Foundation (Siddha Yoga Dham Associates) was set up by Muktananda to handle the financial and organizational aspects of the movement. This body began to make decisions that were formerly handled only by Muktananda. The SYDA Foundation continues in this organizational capacity with its international headquarters located at Shree Muktananda Ashram in South Fallsburg, New York.

In the mid-1990s, a further decentralization of decision making occurred. For many years the staff of Shree Muktananda Ashram handled organizational details ranging from the dissemination of publications to the training of center leaders to run meditation centers around the world. Until the mid-1990s every question raised in various centers—small or large—was directed to the "Centers' Office" in South Fallsburg. This changed when a regional system was set up, first in the United States, then in Europe, and, in 1999, in India. Regional teams were formed to oversee different areas, such as finance, programming, public relations, etc. In addition, teams were set up to run meditation centers that were previously under the direction of just one person. Members of these center teams generally rotate every two years. In 2000, a chief executive officer and a chief operations officer were added to the top of the organizational structure. Leadership is also shared through a recent initiative in which leaders in different areas are called together to create principles to guide the dissemination of knowledge and practice in their particular area. As of this writing, two groups have been formed: one in the area of music and another in the area of leadership.

Several philanthropic and educational organizations are associated with Siddha Yoga. The Prison Project brings the practices of Siddha Yoga into eight hundred prisons worldwide. *Prasad* offers nutrition to Indian children and free medical and dental care to sixty thousand rural Indian villages each year, as well as cataract surgery camps in Mexico and India. The Muktabodha Indological Research Institute was founded under the guidance of Gurumayi to preserve and disseminate the religious heritage of India through sponsoring research by Indological scholars and publishing new scholarly research.

In my interviews with Siddha Yoga devotees, many expressed the conviction that the institution, far from being a bureaucratic monolith, was in fact accessible and personal, offering a sense of being a part of a lively, engaged community. With the new structure of the community, opportunities abound for members to express their concerns openly and authentically. Questions or suggestions can be directed to the local team, from there to the regional team, and from there to the national team; answers then work their way back down the network. Technology also helps in the communication process; for example, an e-mail address was created that receives comments and suggestions for the CEO. Suggestions that come from local centers or individuals are sometimes shared in global community meetings. The open communication makes people feel a part of the process of change and growth. This forthrightness extends into the area of finances. In the past, finances of the movement were not discussed openly. Even at the local level, the finances of meditation centers were not revealed. However, today financial statements—replete with pie and bar graphs that indicate how much money is received from different sources and how the money is used—are available to Siddha Yoga students.

The main criticism that has been expressed by some former ashram staff about the current structure of the organization is that full-time staff are overworked and underpaid. Traditionally in India, serving a guru was considered not only an honor, but also the fastest route to enlightenment. No price was considered too high to pay for this privilege. However, a new sensibility seems to be emerging in the Siddha Yoga organization. In this case, those in the employ of the organization often carry expectations of the rewards and benefits that are typically found in mainstream corporate structures. This sensibility, imported into Siddha Yoga by a modern, sophisticated clientele, reveals another intriguing interface between a contemporary religious movement and its broader cultural context.

THE FUTURE OF SIDDHA YOGA

The number of participants in Siddha Yoga is not rising, nor is it holding steady. There are a number of possible reasons for this. One is the change of tide in interest in Eastern meditative traditions: The fervor of the sixties and seventies is gone. The age of participants is rising, with the average age in the North American region being forty to fifty. Although there are families who practice Siddha Yoga together, many of the children in these families do not become devotees themselves. Another reason for the lack of growth is that people who practice Siddha Yoga are, for the most part, not the proselytizing type. As I interviewed twenty practitioners of Siddha Yoga, none of them expressed interest in talking about their path with others.

With the reduction in numbers and the economic downturn, financial support has also dwindled. As a result, some facilities that are run at enormous cost will be shut down. The emphasis now is on developing resources within areas around the world rather than relying heavily on central gathering places such as Shree Muktananda Ashram.

In the coming years the model of the guru-disciple relationship will continue to change as the emphasis shifts from being in the physical presence of Gurumayi to imbibing her teachings on a daily basis wherever one may be living. In November 2001, the CEO of the SYDA Foundation revealed a recently developed plan, during a "global meeting," to divide the world into seven strong administrative teaching regions in order to provide a clear path of education for devotees from "A–Z, initiation to enlightenment." The regions are India, Europe, North America, Mexico, South America, the Asian Pacific, and Africa.

Staff development will draw mostly from people within the region, although swamis and other teachers will travel to various centers. The CEO commented that appropriate adjustments would be made to accommodate the customs of the regions. It will be interesting to see in the upcoming years how these adjustments to local customs will play out and how many of the Indian customs that have traveled with Siddha Yoga will remain. Currently, there is quite a bit of uniformity so that if one were to visit a center for Siddha Yoga in India, in the United States, in Australia, or in South Africa, one would find the format of the programs, as well as the culture of the center, to be very similar. Certain Indian customs, such as taking off one's shoes before entering a designated holy area, or the seating of men and women on separate sides of the room, have traveled with Siddha Yoga. Vegetarianism has also accompanied the spread of Siddha Yoga—although recently, the use of eggs in baking has been initiated in some regions. Perhaps some of these customs will change as Siddha Yoga becomes more regionalized.

All religions adapt to local customs when geographically dispersed. However, the growth of communication technologies tends to homogenize cultural differences somewhat. This means that Siddha Yoga, as it continues to take advantage of these new technologies, may not "regionalize" as much as it would without the technologies. How much it varies from one region to another will also depend partly on how much independent innovation is encouraged by Gurumayi and the SYDA Foundation. In any case, if this movement is to retain the name "Siddha Yoga," its central focus will also continue to be the belief that human beings can realize spiritual perfection—perhaps with an evolving understanding of what "spiritual perfection" means—through receiving initiation and guidance in *sadhana* from the head of the lineage.

NOTES

1. Today this ashram is called Gurudev Siddha Peeth.

2. Weekly question and answer sessions from 1971 to 1974 are recorded in five volumes called *Satsang With Baba: Questions and Answers with Swami Muktananda*, (Oakland: SYDA Foundation, 1974, 1976, 1977, 1978, 1978).

3. Siddha Yoga is the name that Muktananda gave to the practices and teachings he espoused, and Gurumayi continues to use this name. Douglas Brooks defined Siddha Yoga as "the distinctive body of teachings, practices, and interpretations that follow from Swami Muktananda's spiritual intention to sustain his own lineage's transmissive power." *Meditation Revolution* (South Fallsburg, NY: Agama Press, 1997), xxvi. Brooks derives this definition in part from a "Constitution of Siddha Yoga" drawn up by Muktananda in 1961 outlining the rules for lineage succession, as well as the guru of this lineage's right to extend the name of Siddha Yoga.

4. One of these gurus, Gurumayi's brother, will be discussed in more detail later in the chapter. Others who claim descent from Muktananda include: Swami Shankarananda, head of the Shiva Ashram near Melbourne, Australia; Master Charles, founder of the Synchronicity Foundation in the Blue Ridge Mountains of Virginia;

Swami Chetananda, guru of The Nityananda Institute in Portland, Oregon; Swami Shambavananda, leader of the Shoshoni Retreat Center in Colorado; Gabriel Cousins, head of Tree of Life spiritual and physical healing center in Patagonia, Arizona; and Adi Da in Fiji, who is believed by his followers to be an incarnation of God (*avatar*).

5. See Muktananda, *Bhagawan Nityananda of Ganeshpuri* (South Fallsburg, NY: SYDA Foundation, 1996). Swami Durgananda outlines what is known of Nityananda's life in her chapter, "Without Talking, He Gave Instructions: Bhagawan Nityananda of Ganeshpuri," *Meditation Revolution* (South Fallsburg, NY: SYDA Foundation, 1997). In a footnote to this chapter, she states (595) that Nityananda's relationship to Ishwara Iyer was verified in 1995 by Swami Anantananda's interviews with Iyer's relatives and neighbors.

6. Sarah Caldwell, "The Heart of the Secret: A Personal and Scholarly Encounter with Shakta Tantrism in Siddha Yoga," *Nova Religio: Journal of Alternative and Emergent Religions* 5, no. 1 (2001): 22.

7. These statistics were gathered by the SYDA Foundation in 2002. There appears to be a decline in numbers since then.

8. Abhinavagupta (tenth century) wrote about *shaktipat* in the *Tantraloka*. Other primary texts that discuss *shaktipat* are the *Tirumantiram, Yogavasistha,* and *Kularnava Tantra.* For contemporary explanations of *shaktipat*, see Deba Brata SenSharma, *The Philosophy of Sadhana* (Albany: State University of New York Press, 1990); Swami Shivom Tirth, *A Guide to Shaktipat* (Paige, TX: Devatma Shakti Society, 1985); Swami Vishnu Tirth, *Devatma Shakti*, 5th ed. (Rishikesh: Yoga Shri Peeth Trust, 1980); Paul Muller-Ortega, *"Shaktipat," Meditation Revolution* (South Fallsburg, NY: Agama Press, 1997), 407–44; and almost any copy of *Darshan,* a SYDA Foundation monthly magazine, which features articles about *shaktipat* written by people who have experienced it.

9. While there is much speculation in modern psychology about the relationship between mind and body, Siddha Yoga draws on the philosophical tradition of Vedanta that addresses the relationship between four bodies: the physical, subtle, causal, and supracausal. For a description of spiritual bodies and *chakras* as they are understood in Siddha Yoga, see Swami Kripananda, *The Sacred Power* (South Fallsburg, NY: SYDA Foundation, 1995); Swami Durgananda, *The Heart of Meditation* (South Fallsburg, NY: SYDA Foundation, 2002); and Swami Muktananda, *Kundalini: The Secret of Life* (South Fallsburg, NY: SYDA Foundation, 1980). Lilian Silburn, *Kundalini: Energy of the Depths* (Albany: State University of New York Press, 1988), is also helpful.

10. Paul Muller-Ortega notes that references are found "in such geographically distant and chronologically disparate texts as the *Tirumantiram,* the *Yogavasishtha,* the *Kularnava Tantra,* the *Tantraloka,* and Jnaneshwar's commentary on the *Bhagavad Gita…*" (diacritical marks deleted). Muller-Ortega, "*Shaktipat,*" 416.

11. For a clear exposition of Abhinavagupta's work on *shaktipat*, particularly the different levels of intensity with which it can occur and the corresponding types of disciplines that ensue, see Deba Brata SenSharma, *The Philosophy of Sadhana*.

12. Muktananda, *Play of Consciousness*, 3rd ed. (South Fallsburg, NY: SYDA Foundation, 2000), 74.

13. A person who has gone through a series of preliminary practices is said to be *adhikarin,* or qualified to receive initiation. A person then undertakes a spiritual

discipline (*sadhana* or *upaya*) appropriate to the strength of *shaktipat* s/he received. For more on the system of *upaya*, or levels of Tantric practice, see Mark Dyczkowski, *The Doctrine of Vibration* (Albany: State University of New York Press, 1987), 163–218; and Sen Sharma, *The Philosophy of Sadhana*, 105–56.

14. *Shaktipat* initiation should not be confused with the initiation (*diksha*) practiced in Indian traditions that prepares a person to enter a life of ritual performance, which is not necessarily accompanied by a transmission of spiritual power, as occurs in *shaktipat*. Even though ritual traditionally accompanied *shaktipat* initiation as well, from the time of Abhinavagupta, texts indicate that this transmission sometimes occurred casually through simple contact between a guru and an aspirant, and could also occur in dreams. However, with the modern day Siddha Yoga lineage, "casual" transmission became the norm.

15. Babu Shetty in Swami Durgananda, "To See the World Full of Saints," *Meditation Revolution*, 19.

16. *Malini Vijaya Tantra,* a text of Kashmir Shaivism, describes nine degrees of *shaktipat* ranging from very intense to mild.

17. The texts of Kashmir Shaivism describe four ways in which *shaktipat* can be given: through look, touch, mantra, and the guru's will. The following incident, related by Swami Kripananda, a monk of Siddha Yoga, illustrates *shaktipat* through the guru's will: "Years ago in Gurudev Siddha Peeth, a man went up to Baba and showed him a photograph of a group of people. He pointed to a particular woman in the photo and said, 'Baba, this is my wife. Could you please give her *shaktipat?*' Baba studied the photograph for a few moments and then said, 'Yes, she will get it in three days.' Several weeks later the man received a letter from his wife, who was at their home in California. A curious thing had happened to her, she said. She had been washing dishes at her kitchen sink one day when she was suddenly gripped by a powerful force and her body began to perform spontaneous hatha yoga postures." *The Sacred Power,* 37–38.

18. While it might make *shaktipat* more tangible for people who pay the fee, the IRS does not consider it so. Since it is not a "course" in which some knowledge or skill is exchanged, but only some intangible "spiritual energy," the IRS considers the fee a tax deductible donation.

19. See his "Introduction," *Theravada Buddhism* (New York: Routledge, 1988), 1–31.

20. Most of the people that were initiated into *sannyas* by Muktananda have renounced their vows for one reason or another.

21. There is no data to support this claim, as demographic information is not collected by the SYDA Foundation. It comes from my own observations of visiting different Siddha Yoga ashrams and meditation centers.

22. The cobra is a classic symbol of *kundalini* awakening.

23. Swami Muktananda, *The Perfect Relationship* (South Fallsburg, NY: SYDA Foundation, 1979), 5.

24. Ibid., 66.

25. *Leaving Siddha Yoga: An Open Letter About Siddha Yoga (SYDA)—Criticism By Former Members.* Available from World Wide Web: (http://members.aolcom/_ht_a/shawdan/open_letter.htm?mtbrand=AOL_US).

26. Muktananda, *Play of Consciousness*, 280.

27. Deloris Gaskins, "And That's the Truth of Things," *Darshan*, vol. 123 (South Fallsburg, NY: SYDA Foundation).

28. There have been mixed messages about the extent to which inner perfection should be reflected in "perfectly lived lives" in Siddha Yoga. Muktananda once stated, "The Guru should possess every virtue," and he elaborated upon these virtues. *The Perfect Relationship*, 10. Elsewhere, however, he describes saints and *siddhas* who had attained enlightenment, but they retained addictions. Similarly, he did not accept the *siddha* Zipruanna as his guru because he went about naked; he preferred to accept a clothed guru because, "I was one of the modern generation." *Satsang With Baba*, Volume One, 29. At the same time, his guru Nityananda had some bizarre behavior not fitting the norms of the "modern generation."

29. In an interview with Lis Harris, Nityananda said he never denied these allegations. "O Guru, Guru, Guru," *New Yorker*, November 14, 1994.

30. For an in-depth, though not conclusive, article on the allegations of sexual misconduct made against Muktananda, see Caldwell, "The Heart of the Secret."

EIGHT

OSHO, FROM SEX GURU TO GURU OF THE RICH

The Spiritual Logic of Late Capitalism

HUGH B. URBAN

> I always spend before I get. Just the idea that some money is coming and I tell my people: Spend! Because who knows about tomorrow? Spend today. . . . And money keeps on coming. . . . I have started believing that existence takes care, even of an expensive man like me.
>
> —Osho, *Autobiography of a Spiritually Incorrect Mystic*

FEW RELIGIOUS LEADERS of the last century have been as controversial, scandalous and yet also financially successful as the infamous "Sex Guru" and "Guru of the Rich," known in his early years as Bhagwan Shree Rajneesh and in his later life simply as "Osho." Born in India in 1931, Rajneesh developed a radically iconoclastic brand of spirituality that became enormously popular first in India and then in the United States beginning in 1981. Notorious for his crazy-wisdom shock tactics and his collection of ninety-three Rolls Royces, Rajneesh enjoyed a brief but extremely lucrative career in the United States until his arrest and deportation in 1986. Remarkably, however, Rajneesh would become even more popular upon his return to India, where he was reborn as "Osho" and founded a new universal religious community for an affluent international audience. As such, Osho-Rajneesh is a striking example of the transnational flows and global circulation of religious ideas (as well as economic capital) throughout the planet at the turn of the millennium.

In this chapter, I will examine the Bhagwan's complex global journey from East to West and back again, tracing his rapid rise to international fame, his rapid fall into scandal and his new apotheosis as Osho. The primary reason for his success, I will suggest, is that he created a spiritual message that is remarkably well in tune with the current socioeconomic situation, which has variously been dubbed postindustrial society, disorganized capitalism, or "late capitalism." As Paul Heelas has argued, many New Age and new religious movements are by no means opposed to the mainstream values of modern Western society; on the contrary, they often affirm and sanctify many central ideals of individualism, freedom, and progress, providing a kind of "celebration of the self and a sacralization of modernity." Many new religions—for example, the Church of Scientology—are also quite compatible with modern capitalism and consumerism, easily adapting the corporate structures of other secular businesses in the services of a spiritual organization.[1]

Nowhere is this more apparent than in the case of Osho-Rajneesh. Preaching an explicitly iconoclastic form of "religionless religion" that rejects all fixed institutions even as it borrows freely from a wide array of spiritual traditions, Osho-Rajneesh offered a fluid, flexible form of spirituality that could be adapted easily to the shifting demands of his spiritual market. Thus, two of the most powerful themes running throughout his teachings are also two of the most central concerns of late capitalist consumer culture—namely, sex and money. And the genius of Osho-Rajneesh was precisely to create a religious path that could magically combine the enjoyment of sexuality, the pursuit of wealth, and the goal of spiritual transcendence. In his early teachings in India and the United States, Rajneesh had advocated a form of "Neo-Tantra"—a radically iconoclastic brand of spirituality that would liberate his followers from the prudish repression of modern society, by integrating the desire for sensual pleasure with the quest for spiritual experience. Indeed, we might say that Rajneesh is a striking reflection of the increasing preoccupation with sexuality in the twentieth century as a whole; he is a particularly clear illustration of what Michel Foucault has called the "repressive hypothesis," or the belief that Western society has severely repressed and denied sexuality and that what is most needed now is an ecstatic liberation of our true sexual nature.[2]

At the same time, Rajneesh also created a path that could integrate the urge to spiritual transcendence with the desire for material wealth and prosperity. Thus, his ideal of the perfect human state is "Zorba the Buddha," the person who weds the spirituality of the Buddha with the materialism of Zorba the Greek. Later, upon his return to India, Osho's iconoclastic brand of Neo-Tantra would gradually be transformed and combined with a wide array of other spiritual traditions—from Sufi dance to Jewish Kabbalah and Zen paint-ing—and marketed as a universal "religionless religion" for a transnational audience of spiritual seekers. Under the auspices of the Osho Commune Inter-national, his once controversial ideas have been miraculously transformed into a powerful new message for a transnational age.

Likewise, in its organizational form, the Rajneesh movement also devel-oped an extremely effective and profitable corporate structure that was also well suited to the economic situation of late capitalism. Already by the 1980s, the movement had evolved into a complex, interlocking network of corpora-tions, with an astonishing number of both spiritual and secular businesses worldwide, offering everything from yoga and psychological counseling to cleaning services. Meanwhile, the new Osho Commune International had emerged as an efficient transnational enterprise, with centers in more that one hundred countries linked through its "Global Communications Department." In sum, adapting Fredric Jameson's phrase, we might say that Osho-Rajneesh and his movement embody the "spiritual logic of late capitalism."[3]

After a brief review of Rajneesh's early career, I will then look more closely at his central doctrine of "Neo-Tantrism," with its unique combination of spirituality, sexuality, and capitalism. Finally, I will look at his surprising rebirth as Osho and the powerful new transnational movement that has emerged since his death. To conclude, I will suggest that the phenomenon of Osho raises some of the most difficult questions for the study of Indian *Maha-gurus* and religious movements in our own uniquely transnational era. Above all, it raises the question, Is this simply another example of the Coca-coloniza-tion of the world and the McDonaldization of religion under the impact of American-style consumer capitalism? Or is this, rather, one more example of the ongoing, natural adaptation of religious traditions to new historical, social, and economic situations?

THE EARLY CAREER OF BHAGWAN SHREE RAJNEESH

I Am The Messiah America has Been Waiting For.
—Bhagwan Shree Rajneesh

Born in 1931 in the village of Kuchwada, Madhya Pradesh, to a family of twelve whose parents died at an early age, Rajneesh Chandra Mohan was raised by his grandparents, an elderly, wealthy Jain couple. From a very early age, Rajneesh reports having various ecstatic experiences, finally achieving "full enlightenment" at age twenty-one. While at college at Jabalpur, the young Rajneesh suffered a traumatic period of depression, anorexia, and attempted suicide; yet he finally emerged from his crisis in an intense spiritual break-through to Self-realization—"an inner explosion," as he put it, in which he left his body and realized his true inner nature.[4]

After receiving his master's degree in 1957, Rajneesh taught philosophy for nine years at the University of Jabalpur. In 1967, however, he decided he could no longer keep his enlightened knowledge to himself, and so he left the academic world to gather disciples and teach the spiritual life. His rather radical teachings quickly aroused enormous controversy in the Indian community, as he urged his disciples to indulge all their physical desires, even as he parodied national heroes such as Mahatma Gandhi (whom he ridiculed as a masochistic chauvinist pervert).[5] By 1971, Rajneesh had begun to call himself "Bhag-wan"—a variant of Bhagavan, Blessed One or God—and built himself an ashram in Pune, where he hoped to begin a new utopian community as the seed of a new civilization. Bhagwan's highly lucrative New Civilization, how-ever, soon came into increasing financial and legal problems with the Indian government. In 1981, Bhagwan and his devotees were forced to flee the coun-try, trailed by some five million dollars in debts and a host of police and tax collectors.

Announcing himself as "the Messiah America has been waiting for," Rajneesh took refuge in the United States—the land, as he described it, of freedom, opportunity, and unfettered capitalism. After a brief stay in a New Jersey mansion, he and his now large following bought a sixty-four thousand acre ranch at Big Muddy, Oregon, which they dubbed their own new city and ideal society, "Rajneeshpuram," or Rajneesh's town. Quickly growing into a remarkably lucrative financial complex, Rajneeshpuram amassed some $120 million in revenues in its short four-year existence. Meanwhile, Rajneesh's fol-lowing had spread throughout the United States, Europe and India, claiming more than twenty-five thousand members at its peak, and growing into an enormously diverse, multifaceted international business complex (see below).[6]

Ironically, as its numbers and wealth rapidly grew, this seemingly "anti-authoritarian" movement began to assume a fairly rigid institutional structure of its own. Particularly in the later years of the movement in Oregon, it devel-oped a complex hierarchy under the control of Rajneesh's secretary, Sheela, and her female inner circle (dubbed the "Ma-Archy"). Eventually, Sheela and her associates would largely displace Rajneesh himself as the ruling force of the commune, transforming it into an increasingly rigid and profit-oriented movement. Under Sheela's guidance, Rajneeshpuram became an extremely tightly controlled and highly guarded community, with its own "Peace Force" officers, where members were divided hierarchically by colored armbands and surveillance cameras were set up to identify potential dissidents. Meanwhile, ordinary members or *sannyasis* were often forced to work long hours with no pay and little food. As some observers concluded, Rajneeshpuram had become "the closest thing to an Eastern bloc experience in the United States."[7] Rajneesh himself would later claim that he had actually allowed Sheela to take command in order to give his disciples "a little taste of what fascism means" and thereby to contrast that with his own nontotalitarian form of teaching.[8]

Not surprisingly, the group soon also came into conflict with its American neighbors. The more it grew, the more the Rajneesh community began to encroach upon the nearby retirement community of Antelope. Because of their overwhelming numbers, which eventually surpassed those of the local residents, the Rajneeshis were able to engineer the political takeover of Antelope through the election of ashram residents to nine of ten official posts in town. Eventually, as tensions with the local community grew, Rajneesh members would resort to more aggressive, even guerrilla warfare strategies, such as dumping animal parts on the lawns of local officials, mailing sexual devices to courthouse clerks, and distributing salmonella bacteria in local restaurants and grocery stores.[9]

By 1985, the community had also come under investigation by the U.S. government, specifically around the issue of the interlock of the Rajneesh Church and the city of Rajneeshpuram and its claim to tax exempt status. Finally in 1986, the State Attorney General decided that Rajneeshpuram violated the church-state separation clause of the Constitution. Rajneesh and his disciples, meanwhile, had also come under investigation for a shocking array of criminal charges, which included counts of electronic eavesdropping, immigration conspiracy, lying to federal officials, harboring fugitives, criminal conspiracy, first degree assault, attempted murder, burglary, racketeering, and arson. The movement, the attorney general concluded, had become "sociopathic."[10] Deported from the United States and refused entry into virtually every country to which he applied, Rajneesh finally returned to Pune.

NEO-TANTRISM AND RELIGIONLESS RELIGION: RAJNEESH'S EARLY TEACHINGS

> Tantra is not revolutionary; it is rebellious. Rebellion means individual . . . it is just going beyond society. . . . It is for freedom—freedom to be.
>
> —Osho, *The Tantric Transformation*

In itself, Rajneesh's early philosophy was an ingenious synthesis of philosophical and religious ideas drawn from an enormous array of sources. His vast body of writings is itself a kind of "postmodern pastiche," an eclectic mélange of ideas drawn from a remarkable range of sources, from Plato to Shankara to Lao Tzu to Sartre; however, he had a special fondness for the more radical figures such as Nietzsche, Gurdjieff, and Crowley. As one observer put it, his teachings are a "potpourri of counter-culturalist ideas: strive for love and freedom, live for the moment, self is important, you are okay . . . the fun ethic, God is within."[11] An explicitly self-parodying, self-deconstructing guru, Rajneesh claimed that his entire teaching was itself nothing more than a joke, a farce or a game—the ultimate game: "Nothing is serious. Even your disappointments are laughable. To become a Sannyasin is to enter the ultimate game. . . . [I]t is a play . . . it is the ultimate game. . . . You have played at being a husband, wife, mother, being rich, poor. . . . This is the last game. Only you are left."[12]

Part of the remarkable success of Rajneesh's teaching, I would suggest, was precisely the fluidity and flexibility of his message, which could be adapted— like *upaya* or "skillful means"—to the particular needs of particular audiences. The primary model of Rajneesh's style of guru-ship is that of the Proteus or shape shifter, who "defies identification thorough his power to change appearance."[13] As Rajneesh described himself: "I am consistently inconsistent. . . I live in the moment and whatsoever I am saying right now is true for this moment. . . . I don't think of the future at all."[14] As such, his uniquely protean, shifting message could freely be directed toward the specific desires of his spiritual consumers. As Lewis Carter observes, "Rajneesh was unencumbered by tradition and willing to experiment with techniques till he found those which were most successful. . . . The movement became demand-driven."[15]

Rather than a religion in the conventional sense, Rajneesh taught a radically iconoclastic brand of spirituality—"an antinomian philosophy and moral anarchism."[16] As a "religionless" religion or antireligion, his was a path beyond conventional morality, beyond good and evil, and founded on the explicit rejection of all traditions, doctrines, and values. "Morality is a false coin, it deceives people," he warns. "A man of real understanding is neither good nor bad. He transcends both."[17] For Rajneesh, the cause of all our suffering is the distorting socialization or "programming" of cultural institutions, such as family, schools, religion, and government. All metanarratives or overarching theories about the universe are only so many fictions, imaginary creations used by those in power to dominate the masses. True freedom can be achieved only by deconstructing all metanarratives, liberating oneself from the confining structures of the past. One must be deprogrammed and de-hypnotized:

> You are programmed by family, acquaintances, institutions. Your mind is like a blackboard on which rules are written. Bhagwan writes new rules on the blackboard. He tells you one thing is true and next the opposite is true. He writes and writes on the blackboard of your mind until it is a whiteboard. Then you have no programming left.[18]

In order to help his disciples achieve this state of deprogramming and liberation, Rajneesh taught a variety of yogic, meditative, and other disciplines.[19]

Most of these, we might note, came at some cost; at the Oregon Ranch, prices ranged from $50 for a one-day introduction to Rajneesh meditation to $7500 for a complete three-month rebalancing program.

Among the most important of these spiritual techniques was Rajneesh's unique brand of "Neo-Tantra." As it is defined by most historians of religions today, Tantra or Tantrism is a highly complex and diverse body of traditions that spread throughout the Hindu, Buddhist, and Jain communities since at least the fourth or fifth century. Above all, Tantra is characterized by its highly esoteric and deliberately transgressive form of practice, which involves consumption of normally prohibited substances (such as meat and wine) and, in some cases, sexual intercourse in violation of class.[20] Rajneesh, however, was one of the most important figures in the transmission of Tantra to the modern Western world, where it has been popularized, redefined, and quite radically transformed in a very different cultural context. As he defines it, Tantra is the ultimate nonreligion or antireligion, a spiritual practice that does not demand rigorous ritual or morality but instead frees the individual from all such constraints. "Tantra is freedom—freedom from all mind-constructs, from all mind-games. . . . Tantra is liberation. Tantra is not a religion. . . . Religion is a mind-game. . . . Religion gives you . . . a discipline. Tantra takes all disciplines away."[21] In this sense, Tantra is the ultimate form of rebellion for an age in which political revolution is no longer practical or relevant; it is not the rebellion of the masses against the state, but rather of the individual against modern society as a whole:

> Tantra is a rebellion. I don't call it revolutionary because it has no politics in it. . . . It is individual rebellion. It is one individual slipping out of the structures and slavery. . . . The future is very hopeful. Tantra will become more and more important. . . . [N]o political revolution has proved revolutionary. All political revolutions finally turn into antirevolutions. . . . Rebellion means individual. . . . It is for freedom—freedom to be.[22]

In strong contrast to established social institutions, Tantra does not deny life or the body; rather, it is the ultimate affirmation of passion, physicality, and pleasure. It is the supreme "Just Do It!" religion, which celebrates life in all its transience and contingency: "Tantra accepts everything, lives everything," Rajneesh declares, "This is what Tantra says: the Royal Way—behave like a king, not like a soldier. . . . Why bother about tomorrow? This moment is enough. Live it!"[23] Even the sinful and perverse side of life, even the most selfish and immoral sides of the ego, must be accepted as innately divine. Far from imposing moral restraints, Tantra celebrates human nature in all its most flawed, weak, even seemingly "evil" dimensions: "Tantra says—If you are greedy, be greedy; don't bother about greed"—

Tantric acceptance is total, it doesn't split you. All the religions of the world except Tantra have created split personalities, have created schizo-phrenia. . . . They say the good has to be achieved and the bad denied, the devil has to be denied and God accepted. . . . Tantra says a transformation is possible. . . . Transformation comes when you accept your total being. The anger is absorbed, the greed is absorbed.[24]

Above all, Tantra centers around the power of sex—a power that is at once the most intense force in human nature and also the one most severely dis-torted by Western society. Because the traditional Christian West has suppressed sexuality, Rajneesh argues, it is sexuality that must be liberated if modern stu-dents are to actualize their innermost Self fully:

Freud . . . stumbled only upon the repressed sexuality. He came across repressed people. Christian repression has made many blocks in man where energy has become coiled up within itself, has become stagnant, is no longer flowing.

The society is against sex: it has created a block, just near the sex center. Whenever sex arises you feel restless, you feel guilty, you feel afraid. . . . That's why I teach dynamic methods: they will melt your blocks.[25]

As the strongest power in human nature, sex also becomes the strongest spir-itual force when it is fully integrated and absorbed. "Sex has to be absorbed, then it becomes a tremendous force in you. A Buddha . . . a Jesus, they have such a magnetic force around—what is that? Sex absorbed."[26] Thus, many of Rajneesh's practices involved group sex—or "therapy intensives," which were "designed to bring about a catharsis followed by transformation of consciousness."[27]

The ultimate aim of Tantric practice is precisely to achieve this full self-acceptance, to love ourselves wholly and completely, with all our sin, vice, greed, and sensual desires, and to realize that we already are "Perfect." Once we accept our sensual, desiring nature, once we release the pent-up sexual side of ourselves, we discover that we are already divine. We already possess truth, free-dom, and infinite power within ourselves. We already are "God"—

This is the most fundamental thing in Tantra, that it says you are already perfect. . . . Perfection does not have to be achieved. It simply has to be realized that it is there. Tantra offers you enlightenment right here and now—no time, no postponement.[28]

Ecstasy is your very nature. You are truth. You are love. You are freedom. . . . You are already there. . . . If you can stop all doing for a single moment the energy converges and explodes. . . . Then you become a god.[29]

It is not difficult to see why Rajneesh's version of Tantra was so appealing to a Western audience of the 1970s and '80s. Promising absolute freedom and instant deification, even while allowing physical indulgence and sensual pleasure, Neo-Tantra would seem to be a spiritual expression of the "Me Generation" of the '70s and the "Power Generation" of the '80s. "Rajneesh offered everything Westerners imagined Tantra to be: a free love cult promising enlightenment, an exciting radical community. Rajneesh slipped comfortably into the role of 'Tantra Messiah'. . . . Largely because of Rajneesh, Tantra reemerged as a New Age Cult in the 1970s and 80s."[30]

In this sense Osho-Rajneesh is a striking example of a larger shift in Western attitudes toward sexuality in the latter half of the twentieth century. As Foucault has argued, it is a misconception to suppose that the history of sex in the West is a progressive narrative of liberation from Victorian repression and prudery. In fact, Foucault suggests we have not so much "liberated" sex in any radical way, but rather simply continued a long history of preoccupation with and discourse about sexuality, which has been described, debated, classified, and categorized in endless, titillating detail. "What is peculiar to modern societies," he writes, "is not that they consigned sex to a shadow existence, but that they dedicated themselves to speaking of it ad infinitum, while exploiting it as the secret."[31] Thus, as Jeffrey Weeks observes, the late twentieth century has been characterized not so much by a sexual revolution; rather, what has happened is something more like a "commodification of sex," as part of the larger socio-economic process of the expansion of capitalism to all domains of modern culture: "Sex had long been something you were. By the 1950s it was also something you could buy, not just in the traditional form of prostitution, but in the form of glossily marketed fantasy. . . . Not only was sex an area that could be colonized by capitalism, it was also one that could expand ever more exotically."[32] This is much the same kind of commodification of sex, I think, that we see in the case of Osho-Rajneesh, who was one of the key figures in the remarkable transformation of "Tantra" from a highly esoteric and elaborate ritual tradition into an extremely popular and widely marketed spiritual commodity for a Western audience.

ZORBA THE BUDDHA

I sell happiness. I sell enlightenment.
—Rajneesh, Interview with
Mike Wallace of *Sixty Minutes*

As the ideal wedding of sensuality and spirituality, Rajneesh's neo-Tantric path also offered the perfect integration of this-worldly materialism and otherworldly transcendence. Indeed, not only was Rajneesh unopposed to the accumulation of wealth, but he even saw it as the natural manifestation of spiritual attainment. With his ideal of "Zorba the Buddha," he conceived of a new kind of perfect man or total being, who would combine the spirituality of the Buddha with the sensuality and materialism of Zorba the Greek.

> My concept of the new man is that he will be Zorba the Greek and he will also be Gautama the Buddha. . . . He will be sensuous and spiritual— physical . . . in the senses, enjoying the body . . . and still a great con- sciousness. He will be Christ and Epicurus together.[33]

Indeed, Rajneesh was an ardent defender of American-style capitalism— which he saw as the expression of individual self-determination and free will—and an outspoken critic of socialism—which he saw as the symptom of laziness of the masses and the jealousy of the have nots: "[T]he creation of wealth is the task of genius. . . . Socialism is the jealousy of the masses, of the have-nots against the few who succeed in doing something for mankind."[34] As Rajneesh put it, in his typically unapologetic style, "I don't condemn wealth. Wealth is a perfect means which can enhance people in every way and make life rich in all ways. The materially poor can never become spiritual."[35] More- over, "People are unequal and a fair world has to give people full freedom to be unequal. Capitalism has grown out of freedom. It is a natural phenome- non."[36] The Neo-Tantric path, for Rajneesh, is the unique path that does not separate, but actually integrates and synthesizes the quest for spiritual liberation with the desire for material wealth. Rather than denying the physical senses or even material greed, Tantra seeks the active wedding of worldly enjoyment and spiritual liberation: "Tantra has a very beautiful thing to say and that is: First, before you start serving anybody else, be absolutely selfish. How can you serve anyone else unless you have attained your inner being? Be absolutely selfish!"[37]

In the American media, Rajneesh was most infamous and most widely criticized for his own rather rich tastes—above all, for his collection of Rolls Royces, in which he was frequently seen riding comfortably past masses of adoring devotees. Yet Rajneesh seemed quite unapologetic about his taste for the finer things of life and saw no contradiction, for the truly liberated and realized individual, between material wealth and spiritual freedom. As he later explained his penchant for expensive automobiles, "People are sad, jealous and thinking that Rolls-Royces don't fit with spirituality. I don't see that there is any contradiction. . . . In fact, sitting in a bullock cart it is very difficult to be meditative; a Rolls Royce is the best for spiritual growth."[38] Indeed, far from opposing spiritual authority to capitalist economics, Rajneesh made the accu- mulation of material wealth the expression and manifestation of his charisma. As the American media never tired of pointing out, Rajneesh was an extreme example of conspicuous consumption—a gross display of material wealth and a shameless flaunting of gold jewelry, expensive hats, and electronic gadgets. Material wealth did not detract from his status as spiritual leader; on the contrary, it was the natural confirmation of his charismatic power.

SPIRITUAL CHARISMA AND DISORGANIZED
CAPITALISM: THE CORPORATE STRUCTURE
OF THE RAJNEESH MOVEMENT

> There is no organization around me. Whatever you see is no organization, it is simply functional; it is just like the post office.
> —Bhagwan Shree Rajneesh

One of the most astonishing features of the early Rajneesh movement was its remarkable success as a business enterprise—or more accurately, as a complex network of interrelated enterprises spread throughout the world, operating on a variety of levels. The success of Rajneesh's enterprise, I would suggest, is based on the same eclectic principles as his spiritual teachings: first, radical pluralism and eclecticism, allowing a wide range of organizational structures; and second, a kind of de-institutionalized, decentralized authority, which at the same time paradoxically reasserts a new kind of hierarchical power. Thus, the Rajneesh movement might be called a kind of "charismatic variant of a multinational corporation."[39]

The structure of the early Rajneesh movement appears to have been particularly well suited to the complex and volatile economic situation of the last decades of the twentieth century. Precisely because Rajneesh explicitly rejected all dogmatic authority and presented such a radically flexible, fluid form of spirituality, his teachings meshed seamlessly with the constantly fluctuating market of late capitalist society. Having effectively deconstructed all other institutional authority, this made possible a radically fluid, flexible, and adaptable business structure, one based not on centralized direction or fixed rules but rather on economic opportunism and organizational diversity. The only law, it seems, was what worked; the only constant is what makes money. "Sannyasins were encouraged to experiment with any business or organizational form which offers convenience," Carter observed. "Sannyasins required no justification for their enterprises save that they be profitable."[40]

With the help of some sophisticated legal and business management, the movement established a complicated system of parent companies and subsidiaries.[41] Three separate but mutually reinforcing organizations were formed, which supported one another in a complex interlocking structure. The parent organization, the Ranch Church or Rajneesh Foundation International (RFI), was managed through the Rajneesh Investment Corporation (RIC), and

Rajneesh Neo-Sannyasin International Corporation (RNSIC). The RIC was a for-profit corporation to which ownership of the ranch was transferred and which then served as the depository for funds taken from other centers around the world. The RNSIC, or "commune" on the other hand, was established as an independent corporation to provide subsistence for members who donated their labor to the construction of the ranch. Through the interlocking of these three corporations, and through their skillful combination of religious (and tax exempt) and secular enterprises, the movement was able to maintain a uniquely fluid structure; it was thereby able to transfer funds rapidly and easily while maintaining the facade of a separation of church and state and paying as little tax as possible. For example, when Rajneesh's appetite for Rolls Royces began to exceed the ordinary needs that a religious leader might be expected to have, the solution was to create an entity separate from the church called the "Rajneesh Modern Car Trust" to hold the titles. And so it went—"not according to a grand scheme, but in an adaptive, expedient, ad hoc fashion."[42]

In a remarkably short time, the Rajneesh center at Big Muddy became an immensely successful enterprise. Through its various meditation workshops, training seminars, lectures, and conferences, costing anywhere from $50 to $7500, the organization quickly accumulated a vast amount of wealth. Between 1981 and 1986 an estimated $120 million poured into the Ranch. As former disciple Hugh Milne recounts, "Money making, collecting donations . . . and legal work became the chief activities. . . . Bhagwan said that in the new commune we would grow money on trees. . . . Bhagwan was quite open about the fact that the primary object was to make money."[43]

By no means content to limit its operations to the United States, the Rajneesh Church soon began to spread worldwide, in a rapid proliferation of ancillary businesses, such as spiritual institutes, therapy and meditation centers, discotheques, restaurants, and a vast array of books, tapes, and videos. Twenty major corporations were created worldwide, with twenty-eight bank accounts, including twelve in Switzerland. As Carter suggests, this global network had charismatic organizational structure; rather than a fixed corporate organization with permanent structures, the Rajneesh corporation adapted quickly to the changing needs of different contexts. The individual businesses within the Rajneesh Foundation served as "empty forms " or fluid structures that might be a discotheque one week, a yoga center the next, or a health food store the next, depending on the shifting needs of the market: "Corporate identities are used as disposable devices . . . created as a need of the moment arises and discarded . . . specialized corporations of limited life span can be created to provide vehicles for new activities or transfers of assets."[44]

In sum, Rajneeshism as a business enterprise was based on the same paradoxical yet remarkably effective principles as his spiritual teachings. Like his philosophy, his business enterprise was not a fixed, consistent system, but a protean, fluid, constantly shifting network, which could adapt easily to the shifting demands of his consumer market.

OSHO — THE APOTHEOSIS OF A
FALLEN NEW AGE GURU

Why do I contradict myself? I am not teaching a philosophy here. The philosopher has to be very consistent—flawless, logical, rational. . . . I am not a philosopher. I am not here giving you a consistent dogma to which you can cling. My whole effort is to give you a no-mind.

—Osho

The most surprising aspect of the Rajneesh phenomenon lies not so much in his scandalous career in America, but in his remarkable apotheosis upon his return to India. A truly global guru, Rajneesh made the journey from India to America and back to India again, now achieving even more success in his homeland, in large part because of his status as an international figure that had a massive U.S. and European following. His followers were not only able to rationalize the disastrous scandal in the United States, but even to make Rajneesh a heroic martyr who had been unjustly persecuted by the oppressive imperialist U.S. government: "[The Ranch] was crushed from without by the Attorney's General's office . . . like the marines in Lebanon, the Ranch was hit by hardball opposition and driven out."[45]

As part of his transfiguration in India, he would also reject his former Hindu title of "Bhagwan Shree Rajneesh," an appellation that had asserted his divine, god-man status. "Enough is enough! The joke is over," he declared.[46] Instead, he adopted the more universal title of "Osho"—a title that, according to some, derives from the Japanese term for master, and according to others, from the "oceanic experience" described by William James. His message, too, became increasingly universal, more palatable and marketed to a global consumer audience. "My message is too new. India is too old, ancient, traditional. . . . In fact, I am not an Indian. . . . I belong to no nation. My message is universal."[47] As author Tom Robbins describes it, Osho's message is really a more simple, universal one of humor, irony, and laughter. Even his seemingly excessive consumption and crazy wisdom behavior in the United States were only his own form of "cosmic comedy" aimed at helping us to laugh at ourselves: "Jesus had his parables, Buddha his sutras . . . Osho has something more appropriate for a species crippled by greed, fear, ignorance and superstition: he has cosmic comedy. What Osho is out to do, it seems to me, is pierce our disguises, shatter our illusions . . . and demonstrate the . . . tragic folly of taking ourselves too seriously."[48] Yet at the same time, interestingly enough, Osho also down-played the more objectionable aspects of his earlier message, transforming his radical brand of Neo-Tantrism into a kind of universal global religion of Love. Thus, his *Autobiography of a Spiritually Incorrect Mystic* makes only brief reference to Tantra or sexual practices, and even then only in the most defensive terms: "I have never taught 'free sex.' What I have been teaching is the sacredness of sex. . . . This is the idiotic Indian yellow journalism that has confined my whole philosophy to two words. . . . What they have been doing all along is misin-forming people."[49]

Osho died in 1990, after just a few years back in Pune. According to many devotees, he had actually been "poisoned in Ronald Reagan's America" (given thallium during his period of incarceration in the American prisons) because of his radical, threatening, and subversive teachings.[50] Remarkably, however, Osho has only grown in popularity in the years since his death. Indeed, he seems to have published more books and received more acclaim as a disem-bodied photograph or video image than he ever did while still incarnate. The Pune center, meanwhile, has grown into a successful and now globalized spiri-tual organization, the "Osho Commune International." Linked through its "Global Connections Department," the Commune runs an intricate network of centers and activities worldwide, including "Osho International" in New York, which administers the rights to Osho's works. Describing itself as the "Esalen of the East," the Osho Multiversity in Pune teaches a dizzying array of spiritual techniques drawn from a smorgasbord of traditions: Astrology Train-ing, Feldenkraus body work, Crystal Energy, Acupuncture, neo-Zen, Hypnosis Love and Relationship, Primal Deconditioning, Pulsation-Reichian Bioenergy, Primal Deconditioning, and Shamanic Energy Work are but a few of the many courses offered. With an explicitly universal religious vision, the new Osho commune has taken Rajneesh's Neo-Tantric "religionless religion," combined it with a host of other more generic New Age ideals and marketed it to a global audience of spiritual consumers. As we read in a recent advertisement for the commune,

> Osho Commune International . . . continues to attract thousands of visi-tors per year from more than one hundred different countries around the world. . . . The resort meditation programs are based on Osho's vision of a qualitatively new kind of human being who is able to participate joyously in everyday life and to relax into silence. Most programs take place in modern air-conditioned facilities and include everything from short to extended meditation courses, creative art, holistic health treatments, per-sonal growth and the "Zen" approach to sports and recreation.[51]

The commune is thus promoted as a kind of spiritual oasis amidst the growing confusion of modern life, a unique sacred space where one can discover one's own self and unite the desires of both body and mind in a beautiful resort environment. As *Elle* magazine put it, "Every year thousands of people visit this luxurious resort. . . . The atmosphere is really like a fairy tale. A paradise where all your emotional, bodily and spiritual needs are met." In sum, the character of Rajneesh has undergone an incredible apotheosis in his later years, particularly after his death: he has been transfigured from a shocking, scandalous Tantric sex guru into an international icon for a high tech global movement and business enterprise.

THE SPIRITUAL LOGIC OF LATE CAPITALISM

> The days of the nations are over, the days of divisions are over, the days of the politicians are over. We are moving in a tremendously new world, a new phase of humanity—and the phase is that there can only be one world now, only one single humanity. And then there will be a tremendous release of energies.
> —Osho, *Autobiography of a Spiritually Incorrect Mystic*

The enigmatic figure of Osho-Rajneesh has thus brought us full circle, from East to West and back again, in a remarkable transnational exchange of spiritual ideas and economic capital. As such, he is a powerful illustration of what F. Max Müller more than a century ago called "that world-wide circle through which, like an electric current, Oriental thought could run to the West and Western thought return to the East."[52] For it appears that he was able to create a spiritual path that was remarkably well suited to the uniquely global socioeconomic situation at the close of the twentieth century—namely, the particular cultural and economic formation that has been variously dubbed "post-industrialism" (Bell), "post-Fordism" (Harvey), or "disorganized capitalism" (Offe).[53] Yet whatever its name, most observers agree, the contemporary global economic system is by no means "postcapitalist." On the contrary, it is hyper-capitalist, or, in Ernest Mandel's terms, a purer form of capitalism than any seen before, one that allows for the most powerful application of capitalist principles to all aspects of human life. Since at least the early 1970s, there has been a shift from the "Fordist" economics of modern industrial capitalism, to a more pervasive process of "flexible accumulation." In the global marketplace of postmodernity, funds can be transferred and exchanged instantaneously, from any point on the planet, through a network of constantly shifting, increasingly flexible corporate structures and modes of consumption.[54]

At the same time, late capitalism has gone hand in hand with a series of marked shifts on the cultural level. As Fredric Jameson summarizes it, the "cultural logic of late capitalism" is characterized by a general loss of faith in any grand, totalizing, or unifying view of the world or human history (a death of "metanarratives," to use Lyotard's phrase) and a concomitant sense of intense fragmentation, pluralism or "heteroglossia," which mirrors the bewildering diversification in consumer society itself.[55] Instead of the construction of any unifying metanarrative, the dominant logic of late capitalism is thus one of "pastiche" and "bricolage"—the freewheeling syncretism of diverse elements drawn from disparate historical and cultural eras, patched together largely by the whim of the individual consumer. Today, we "no longer produce monumental works of the modernist type but ceaselessly reshuffle the fragments . . . of older cultural productions, in some new . . . bricolage: metabooks which cannibalize other books."[56] And instead of the ideal of unity, order, or harmony, the late capitalist aesthetic is that of physical intensity, shock value, immediate gratification, and ecstatic experience. As Terry Eagleton observes, "Its stance toward cultural tradition is one of irreverent pastiche and its contrived depthlessness undermines all metaphysical solemnities . . . by a brutal aesthetics of squalor and shock."[57]

The final and most obvious aspect of late capitalism, however, is the progressive extension of the logic of the marketplace to all aspects of culture. In the "market-like conditions of modern life," as Jürgen Habermas puts it, everything tends to become a commodity that may be bought and sold, from art to politics to religion itself.[58] Now forced to compete in the commercial marketplace alongside other secular businesses and industries, religion itself tends to become yet another consumer product within the supermarket of values. The religious believer, meanwhile, is free to choose from a wide array of possible beliefs and to piece together his or her own personalized spiritual pastiche:

> Max Weber's metaphor . . . of religion striding into the marketplace of worldly affairs and slamming the monastery door behind, becomes further transformed in modern society with religion placed very much in the consumer marketplace. . . . Individuals [are] able to select from a plurality of suitably packaged bodies of knowledge in the super-market of lifestyles. . . . The tendency in modern societies is for religion to become a private leisure pursuit purchased in the market like any other consumer lifestyle.[59]

Finally, as the logic of the marketplace has spread to all facets of human life, it has also brought with it some fundamental shifts in our attitudes toward the body, physical pleasure, and desire. As Bryan S. Turner, Mike Featherstone, and others suggest, there has been a basic shift from the early capitalist attitude based on the Protestant work ethic, thriftiness, and innerworldly asceticism, to a late capitalist attitude based on mass consumption, physical pleasure, and hedonistic enjoyment. In consumer culture the human body ceases to be a vessel of sin or an unruly vessel of desires that must be disciplined and mastered—rather, the body is proclaimed as ultimate source of gratification, enjoyment, and fulfillment. As Turner puts it, "In the growth of a consumer society with its emphasis on the athletic/beautiful body we see a major transformation of values from an emphasis on the control of the body for ascetic reasons to the manipulation of the body for aesthetic purposes."[60] In short, as Featherstone concludes, "the new consumptive ethic . . . taken over by the advertising industry, celebrates living for the moment, hedonism, self-expression, the body beautiful, freedom from social obligation."[61]

All of these general cultural aspects of late capitalism, I would argue, are strikingly apparent in both the teachings and the organizational structure of the Osho-Rajneesh movement. A spiritual Proteus and an incredibly eclectic thinker, he was capable of adapting his message to the particular needs of his followers in a fluid, flexible way. Rejecting all the great metanarratives of mainstream religion, society, and politics, he conceived his own kind of "postmodern bricolage," drawing freely on all the sacred traditions of the world, while at the same time catering it to the specific needs of his audience.

At the same time, he was also able to create an expansive, largely decentralized but intricately interconnected network of spiritual enterprises, extending in an equally flexible web of both secular and religious centers throughout the world. He was, moreover, quite unashamed of the fact that his message had both a spiritual and material aim, and he saw no contradiction between the pursuit of the sacred and the pursuit of wealth. On the contrary, it was precisely his aim to unite the desire for transcendence and desire for economic capital in his ideal of the new Superman, Zorba the Buddha. And finally, Osho-Rajneesh is also a powerful example of the preoccupation with the body and sexuality in late capitalist consumer culture. In this repressive modern world, Osho tells us, the intense energy of sexual pleasure is precisely what is most in need of liberation; and it is the most powerful means to realizing our inherent Godhood, through the ecstatic sensual-spiritual experience of "Buddha's inner orgasm."

Yet as Foucault points out, it is not so much the case that modern society has really "liberated" sexuality in any radical way; rather, we have only continued a long history of preoccupation with and discourse about sexuality, which has been described, debated, classified, and categorized in endless, titillating detail, while being exploited as "the secret." Yet what we have done is to push sex to the furthest possible extremes—to extremes of transgression and excess, not resting until we have shattered every law, violated every taboo: "The 20th century will undoubtedly have discovered the related categories of exhaustion, excess, the limit and transgression—the strange and unyielding form of these irrevocable movements which consume and consummate us."[62]

CONCLUSIONS: INDIAN MAHAGURUS — KARMA COLA
OR COUNTER-HEGEMONIC RESISTANCE?

> When East meets West all you get is the neo-Sannyasi, the instant
> Nirvana. . . . You have the karma, we'll take the Coca Cola, meta-
> physical soft drink for a physical one.
>
> —Gita Mehta, *Karma Cola*

> I thought when I first visited the Orient that I would find myself
> witnessing the West in conquest of the East, armies of its invaders
> bearing their cultural artifacts across the plains of Asia. Yet . . . I
> began to suspect that none of the countries I had seen . . . could
> ever be fully transformed by the West. Madonna and Rambo might
> rule the streets, and hearts might be occupied with dreams of
> Cadillacs . . . but every Asian culture seemed . . . too canny to be
> turned by passing trade winds from the West.
>
> —Pico Iyer, *Video Night in Kathmandu*

To close, I would like to suggest that the phenomenon of Osho-Rajneesh sheds
some important light on a number of critical issues for the study of religions in
the context of transnationalism and globalization at the turn of the millennium.
Above all, he forces us to ask the difficult question of whether South Asian religious traditions are inevitably doomed to undergo the fate of westernization
and commercialization as they move into the modern world system. Are they
doomed, in a sense, to become Coca-colonized and McDonaldized into yet
another franchise in the global marketplace of cultures?

In his monumental study of the cross-cultural intellectual exchange
between India and Europe, Wilhelm Halbfass seems to have arrived at a fairly
pessimistic answer to these questions. What we have witnessed in the modern
era, Halbfass believes, is the progressive "Europeanization of the world"—that
is, the domination of the globe by Western culture, ideology, and discourse, to
such a degree that other cultures can now only define themselves through the
categories that have already been imposed by the West:

> In the modern planetary system, Eastern and Western cultures can no
> longer meet one another as equal partners. They meet in a Westernized
> world, under conditions shaped by Western ways of thinking.
>
> [F]or the time being there is no escape from the global network of
> Europeanization and no way to avoid the conceptual and technological
> ways . . . of communication and interaction that the European tradition
> has produced.[63]

However, it seems to me that the real danger today is no longer the
threat of the "Europeanization" of the world; indeed, it is no longer even the
threat of "Americanization." Surely we are now living in a very different sort

of global economy where such boundaries no longer have much meaning. Rather, the real threat today is the spread of consumer capitalism and the domination of the global marketplace over all local economies, polities, and cultural forms—a process that is no longer dominated by the West, no longer a matter of either "occidentalization" or "orientalization," but a far more complex product of transnational capitalism. To many observers, we seem to be living more and more in "one McWorld tied together by communications, information, entertainment and commerce," that remains "caught between Babel and Disneyland."[64]

Thus, many authors are quite cynical about the encounter between East and West in the age of global capitalism. As Gita Mehta suggests, India has now been subjected to the complete penetration of American mass marketing, and now any encounter between East and West will only result in the worst of both worlds. While India seeks the materialism and technological power of the West, the West seeks the exoticism, eroticism, mysticism, and cheap drugs of the East. Both end up with empty distorted phantasms reflecting their own repressed desires:

> It is unlikely that either the Occidental or the Easterner has the stamina to survive the exchange of views, yet both insist on trying, and both use irrelevant language to camouflage the contradictions. . . . [T]he Easterner . . . calls what fascinates him in the West economic necessity, technology, historical imperative. . . . The Occidental . . . calls what fascinates him in the East the transcendence of economics and technology. . . . The Westerner is finding the dialectic of history less fascinating than the endless opportunities for narcissism provided by the wisdom of the East.[65]

Tantra in the style of Osho-Rajneesh, Mehta concludes, is the epitome of this superficial cross-cultural exchange: The result is the neo-Tantric or "neo-sannyasin" who seeks instant nirvana (enlightenment) and soda-pop enlightenment. "The Tantrics would be surprised to learn that the taboos they believe should only be broken by the initiate, lest they boomerang against the practitioner, are now being used as a means of getting rid of one's hang ups."[66]

In contrast to these pessimistic visions of "global monoculture" and "Coca-colonization," however, others have suggested the more hopeful possibility of local resistance and indigenous critique. As Marshall Sahlins argues, indigenous peoples are never simply dupes of Western capitalism who passively absorb consumer ideology or the logic of the marketplace without reflection or agency; instead, they appropriate and transform them according to the logic of their own local culture: "Western capitalism has loosed on the world enormous forces of production, coercion and destruction. Yet precisely because they cannot be resisted, the goods of the larger system take on meaningful places in the local scheme of things."[67] Hence, some, like Pico Iyer, argue that what we are witnessing today is not so much the relentless imposition of global capitalism onto all aspects of human culture; rather, we find a more dynamic process of "the spread of America's pop-cultural imperialism throughout the world's ancient civilizations" and the simultaneous "resistances put up against the Coca-colonizing forces."[68]

My own view here is somewhat more complex and ambivalent—at once more optimistic than Halbfass's narrative of inevitable Europeanization of the earth, and yet also more pessimistic than Sahlins's narrative of valiant indigenous resistance against the onslaught of global capitalism. With Sahlins, I would like to highlight, even celebrate, the power of non-Western cultures to appropriate, transform, and deform the forces of global capitalism, to adapt them on their own terms, according to their own cultural logic. Yet it seems to me that the rules of the game are still largely determined, conditioned, and structured by the logic of the global capitalist market. In contrast to Halbfass, I would argue that this is no longer a simple matter of Orient versus Occident or the Europeanization of the world, but rather the more complex expansion of transnational capitalism—which is surely now no longer simply Western, but as much Japanese and Indian as American—to all points of the globe and all aspects of human interaction.[69] Thus, any resistance tends to become resistance to the market, a deformation of capitalism, and yet still largely ruled by the laws of the marketplace, still unable to imagine another space outside of global capitalism. And if "resistance" means nothing more than adding an Indian "curry" flavor of "Chicken McNuggets" to the McDonald's menu,[70] it seems a fairly pathetic form of resistance.

But perhaps the value of reflecting upon a radically deconstructive, ironic, and self-parodying figure such as Osho is that he might force us to rethink and deconstruct some of our own most basic assumptions. If Osho were alive today, he might well have challenged us to look more closely at ourselves and to critique the basic values of late capitalist consumer culture itself. After all, as Osho explained his own mission, his goal all along has been to try to shock us out of our comfortable slumbers and self-contented illusions. This is possibly the greatest lesson to be learned from extreme, paradoxical, and irreverent characters such as Osho-Rajneesh; for they force us to reflect critically upon ourselves and to take seriously the strange spiritual logic and cultural contradictions that run through our own increasingly plural, fragmented, and yet strangely interconnected world.

NOTES

1. Heelas, *The New Age Movement: The Celebration of the Self and the Sacralization of Modernity* (Oxford: Blackwell, 1996). On Scientology and its unique fit with capitalism, see Roy Wallis, *The Road to Total Freedom: A Sociological Analysis of Scientology* (London: Heinemann: 1976).

2. Foucault, *History of Sexuality, Volume I: An Introduction* (New York: Vintage, 1978), 35.

3. Fredric Jameson, *Postmodernism: Or, the Cultural Logic of Late Capitalism* (Durham: Duke University Press, 1991).

4. For Rajneesh's biography, see Urban, "Zorba the Buddha: Capitalism, Charisma, and the Cult of Bhagwan Shree Rajneesh," *Religion* 26 (1996): 161–82; and Susan J. Palmer and Arvind Sharma, *The Rajneesh Papers: Studies in a New Religious Movement* (Delhi: Motilal Banarsidas, 1993). More popular accounts by disciples and ex-disciples include: Yati, *The Sound of Running Water: A Photobiography of Bhagwan Shree Rajneesh* (Poona: Rajneesh Foundation, 1980); Milne, *Bhagwan: The God that Failed*; James Gordon, *The Golden Guru: The Strange Journey of Bhagwan Shree Rajneesh* (New York: Viking, 1987).

5. Georg Feuerstein, *Holy Madness: The Shock Tactics and Radical Teachings of Crazy-Wise Adepts, Holy Fools, and Rascal Gurus* (New York: Paragon House, 1990), 65.

6. See Lewis Carter, *Charisma and Control in Rajneeshpuram: The Role of Shared Values in the Creation of a Community* (Cambridge: Cambridge University Press, 1990), 77–78.

7. Judy and John Kaplan Mills, *Spokane Spokesman Review* (1983). For a good discussion of Sheela's increasing control over the movement and her various criminal activities, see Carter, *Charisma and Control*, 94–96, 102–105, 132–35. For Osho's own retrospective views on Sheela, see *Autobiography*, 253–57.

8. Osho, *Autobiography of a Spiritually Incorrect Mystic* (New York: St. Martin's, 2000), 255.

9. See Hugh Milne, *Bhagwan: The God that Failed* (New York: St. Martin's, 1986), 221ff.

10. Carter, *Charisma and Control*, 225, 237.

11. Bob Mullan, *Life as Laughter: Following Bhagwan Shree Rajneesh* (Boston: Routledge, 1983), 44.

12. Rajneesh, *The Art of Dying.* "I am not here to impose any religion on you. I am here to make you completely weightless—without religion, without ideology. . . . There is no need of any religion, there is no need of any God, there is no need of any priesthood . . . I trust in the individual categorically." Quoted at the Osho.com Web site: (www.osho.com/Main.cfm?Area=Magazine).

13. Carter, *Charisma and Control*, 37.

14. Vasant Joshi, *Awakened One: The Life and Work of Bhagwan Shree Rajneesh* (San Francisco: Harper and Row, 1982), 165.

15. Carter, *Charisma and Control*, 112–13.

16. Feuerstein, *Holy Madness*, 67.

17. Rajneesh, *Tantra the Supreme Understanding* (Poona: Rajneesh Foundation, 1975), 55, 6.

18. A Sannyasin informant, cited in Carter, *Charisma and Control*, 48. As Osho puts it, "You are certainly brainwashed, I use a dry cleaning machine. . . . And what is wrong with being brainwashed? Wash it every day, keep it clean. . . . Everybody is afraid of brainwashing. I am in absolute favor of it. . . . It is just an up to date religious laundry." Osho, *Autobiography*, 133–34.

19. One of the most popular early techniques was "Dynamic" or "Chaotic Meditation." As a kind of "microcosm of Rajneesh's outlook," its explicit aim was to "shock habitual patterns of thought and behavior" and so open the individual to ecstatic freedom. After an initial stage of concentration and yogic breathing, the chaotic meditation would culminate in an ecstatic, uncontrolled state of "letting the body go, without restrictions," through dancing, laughing, shrieking, or rolling on the ground. Rajneesh, *The Mystic Experience* (Delhi: Harper and Row, 1977), 72ff.

20. For a general discussion of Tantra, David Gordon White, ed., *Tantra in Practice* (Princeton: Princeton University Press, 2000).

21. Osho, *The Tantric Transformation*, (Shaftesburg: Element, 1978), 4. On the transformation of Tantra in the modern Western context, see Hugh B. Urban, "The Cult of Ecstasy: Tantra, the New Age, and the Spiritual Logic of Late Capitalism," *History of Religions* 39 (2000): 268–304.

22. Osho, *The Tantric Transformation*, 6–7.

23. Rajneesh, *Tantra the Supreme Understanding*, 93, 157.

24. Ibid., 190, 98–99.

25. Rajneesh, *Yoga: The Alpha and the Omega* (Poona: Rajneesh Foundation, 1981), 157, 21. As Susan J. Palmer comments, "Rajneesh's philosophy and commune life validate the role of lover and present a sexually promiscuous lifestyle as a spiritual path. Rajneesh offers a highly elaborated theology of sexual love." "Lovers and Leaders in a Utopian Commune," in Palmer and Sharma, *The Rajneesh Papers*, 127.

26. Rajneesh, *Tantra the Supreme Understanding*, 100.

27. Feuerstein, *Holy Madness*, 70. "The Rajneesh therapy groups that aspiring initiates were obliged to participate in employed various techniques which encouraged members to release inhibitions. . . . Sexual feelings were interpreted as charismatic indications of Bhagwan's presence 'flowing' between his disciples." Palmer, "Lovers and Leaders in a Utopian Commune," 111.

28. Rajneesh, *Tantra the Supreme Understanding*, 100.

29. Rajneesh, *The Goose is Out* (Poona: Rajneesh Foundation, 1982), 286.

30. Nik Douglas, *Spiritual Sex: Secrets of Tantra from the Ice Age to the New Millennium* (New York: Pocket Books, 1997), 15.

31. Foucault, *History of Sexuality, Volume I: An Introduction* , 35; cf. Foucault, *Religion and Culture*, ed. Jeremy R. Carrette (New York: Routledge, 1999), 117.

32. Jeffery Weeks, *Sexuality and its Discontents: Meanings, Myths, and Modern Sexualities* (London: Routledge and Kegan Paul, 1985), 23, 24.

33. Osho, *Autobiography*, 217. "I teach a sensuous religion. I want Gautama the Buddha and Zorba the Greek to come closer and closer; my disciple has to be Zorba-the-Buddha. Man is body-soul together. Both have to be satisfied." Rajneesh, quoted in Joshi, *Awakened One: The Life and Work of Bhagwan Shree Rajneesh*, 1.

34. Mullan, *Life as Laughter*, 48.

35. Rajneesh, quoted in Laurence Grafstein, "Messianic Capitalism," *The New Republic* 20 (1984).

36. Rajneesh, *Beware of Socialism!* (Rajneeshpuram: Rajneesh Foundation, 1984), 15, 19.

37. Ranjeesh, *Tantra the Supreme Understanding*, 109–10. "Tantra creates a totally new religion. . . . [I]ts God is so vast the world can be included. . . . If it is God who has created your body, your sexuality, your sensuality, then it cannot be against God." Osho, *The Tantric Transformation*, 260.

38. Osho, *Autobiography*, 157.

39. Carter, *Charisma and Control*, 72.

40. Ibid., 283 n. 38.

41. Milne, *Bhagwan: The God that Failed*, 245.

42. Gordon, *The Golden Guru*, 116.

43. Milne, *Bhagwan: The God that Failed*, 245.

44. Carter, *Charisma and Control*, 77.

45. Swami Anand Jina, "The Work of Osho Rajneesh: A Thematic Overview," in Palmer and Sharma, *The Rajneesh Papers*, 54.

46. *Osho, Never Born, Never Died*. Available from World Wide Web: (http://www.sannyas.net/osho02.htm).

47. "The Laughing Swamis," 78.

48. Tom Robbins, quoted on the "Osho.com" Web site.

49. Osho, *Autobiography*, 132.

50. Ibid., 268–69.

51. Appendix to Osho, *Autobiography*, 294; see also Jina, "The Work of Osho Rajneesh," 55; Palmer and Sharma, "Epilogue" to *The Rajneesh Papers*, 161.

52. Müller, *Biographical Essays* (New York: C. Scribner's Sons, 1884), 13.

53. On the concept of late capitalism, see Ernest Mandel, *Late Capitalism* (London: NLB, 1975); Fredric Jameson, *Postmodernism: Or, the Cultural Logic of Late Capitalism*; Daniel Bell, *The Coming of Post-Industrial Society* (New York: Basic Books, 1973); Claus Offe, *Disorganized Capitalism* (Oxford: Oxford University Press, 1985); David Harvey, *The Condition of Postmodernity* (London: Blackwell, 1989).

54. As Harvey summarizes, "modernist" or "organized capitalism," which predominated up to the 1970s, may be characterized as: profit-centered big business, centralization of industrial banking, and regulated national markets; complex managerial hierarchies; a concentration of capitalist relations with relatively few industries; and monopolistic corporate power. Late or disorganized capitalism, on the other hand, may be characterized as: a deconcentration of corporate power away from national markets; increasing internationalization of capital; increasing independence of large monopolies from state regulation; cultural fragmentation and pluralism; a decline of industrial cities and a deconcentration from city centers to peripheral areas; and entrepreneurial individualism. Harvey, *The Condition of Postmodernity*, 291–98.

55. Jameson, "Postmodernism and Consumer Society," in *The Anti-Aesthetic: Essays on Postmodern Culture*, ed. Hal Foster, (New York: New Press, 1998), 99. As Terry Eagleton comments, "We are now in the process of awakening from the nightmare of modernity, with its manipulative reason and fetish of totality, into the laid back pluralism of the postmodernism, that heterogeneous range of . . . language games which has renounced the urge to totalize." "Awakening from Modernity," *Times Literary Supplement* February 20 1987, cited in Harvey, *The Condition of Postmodernity*, 9.

56. Jameson, *Postmodernism: Or, the Cultural Logic of Late Capitalism*, 96; cf. Harvey, *The Condition of Postmodernity*, 54.

57. Eagleton, "Awakening from Modernity"; cited in Harvey, *The Condition of Postmodernity*, 7. See also Jameson, "Postmodernism and Consumer Society," 124.

58. Jürgen Habermas, "Legitimation Problems in the Modern State," *Communication and the Evolution of Society* (Boston: Beacon Press, 1974).

59. Mike Featherstone, *Consumer Culture and Postmodernism* (London: Sage, 1991), 112–13.

60. Bryan S. Turner, *Regulating Bodies: Essays in Medical Sociology* (London: Routledge, 1992), 164–65, 47.

61. Featherstone, *Consumer Culture and Postmodernism*, 114.

62. Foucault, *Religion and Culture*, 69.

63. Halbfass, *India and Europe: An Essay on Understanding*, 339–40, 441–42.

64. Benjamin Barber, *Jihad vs. McWorld: How Globalism and Tribalism are Reshaping the World* (New York: Ballantine, 1992), 4. See also Aijaz Ahmad, *In Theory: Classes, Nations, Literatures* (New York: Verso, 1992); Mike Featherstone, *Undoing Culture: Globalization, Postmodernism, and Identity* (London: Sage, 1995), 8; Arjun Appadurai, "Disjuncture and Difference in the Global Cultural Economy," in *The Globalization Reader*, eds. Frank J. and John Boli Lechner (London: Blackwell, 2000), 322–30. As Aijaz Ahmad has argued, we are perhaps no longer divided into "Three Worlds," nor are we even divided into simple binaries such as "capitalist/pre-capitalist" or "modern/pre-modern"; instead, there is now only one world—that of international capitalism: "One of the many contradictory consequences of decolonization within a largely capitalist framework was that it brought all zones of capital into a single integrated market, entirely dominated by this supreme imperialist power." *In Theory: Classes, Nations, Literatures*, 21.

65. Gita Mehta, *Karma Cola: Marketing the Mystic East* (New York: Simon and Schuster, 1979), 106.

66. Ibid., 157; cf. p. 107. Mehta cites Rajneesh, Muktananda, and various other neo-Tantric gurus as key examples of this cross-cultural confusion.

67. Sahlins, "Cosmologies of Capitalism: The Trans-Pacific Sector of 'The World System," *Proceedings of the British Academy* 74 (1988), 4. A similar argument is made by John and Jean Comaroff, eds., *Modernity and its Malcontents: Ritual and Power in Postcolonial Africa* (Chicago: University of Chicago Press, 1993), xi–xii.

68. Pico Iyer, *Video Night in Kathmandu and Other Reports from the Not-so-far East* (New York: Knopf, 1988), 5.

69. As Appadurai observes, "the United States is no longer the puppeteer of a world system of images but is only one node of a complex transnational construction of imaginary landscapes." *Modernity at Large: Cultural Dimensions of Globalization* (Minneapolis: University of Minnesota Press, 1996), 31.

70. Some authors seem more hopeful about this sort of local adaptation of the global market: "regions respond to similar economic constraints in different ways. Countries still have great leeway in structuring their own polities; the same television program means different things to different audiences; McDonald's adapts its menu and marketing to local tastes." Frank J. and John Boli Lechner, *The Globalization Reader* (London: Blackwell, 2000).

NINE

RIDING THE DAWN HORSE

Adi Da and the Eros of Nonduality

JEFFREY J. KRIPAL

> As certainly as God is, God will be known. . . . It is like the Dawn
> Horse vision that I have described to you. There was this Siddha
> [perfected master] whose *Siddhi* [superpower] was to manifest
> things from nothing. His disciples lined up before him, and he just
> sat there. At some point they all saw that he had done it, funda-
> mentally, and they all left. But nothing had appeared yet. Franklin
> sat around for awhile, and all of a sudden this horse appeared in the
> middle of the room.
>
> —Bubba Free John, *Garbage and the Goddess*

THE MOUNTAIN OF ATTENTION SANCTUARY is just down the road from
Middletown, California, one of those small mountain communities that lay up
the road a torturous two and a half hour drive from the Golden Gate Bridge.
The Sanctuary is one of three ashrams belonging to Adidam, an American
siddha guru tradition deeply influenced by Hindu and Buddhist systems of
thought and practice, particularly in their Tantric nondual forms, and centered
on the charismatic person and teaching of Ruchira Avatar Adi Da Samraj
(born Franklin Jones, 1939, in Long Island, New York), whom I will refer to
henceforth simply as Bubba, as Da, or as Adi Da, depending on the text or historical context I am discussing.[1] By 1997, the twenty-fifth anniversary of the
guru's teaching work, the community could locate ten active communities (in
Seattle, San Francisco, Los Angeles, Ottawa, Boston, Washington, D.C., England, Holland, Australia, and New Zealand), three ashrams (The Mountain of

Attention in Middletown, California, Love-Ananda Mahal in Kauai, Hawaii, and Ruchira Buddha Dham in Naitauba, Fiji), and a small library of publications that includes more than seventy-five monographs written by the guru, six separate magazine runs, and numerous devotional works written by disciples.[2] Since then, moreover, the community has initiated an ambitious source-text publishing project designed to publish in a new format all twenty-three of the guru's source texts: *The Five Books Of The Heart Of The Adidam Revelation*, *The Seventeen Companions Of The True Dawn Horse*, and the master-work itself, *The Dawn Horse Testament of the Ruchira Avatar*. These volumes, although certainly not without their rhetorical, literary, and theological challenges, do rank among the most philosophically sophisticated and doctrinally extensive of all the Western guru literature.

Still, Adi Da is not quite a "great guru," at least in the sense that the present volume is using that expression. It all depends, of course, on what one means by *maha*. If one measures religious greatness by demographics, that is, by the number of active devotees, it is doubtful whether Adi Da would qualify for the term *mahaguru*, since, although his devotee base is quite solid, it has probably never numbered more than a few thousand individuals. If, moreover, one takes the traditional ethnic or racial position that a guru must possess a particular ethnic identity or cultural pedigree (in this case, an Indian one), then Adi Da again hardly qualifies: He was, after all, born Franklin Jones in, of all places, Long Island, New York.

And this is precisely what makes him so important to consider. Here, after all, is a man whose life and teachings display in abundance the charismatic energies, miracle stories, philosophical complexities, and ethical controversies (particularly around the transgressive pedagogy of "crazy wisdom") that we have come to recognize as consistent, if not constant, features of the modern *mahaguru*. And yet he is, if I may put it so colloquially, a white guy. Clearly, Adi Da's very existence and recognized presence within the American guru scene challenges any position that identifies a head count, skin color, or identity politics as reliable standards of religious influence and historical importance. He also offers us the opportunity of what we might call "strong comparison," that is, the possibility that we can learn something more about the phenomenon of the Western guru (not to mention global Hinduism) by looking at both Indian and Euro-American figures with a distinctly comparative eye. Specifically, what is changed, ignored, denied, accentuated, when we move back and forth from an Indian guru to a Euro-American one? And can the reversed orientalism (itself a reversal of a racist colonial discourse) that has always dominated the Western guru scene, with the Indian qua Indian as somehow more spiritual, adequately explain the richness and cross-cultural complexity of the actual historical record? And finally, and perhaps most deeply, is this same reversed orientalism, this insistence on the Indian guru, really faithful to the ontological teachings of these same teachers? Does not the ontological logic of nonduality itself render cultural location and ethnicity irrelevant? Why *not*, then, a *mahaguru* from Long Island? Such opening questions, of course, are largely rhetorical ones. It now remains to be seen how Adi Da and Adidam might help us at least to consider the possibility of such conclusions so poorly posing as questions.

Another feature of Adi Da's person and teaching that renders him an especially interesting subject for our present inquiries (and which complicates much that was said immediately above about orientalist structure) is his quite conscious and careful attempt to locate himself in a lineage of famous guru-figures, beginning immediately with Swami Rudrananda or Rudi, one of his own early gurus (like him, of Euro-American descent), and Swami Muktananda, from whom he took both early instruction and an initiatory transmission, back through Ramana Maharshi to Shri Ramakrishna and Swami Vivekananda. The Western phenomenon of the Indian *mahaguru*, in other words, is integral to Adi Da's own self-understanding and community, and he unmistakably intends to communicate himself as being such a guru, indeed, as the greatest of these great gurus.

In looking at these issues of cross-cultural translation and nonduality, I will focus on a single stubbornly recurring issue in the phenomenon of the Western guru: the erotic. Such a focus is by no means accidental or tangential, particularly here. From the South Asian Tantric perspectives within which so much of Adi Da's teaching is expressed, little of spiritual value can be accomplished until what Adi Da has coined as the emotional-sexual nature of the human being is confronted, incorporated into one's *sadhana* or spiritual practice, and thoroughly worked through. Among the Western theoretical perspectives that lie at the center of religious studies (literary criticism, gender studies, and psychoanalytic theory), human sexuality always deeply encodes social practices, cultural assumptions, identity formation, political structure, and the most secret and important truths of individuals, not to mention every encounter with an Other, including a cross-cultural one. To fuse these two different cultural horizons within a hermeneutical practice such as this, then, is to join a Tantric mystical practice to an intellectual one in an attempt to understand more deeply the erotic processes of cultural encounter and ontological transformation. Such a move is particularly appropriate here, as Adi Da himself, affectionately known to his disciples as "Beloved," long ago came to an analogous conclusion: He has often said that his present incarnation and work could not have been as effective without the earlier cultural and philosophical groundwork laid by Freud's depth psychology.

THE DAWN HORSE

Certainly any number of sexual-textual moments bear this remarkable confession out. Indeed, one of the more interesting aspects of Adi Da and his tradition is the quite public fashion in which they have handled the question of sexuality and its central role in the spiritual life of the community. It is difficult, for example, to imagine a life-long celibate guru when his daughters and his two partners are not only present but ritually privileged during the ritual of *darshan*. Certainly the goal of celibacy is offered as an accomplishment of serious spiritual practice and Adi Da may in fact be celibate now, but never is this celibate goal allowed to smother or deny the centrality of the emotional-sexual nature of human behavior, including and especially religious behavior. Nor has Adi Da avoided the topic of sexuality in his books or conversation. Quite the contrary, he has spoken and written about it at considerable length since he first began teaching and publishing in the early '70s, often in a bawdy, delightfully humorous, even "obscene" way (obscenity, of course, always being a matter of personal taste or preference). Indeed, the first two lines of his very first book, an autobiography entitled *The Knee of Listening*, read thus: "On November 3, 1939, at 11:21 a.m., in Jamaica, New York, I was born Franklin Albert Jones. The sign of my birth is Scorpio, marked by the images of Spirit and of Sex, the eagle and the crab."[3] Apparently, the astrological stage was set for an inevitable drama of extremes.[4]

The challenge of locating the sexual within the tradition here then is quite the opposite of what one often encounters in other guru traditions. Whereas in the latter there is often precious little to go on, much is intentionally censored, concealed, or flat-out denied in various subtle and not so subtle ways, and one must be creative to find what is hinted at or, more likely, break any number of taboos and good graces to begin to think such thoughts, here there is far too much material to read and process in any adequate fashion, much less to fully understand, analyze, and then squeeze into a single essay. The community's rich audio and textual archives, not to mention Adi Da's personal library at the Mountain of Attention, organized according to his seven stage developmental model of the spiritual life, only add to an already dizzying sense of historical vertigo.[5] And then, of course, there are the devotees themselves, many of whom are quite willing to talk about this aspect of their guru and their own devotional lives. Where exactly to begin? And, more importantly, where to end?

I want to organize my own thoughts here around an archetypal animal that appears in a kind of dream-vision, the Dawn Horse[6] of Adi Da's initial vision, which would quickly morph into the name of the community's press (The Dawn Horse Press), the name of the early community (The Dawn Horse Communion), and the title of Adi Da's magnum opus (*The Dawn Horse Testament*). Obviously, we are dealing here with something of an organizing metaphor or shamanic totem, a visionary beginning that is renewed and perfected anew with each new attempt to embody it in institution, text, or symbol.

I have never run across a scriptural reference to the Dawn Horse in the primary texts of Adidam, but I suspect that the image is related to the first verse of the *Brihadaranyaka Upanishad*: "The dawn indeed is the head of the sacrificial horse." That Adi Da has written extensively about his existence as a kind of sacrifice adds to the likelihood that we are dealing here with a creative reworking of this ancient scriptural image. More important than this specula-tion is the guru's use of the image in his own life and writings. In *Garbage and the Goddess*, Da uses the image to explain how the work of those months from March to July of 1974 is in some fundamental sense already accomplished, "like the Dawn Horse."[7] The image, then, participates in that particular onto-logical paradox of radical nonduality that Alan Watts addressed in his brief but important foreword to *The Knee of Listening*.[8] We also see it, for example, in contemplative traditions such as Advaita Vedanta, Japanese Zen, or Tibetan Dzogchen: Nothing can be done to effect that pristine state of consciousness that already is, and yet something must be done in order that it may appear in the phenomenal experience of the aspirant—the path that is not a path.

The symbolism of the Dawn Horse began as a small, prehistoric horse; in later versions, it manifested into a rearing stallion and eventually was given wings. The Dawn Horse's fluid symbolism was constantly being altered by the artists and the publishers, always at the initiation of Adi Da himself. The guru himself is quite clear and open about this. So, too, with my use of the image. I do not claim that my rhetorical use of the symbol of the Dawn Horse as the organizing metaphor of this chapter is completely faithful to the tradition. It is not. Rather, it is best thought of as a kind of "hermeneutical site" or fusion of horizons through which I can best encounter, interpret, and analyze this religious world of meaning. I adopt the symbol here primarily for my own rhetorical purposes, that is, as an implicit visionary marker for the ontological irrelevance of ethnicity, religious identity, or temporal privilege (as if the truth always dwells most fully in the past). Certainly such identities are paramount on the level of politics, cultural history, and civic life, but as features of the socialized ego, that *ahamkara* or "I-maker" that is transcended in so many forms of Indian nondualism, these identities and their politics mean nothing, literally *absolutely* nothing, on the level of the Real. If nonduality is already accomplished (*siddha*), then it is already accomplished, no matter what color of skin one has, what language one happens to speak (or not speak), or what particular family or time period one was born into. Everything else is percep-tual error, social illusion, or religious racism. The white guru from Long Island, in other words, need not be read as yet another example of neocolo-nial misappropriation; he may just as easily be the inevitable end and fulfill-ment of the radical nondual logic. In this sense at least, Adi Da is entirely justified in his claims: He does indeed literally fulfill the promise of the Indian nondual traditions for the West.

Such anyway is my working thesis for the present chapter. Toward this essentially mystical end, I will proceed chronologically through two texts from the earliest period with an eye on the ontological relationship of the mystical and the erotic and the specific yogic techniques that were used in the community to conform a sexually active life to spiritual goals at the time of these texts' production. Having examined in some detail the actual content of these two documents, I will then proceed to offer a few interpretive observations of my own regarding the distinctly American transformations of Tantra. Finally, I will conclude as I began, with the already accomplished appearance of the Dawn Horse. The essay thus duplicates on a structural level the most basic ontological message of the tradition, namely, that the secret of spiritual practice is the realization that one's efforts never effect or cause enlightenment. In Da's words, reality is "always already the case." Appropriately, then, we must end where we began, with the Dawn Horse appearing, as if out of nowhere, this time in the West. Implied, after all, in the "always already" mantra is a third nondual term: "everywhere."

GARBAGE AND THE GODDESS

Garbage and the Goddess was published in 1974 as the third book to appear from the community, following the guru's early autobiography, *The Knee of Listening* (1972), and a companion volume of some of his early talks, *The Method of the Siddhas* (1973). In this third volume, however, the guru had made his first name-change, from Franklin Jones to Bubba Free John. "Bubba," we are told, means "brother" and signals a kind of closeness or intimacy.[9] It also happened to be his childhood nickname.[10] "Free John" was a new rendering of Franklin Jones. The freewheeling style of Bubba's talks and the openness of the community in this third volume certainly bear this out.

In terms of content, the volume's combination of philosophical sophistication, elaborate and delightfully honest descriptions of the devotees' ecstatic and visionary states, simple but effective line drawings, delightful photographs, and often humorous expressions of Bubba make it, in my opinion, one of the most important, interesting, and certainly one of the most entertaining things to come out of the American guru culture. Here is a text in which one can laugh out loud. Indeed, laughter is theologized, for "humor is the bodily confession of God."[11] But humor here is not only a theological principle. It is a funny turn of phase, a photo full of smiles and laughing human beings, even an occasional "offensive" expression.[12]

The book also has a fascinating history. Other than *The Knee of Listening*, the guru's autobiography, no book published by the community has sold as

well and as fast as *Garbage and the Goddess*. Unlike their previous print runs of
five thousand, the press published twenty thousand copies. Despite the text's
rather obvious messages that the "miracles" of Bubba were over, and that the
spiritual life has nothing to do with extraordinary experiences (hence "the
garbage" of the title), people began showing up at the ashram, looking for both
these same extraordinary experiences and the parties portrayed in the book
with such color and warmth. This was not the message the guru or the community wanted to send, and yet clearly on some level that was precisely the
message the book was sending. Ultimately, then, despite the book's commercial
success, the community chose to withdraw the book from the market. Moreover, they gathered as many copies as they could from the bookstores and
burned them. This poignant, deeply ambivalent event captures well the diffi-
culty, perhaps the impossibility, of portraying the religious nature of what were
essentially Tantric methods of transgression and sexual experimentation to a
public audience. What began as a remarkably honest attempt to document a
particularly creative period of the tradition ended, quite literally, in flames. Still,
not every copy was lost, and the book stands to this day as an important record
of these early defining months.

The text itself recounts a four to five month period in the life of the community ending on July 7, 1974. The "last miracles" of the guru were said to be
complete and no longer necessary to the teaching, and the community was
now to take over the task of communicating the guru's message to the world.
July 7, 1974, then, effectively became the birthday of the Dawn Horse Communion,[13] the origin date of the tradition. And indeed, this is the movement
and the message of the book: that, as of now, the extraordinary events of the
early community, so lovingly recounted in the book, are no longer necessary to
the practice.[14] As manifestations of the goddess and her phenomenal world,
dramatic experiences such as *kundalini* phenomena, synchronistic experiences,
numinous dreams, possession states, involuntary bodily movements, shouting, a
miraculous storm, etc.[15] may or may not continue to arise; regardless, they are
nonessential to the realization of Consciousness itself. Baldly put, they are
"garbage" to throw away for the grace of that which is always already the case,
Consciousness itself.

The image of garbage comes from the life of Bubba and his first guru,
Rudi, or Swami Rudrananda. Born Albert Rudolph (1928–1973), Rudi used
to hand Bubba (as Franklin) a greasy bag of garbage whenever he visited.[16]
Through Rudi's teaching, throwing away the garbage became a simple ritual
with a message, namely, that one must ignore the unusual states of mind and
body that often accompany spiritual practice. Throw them away, with the
greasy garbage, and move on. From now on, Bubba's "Force," manifested
through the devotees in the period of miracles, will be replaced by a kind of
pure "Presence."[17] The responsibility for attracting and working with new

devotees now lies with the textual deposit and the "great Community of unreasonably happy men,"[18] both seen as extensions or embodiments of the guru himself.[19] Indeed, in one passage, the community is seen as the Devi, the goddess-consort of Consciousness, or again as an *avatar*, a literal embodiment of the divine on earth.[20]

THE NATURE OF REALITY AND OF NARCISSUS THE EGO

There is no way to interpret any of the tradition's many texts, understand the guru's teaching style, or delineate the relationship between the erotic and the mystical without beginning with the most basic question of all, the question of the nature of reality. For our own purposes, it is perhaps best to begin with the tradition's most recent publication of the twenty-three source texts, each of which includes a common introduction in which the ontology of the tradition is stated in three brief sentences, perhaps following the model of Upanishadic great sayings (*mahavakyas*), which capture the essence of the teaching. Here, anyway, are the three "great sayings" of Adidam:

> There is no ultimate "difference" between you and the Divine.
> There is only the Divine.
> Everything that exists is a "modification" of the One Divine Reality.[21]

In philosophical terms familiar to students of Hindu or Buddhist thought, these sayings indicate a cosmic nondualism with strong affinities to Shakta Tantra, Tibetan Dzogchen, and Zen Buddhism, a nondualism in which the phenomenal world's reality is both affirmed as real and celebrated as sacred, but not made ultimate.

Here there simply is no such thing as an individual cut off from the rest of Reality. The socialized ego, what the guru likes to call the "cult of Narcissus," is a complete fiction: "There is not now, nor has there ever been, nor will there ever be an individual being. There is no such thing. All the cultic ways are strategic searches to satisfy individuals by providing them with various kinds of fulfillment, or inner harmony, or vision, or blissfulness, or salvation, or liberation, or whatever. But the truth is that there is no such one to be fulfilled; literally, there is no such one."[22] But if in reality there is no individual, there also can be no searches, no existential dilemmas, no religiously based salvations (for what could no one possibly be saved from?). Which leads the serious aspirant directly into the paradox of having to look for something that is already present, of having to search for something that is already found—the paradox of the practice that is not a practice.

THE SATURDAY NIGHT MASSACRE AND THE CULT OF PAIRS

How, then, to live in such a nondual world where nothing is really happening, where there is no self and nothing to accomplish, and yet bills to pay and human, that is, individual relationships to manage? Early on, the guru adopted a kind of two-layered esoteric ethic by means of a distinction between what he called "conventional" living, by which he meant conforming to and naively believing in the customs and moral evaluations of one's society, and "functional" living, by which he meant a kind of playful but knowing acceptance of society's rules as necessary for the game of culture.[23] We might think of this latter functional ethic as a kind of two-eyed depth perception—one eye on the world of social custom, the other on Consciousness itself—through which one can see into another dimension, in our metaphor's case, the third one of depth. Or better, we might imagine a kind of "looking out" from Consciousness onto the social world as a kind of theatrical play to enjoy but never to get completely fooled by. I am reminded here of Ramakrishna's teaching about the state of *bhavamukha*, that bifocal perspective subsequent to a mystical state in which one's attention or "face" (*mukha*) is turned toward the "world of existence" (*bhava*) as it looks out from the vantage point of Consciousness—an enlightened "seeing from."

Such an esoteric ethic and the larger ontological world in which it is firmly embedded have major implications for sexual morality and the place of sexual practice in the spiritual life. Some of these implications are drawn out in the first chapter of *Garbage and the Goddess,* which recounts the events of Saturday evening, March 23, at the ashram, a night that became playfully but seriously known as "The Saturday Night Massacre."

During this night and in subsequent ones, Bubba set out his understanding of sexuality. "Sexuality is a phenomenon of nature," we are told. "It exists universally and has no individual form. It is a process prior to personality."[24] As a modification of Consciousness, it should not be equated with something like Freud's id, that is, it is not "some sort of insane animalistic presence in which nothing but mass murder and destruction are hidden." Granted, "the true spiritual process is very wild in many ways, because it is alive. But it is not out of control. It is an absolutely conscious affair. . . ."[25] The reason people fear such a force is because they have conventionally obstructed these energies to such an extent that they are no longer in touch with them[26] and their own intimate connection to the Light that shines infinitely above the head. They assume that they are "the 20 watts" of their little self concepts, of their little psychophysiological egos, and that even these few measly watts will gradually decline until they blip off, like the little light bulb in the refrigerator, at the closing of death. But this is all wrong: "It is not smacked into your body when you are born, frozen there while you live, and then run out when you die. It is a present, ongoing creation."[27] In fact, "there is one Reality, without differentiation. It is full, it is only blissful, there is no danger, and there is no curse."[28] Sounding rather like Freud in *Civilization and Its Discontents*, Bubba goes on to claim that the "cult of this world" is "all about the suppression of ecstasy," and that it is sexuality where human beings most commonly and most profoundly reconnect with the ecstatic experience that we all seek.

The social custom of marriage is an obstacle to the spiritual life because it blocks the flow of this life-energy from circulating among other human beings. "Perhaps the most tight-knit cult is the cult of couples, because in the midst of such pairs, heterosexual or homosexual, the ecstasy of the communicated life-force is ritualized and made exclusive."[29] And for real spiritual practice to begin, sexual energy must be released from the tyranny of social convention and systematic suppression: "If the function of sexuality is obstructed, as it always is in the cultic personality, nothing like the internal and radical spiritual process can take place. The center and process of sexuality must be absolutely free, and this is possible only when the individual understands and realizes his entire complex condition in the always already prior Condition that is Reality, Truth, Self, and God."[30] Sexual freedom, in other words, is ultimately based, not on a kind of libertinism (although there are occasionally elements of this as well), but on a proper ontological understanding of sexuality as something natural, conscious, blissful, and secondary to the prior condition of Consciousness itself, of which these energies, again, are a modification.

The "cult of couples" is a negative thing because it prevents the life-force or "love" from being distributed throughout the sacred community.[31] Marriage reinforces the cultic view of the ego, namely, that it exists and that it is somehow important.[32] It is thus the responsibility of the community to undermine cultic involvement in marriages and all exclusive relationships.[33] All the usual social distinctions are obsolete now; they may function automatically, "but they are not true."[34] Thus the community should feel free to create entirely new forms of social practice, of family, and of generating children.[35] Indeed, at one point, when Bubba returns to his house with a few male disciples and a number of wives (but none of their husbands) and without his four usual female attendants, the editors comment: "By this time it was obvious to everyone that Bubba wasn't just criticizing the forms of our social lives but was also destroying them."[36]

CRAZY WISDOM

Historically speaking, most modern gurus who have employed Tantric practices and ideas in the West have become the object of serious and convincing ethical critique, almost always involving their secret sexualities and false fronts of celibacy. These patterns, moreover, can hardly be explained away as postcolonial distortions or, much worse, as scholarly fictions or ill-intentioned Western projections (the traditional claims of those who prefer polemical scapegoating and identity politics over historical accuracy); quite the contrary, they show every sign of being traditional and well grounded in the indigenous and ancient literatures. As Bernard Faure has so powerfully demonstrated, for example, there is a distinctly "red thread" in the Buddhist Mahayana and Vajrayana traditions that follows a logic of transgression and turns to erotic experience as an inducer of transmoral mystical states, and this no doubt has a great deal to teach us about the sexual scandals that plagued American Buddhist communities in the 1970s and '80s.[37] The exact same thing, of course, could be said about any number of Hindu gurus who have become well known in the West, from Krishnamurti and Swami Muktananda to Bhagwan Rajneesh and Sai Baba. Indeed, in 1985, Jack Kornfield studied fifty-four Buddhist, Hindu, and Jain teachers operating in North America and found that thirty-four of them had had sexual relationships with their disciples.[38]

In this historical American-Asian context, it is hardly surprising that serious ethical charges involving sexual abuse and authoritarian manipulation have been leveled at Adi Da and his community for very similar, if far more open and acknowledged, antinomian practices and ideas. Bay Area journalistic reports from a single month in 1985 are especially salacious,[39] and any full treatment of the erotic within Adidam would need to spend dozens of careful pages analyzing both the accuracy of the reports and the community's interpretation and understanding of the same events, the latter framed largely in the logic of "crazy wisdom," that is, the notion that the enlightened master can employ antinomian shock tactics that appear to be immoral or abusive in order to push his disciples into new forms of awareness and freedom. Perhaps what is most remarkable about the case of Adidam is the simple fact that the community has never denied the most basic substance of the charges, that is, that sexual experimentation was indeed used in the ashrams and that some people experienced these as abusive, particularly in the Garbage and the Goddess Period, even if it has also differed consistently and strongly on their proper interpretation and meaning.

How are we to make at least some sense of such consistent patterns, both in the individual case of Adidam and in the larger *mahaguru* scene? My own sense is that we need to develop a new paradoxical hermeneutic of the guru (or mystic) that does not commit the fallacy of conflating the mystical with the ethical but is, at the same time, willing and able to advance honest and public ethical criticism based on clear, if always culturally relative, moral principles such as the integrity and freedom of the individual human being, the latter of which may or may not find a place in the tradition being studied. In other words, we need to develop models that can embrace the positively ecstatic experiences of the text or believer, the deep and real hurt of the disaffected, *and* the full historical record of the scholar.

Along these same lines, I would also point out that the "crazy wisdom" rhetoric displays in a religious form what I have long argued in more rational, ethical, and historical terms, namely, that there is *no* necessary relationship between the mystical and the ethical (that is, there is nothing contradictory about individuals having profound religious experiences with "immoral gurus"), and that, more radically still, altered or dissociative states of consciousness experienced as spiritual realities are often catalyzed by (which is not at all to say reducible to) explicitly traumatic contexts or acts.[40] If an individual can have a life-altering out-of-body experience in a car wreck (clearly an example of serious physical trauma), why cannot he or she experience the same at the hands or feet of an amoral or transmoral mystic?

Indeed, I would go so far as to say that no fallacy has done more damage to the critical study and public understanding of gurus (or mysticism in general) than the historically and psychologically groundless notion that profound and positive mystical states imply or require some sort of moral perfection or social rectitude on the part of the teacher or text inducing them. As Rudolf Otto taught us long ago, the sacred is *not* the good or the moral; it is rather a *mysterium tremendum et fascinans*, a mystical secret at once terrifying and gorgeous, at once traumatic and terrific. For all its obvious dangers and liabilities, the crazy wisdom tradition at least openly and honestly recognizes this basic metaphysical paradox and struggles with it in a relatively open way. So too should we.

SPIRITUAL CONDUCTIVITY

Finally, before we leave this remarkable document, it is important to treat, however briefly, the text's portrayal of conductivity, the guru's term for the practice of working with the life-energy in the body in order to release it from its usual socially constructed knots and obstructions and get it circulating back up into the Light of Consciousness that is said to shine simultaneously in the Heart and above the cranium. Here, within a subtle mystical physiology indebted to (but not determined by) yogic models of the *chakras* and the channels or *nadis*, the human body is seen as a kind of conductor, a circle of energy that, once released into its natural descending and ascending flow, can "reconnect" the person with the Divine.

I put the expression "reconnect" in scare quotes because Bubba's understanding of conductivity is that it is not a technique of sublimation or repression that somehow effects a shift in consciousness. That is, there is no hydraulics of semen (*retas*), mystical energy (*shakti*), or physiological instinct (*libido*) here, as we see, for example, in the *siddha* traditions of medieval India[41] or in the different drive models of psychoanalysis. Indeed, Bubba goes out of his way to distinguish conductivity from all yogic disciplines of manipulating the psyche or body toward spiritual goals, particularly those forms of practice that were popular in the 1970s under the general rubric of *kundalini yoga*.[42] For him, these kinds of traditions and the experiences they generate can and should be understood for what they are, that is, as he will say much later, brain-based mysticisms[43] that manifest both spiritual and natural phenomena via the brain (instead of the Heart)—interesting and perhaps even useful at a certain stage of religious development, but by no means ultimate.

The Divine is not a manifestation of *Shakti*.[44] The latter, as a function of the Goddess, is again "garbage" to be thrown away. Conductivity, then, is not about producing unusual states of consciousness or working toward some imagined goal; rather, it is "that process generated when the Truth is already enjoyed as the principle and condition of conscious life."[45] Or again, it is not some "transcendental absorption in the functions of the life-force," as we see in yoga, but "understanding the conscious process of radical intuition."[46] Put simply, it is about Consciousness, not natural energies, however pleasurable, fascinating, or even seemingly divine. Once this is understood, the erotic can be located in its proper ontological context, that is, as a playful and conscious manifestation of prior Consciousness, a manifestation that participates intimately in the circle of energy that descends and ascends through the body from and to the Divine. Seen thus, the practice of sexuality becomes, not a religious practice or technique toward some distant goal, but a religious accomplishment or realization of an already present reality: the paradox of the Dawn Horse.

LOVE OF THE TWO-ARMED FORM

We are told in a footnote in *Garbage and the Goddess* that the techniques of conductivity had been described in a text entitled *Devi Yoga: Love of the Two-Armed Form,* but that this text's distribution was restricted to the community.[47] We are told something similar again in a second footnote regarding the "conscious conductivity of the life-force from the prior Light."[48] Four years later in 1978, however, the *Devi Yoga,* literally, "The Discipline of the Goddess," or more likely some later version of it, would be published as *Love of the Two-Armed Form*.[49] Early on, then, we see a tendency in the textual tradition to reveal more and more of the tradition's Tantric techniques and teachings as the years go on. It is clear, however, that even with the publication of *Love of the Two-Armed Form*, which is quite explicit in its discussions of any number of taboo subjects (from mutual masturbation, to the application of finger pressure near the base of the sexual organs in order to prevent orgasmic spasming, to the altering of the heterosexual assumptions of the Asian practices for Western homosexual couples), certain esoteric practices were not discussed in print.[50] Perhaps even these, however, were later addressed in the most recent texts of the tradition, such as the *Ruchira-Tantra Yoga* (literally, The Practice of the Tantra of the "Bright").[51] What we see here is a gradual revealing of the once concealed, a kind of public esotericism.

Love of the Two-Armed Form would appear again in a second edition in 1985. Between these two editions, in the fall of 1979, Bubba Free John would change his name to Da Free John, "Da" from the Sanskrit verb meaning "to give."[52] The second edition is peppered generously with photos of Da at the Taj Mahal and in different devotional settings, of traditional Indian paintings, particularly of Krishna and his milkmaid lovers, and of Japanese erotic prints and a single Tibetan *thangka* (meditative wall hanging). As a constructed group meant to convey some meaning, the photos can be read as a never quite explicit suggestion that the sacralization of sexuality has been primarily an Asian accomplishment. Only India, Tibet, and Japan, after all, are featured. There is no *Song of Songs*, no Kabbalists or Christian bridal mystics here, much less a William Blake, Wilhelm Reich, or Timothy Leary.

According to Da himself, the text itself is a collection of essays and talks produced during a six-year period "of trial and mutual society between myself and hundreds of aspirants to the radical spiritual Way that I Teach."[53] During these six years (1972–1978), the community gave itself to what the guru, following Patanjali's technique of *samyama* (a kind of contemplative "concentration" leading to a direct knowledge of the essence of a thing), calls a "consideration."[54] *Love of the Two-Armed Form* is a collection of those considerations that examined the subject of human sexuality and its relationship to spiritual practice. The central theme of the book is the practice of something called sexual communion, to which we now turn.

WHAT SEXUAL COMMUNION IS NOT

The practice of sexual communion as it is presented in *Love of the Two-Armed Form* is an elaborate collection of sexual techniques first discovered and developed by Franklin Jones in his early adult years and later offered to contemporary Western practitioners, offered within Da's ontological teaching of the "always already" nature of enlightenment. Sexual communion, we are told, possesses the elements "of all traditional religious, yogic, and mystical approaches to Truth," except that "it is not adapted to the conventional dilemma by which men and women pursue Truth." Rather, "it is a free expression of the priorly Enlightened Way of Divine Ignorance."[55] Technically speaking, then, it is not a technique at all, a means toward some future goal; rather, it is the enjoyment of a condition that one already is on some, commonly unconscious, level. One is thus instructed to identify with that prior already awakened Condition and not to get caught in strategic games of arousing and channeling subtle energetic forces, *kundalini*-like phenomena, and other yogic manifestations. Those may or may not arise, but they are not the point; they are secondary, material, and unnecessary manifestations of a deeper spiritual process.

Although the final form of sexual communion is a kind of "motiveless celibacy," the guru is very careful to distinguish the practice from traditional forms of asceticism and celibacy. Granted, in traditional Taoist and Tantric practices of celibacy, as well as in Da's own model of sexual communion, the goal is the "transcendence of degenerative orgasm," that is, the turning around of sexual energies at the sexual base so that they no longer are lost "out" through the sexual organs but invert and turn "in" and "up" toward the brain. Within sexual communion, however, the technique is one of stimulation, prolongation, and transformation of the orgasm, not its conscious suppression, unconscious repression, or systematic (and often misogynistic) denial, as we see in so many forms of traditional celibacy. Interestingly and crucially, it is the Heart, not the mind, that ultimately controls and guides this communion with Life and this spontaneous transformation of the orgasm. Adopting ancient yogic Samkhyan models of thought (*chitta*) and the mind (*manas*) as subtle but entirely natural and material processes, Da locates the true seat of consciousness, not in the brain, but in the Heart, a capitalized term for that pure Consciousness that completely transcends all the worlds but nevertheless manifests itself within the right side of the physiological organ of the beating human heart.

Sexual communion, then, is not based on any fear or rejection of sexual expression. Sexuality here is not somehow "impure" or "sinful," part of that primordial Fall spoken of in Christian mythology as that which exiles us from the Edenic bliss of communion with God. Quite the contrary, sexuality "is or must be realized to be a part of the self-sacrifice or ecstasy of Enlightened or Divine Life."[56] Others may "see sin and violence inside their underwear,"[57] but there is no room for such attitudes among the practitioners of sexual communion, for the "deadening of the sexual response is a deadening of the natural yoga of the body."[58] One might as well train for a long distance race by refusing to eat.

Sinful underwear, of course, is fundamentally a construction of the basic body-spirit or mind-body dualisms of religious history. If the mind or spirit is something separate from the body, then it follows that one must leave or suppress or at least heavily discipline the body to get to the spirit or mind. For Da, however, there simply is no mind separate from the body: The ego or I "is the whole body, high and low, within and without." The usual sense of inwardness, then, and the entire body-as-container sense that comes with it, is ultimately false, something to be left behind in order "to be Radiance without a center."[59] Until one can confess, "I am the body" (instead of the more common "I *have* a body"), sexuality will remain a problem, for one will necessarily experience it as an obstacle instead of as an intimate part of one's own Condition.

To repeat, sexual communion is not a technique, exercise, or discipline that will accomplish anything at all. It will certainly not deliver one from sexuality (nor, of course, will any other practice). Rather, it is the disposition or understanding behind any specific practice that transcends sex; it is the identification with the Heart instead of the self that ultimately liberates.[60] If sexuality is important to the spiritual life, then, it is because it functions as a kind of paradoxical "spiritual riddle," a Zen-like *koan*, if you will, that is produced by the desire and movement of conscious attention that literally creates the sensation of an independent self-consciousness.[61] The final dilemma, in other words, is not God versus sex but God versus the self. In Da's words: "We have not sinned in Eden, but we have been born. Our ultimate fault is not any act within the world, but the primal act or presumption of independent, separate, and separative consciousness—the attitude and strategy of Narcissus."[62] The problem of sex is not sex at all, then, but the self as ego.

Da's understanding of all of this in relationship to the Taoist, Buddhist, and Hindu Tantric traditions is quite sophisticated and displays a very real, but only implicitly acknowledged, indebtedness to academic scholarship on these same traditions. For example, he is quite explicit that, historically speaking, the Asian Tantric systems functioned as "male clubs" that more or less excluded women from their understanding.[63] Not surprisingly, "the whole of this philosophy in all its forms is essentially a male creation,"[64] a fact particularly evident in the traditions' almost total neglect and ignorance of female sexual physiology. How, for example, can there possibly be a reversal of seminal fluid up the spine toward the brain *in a woman*?[65] Hence, Da shifts the discourse away from the internal preservation and circulation of semen, so central to Indic understandings and practices, to the broader, more gender inclusive notion of the conductivity of the Life-Force throughout the human (not male) body. So too with the traditional singular male gaze and its neglect of female subjectivity and agency, a neglect, that in some forms of Taoist (and Hindu and Buddhist) Tantric practice, devolves into a kind of disturbing "sexual 'vampirism'" where the male alone is in control of the esoteric knowledge behind the ritual and feeds off the sexual and orgasmic energies of his female ritual partner.[66]

Distancing himself from such gender-asymmetrical practices and worldviews, Da insists that sexual communion is not a matter of inverting the energy and attention into a private (male) experience. Rather, it is a "whole body process" that is also fully relational. One sacrifices to Infinity "via and in relationship to one's lover."[67] Indeed, the very highest state of religious accomplishment is defined as a kind of total relationship or infinite relativity:

"Enlightenment is relief from the ego contraction, which is the avoidance of relationship."[68] None of this is meant to suggest that traditional Taoist, Hindu, and Buddhist Tantric traditions have nothing to offer contemporary Western practitioners. Quite the contrary, as the photos and artwork of the book make very clear. But one's appropriation or adaptation of these traditions needs to be critical, intelligent, ethically reflexive, and, above all, selective. "There is a principle of the ancient yogic practice that remains true," Da insists, "if we can set aside the body-denying and male-oriented philosophy of such yogas."[69]

WHAT SEXUAL COMMUNION IS

If sexual communion is not a form of asceticism, traditional celibacy, or spirit-body dualism, if it is not an elaborate introversion of libidinal forces, a naïve adoption of an ancient culture's ritual practices, or yet another religious form of misogyny, then what exactly is it?

The book contains literally dozens, if not hundreds, of explicit and implicit definitions. Among the many, we might mention here that sexual communion is said to be "the divine yoga of sexual love,"[70] a "transitional evolutionary process" that guides us into "the fourth or psychic and spiritualizing stage of life" wherein the lower functions are "unified and raised up as a sacrifice to the whole and entire bodily being via the mechanisms of the heart,"[71] there to be "yielded to Infinity."[72] It is a foundation one sets up in order to begin to adapt to the higher functions of the spiritual life.[73] The stakes are certainly high enough, for if something like sexual communion is not realized, one may not ascend to higher levels of structural growth, since the "evolutionary Force" is wasted in the sleep of the body's lower functions of elimination, sexuality, and digestion, an implicit reference to the first three *chakras* or energy centers of some forms of Indian yoga (the hydraulic metaphor returns).

Nor is sexual communion simply a matter of imagined ideals and abstract symbols. Rather, it is a fully physical process that involves chemical processes and biological transformations. If properly stimulated and not prematurely wasted or "thrown out," these energies catalyze all sorts of very real chemical transformations in the body, bestowing it with a surplus of vitality and life, healing it, and providing it with an abundance of creative energy to employ for other human expressions. Sexual communion, that is, conserves and conducts biochemical energy throughout the body in the form of hormones and glandular secretions such as sperm.[74] The latter are said to be stimulated "beyond the degree necessary for ordinary and mediocre functional existence" and are thus available for other uses, such as better health, a longer life, mental power, and spiritual practices.[75] In one place, Da goes so far as to claim that, if we could live long enough, we could see that the cells of the body are biologically, even subatomically, transformed: "Ultimately, the body can even be changed into energy and disappear."[76] There is, in other words, a certain and quite traditional alchemical dimension at work here. Essentially, what we have is a kind of sublimation, but one that works very differently than the Freudian hydraulics model. Rather than a kind of complicated mechanics of impersonal libidinal forces driven by an It (id), here the energies are seen to be literally alive, conscious, and possessing their own spiritual wisdom and teleology. They are catalyzed, if you will, through sexual play, even "yogic masturbation," as a later text will put it,[77] but their proper "control" is not within the ego's purview at all. This is, to repeat, a matter of the Heart, that seat of pure Consciousness that resides in the literal right side of the heart of which all natural energies, including sexual energies, are non-necessary ecstatic manifestations. By "feeling into" the sexual pleasure "to Infinity" via this Heart, the true site of consciousness,[78] the aspirant communes with Life and ultimately with Divinity.

There are, moreover, actual sexual, physiological, and psychological principles or techniques that are described in the texts in considerable detail. To begin with, because sexual communion is first and foremost a relational process, "*every* kind of sexual pleasure" is encouraged.[79] For this text, it is clear that the primary function of human sexuality qua human is not biological reproduction but ecstasy,[80] and the text proceeds to narrate a whole series of techniques that can be used to prolong the pleasure and use the state of arousal toward specifically religious ends.

Interestingly, unlike *Garbage and the Goddess*, where we saw the guru demanding of his disciples a freedom from the cult of couples, here in *Love of the Two-Armed Form*, monogamous marriage or the commitment to a single partner (often spoken of as an "intimate" until today) is offered as the desired norm.[81] Obviously, what is now known as the "Garbage and Goddess period" was just that, a period, a stage in the community's development (or was it just a failed 1970s experiment?). In any case, the process of sexual communion is by now, in the late '70s and mid-'80s "the privileged enjoyment of committed or married lovers," and "marriage is the seal of that profundity, for it is a positive social act, rather than a merely private act."[82] Marriage, far from being a social contract that needs to be violated for the sake of spiritual growth, is now seen as a sign that the partners have chosen spiritual realization over promiscuity, and that they will not exploit their functions and energies.[83]

Moreover, the married state is ontologically superior to that of the ascetic or traditional Indian renouncer. Hence, one section begins with the provocative title, "The Householder's Destiny and the Illusions of Traditional Holiness."[84] Here, we are told that mere asceticism is nothing more than another form of self-possession, and that the aura of holiness that traditionally surrounds such ascetics is a projection, something "granted by our childish self-doubt," guilt, and self-division.[85] And this is patently wrong, for holiness, far from being something generated by world-denial, is something native to the human-divine Condition. Unlike the married householder, who lives in and as this world and Condition, the "ascetic suffers himself as a problem."[86] He is thus forever divided, deluded, caught up in himself within a dualistic illusion of introversion and separation. Only radical relationship and felt love can free him from such a false and deadening ontology. How much better is that polymorphously erotic existence in which the sexual energies are no longer restricted or localized in the genitals but spread throughout the entire body.[87] In such a blissful state, the conditions of life, including sex, are "continuously re-cognized to be only modifications of the Radiant Transcendental Consciousness," which is neither attached to nor detached from the energies "in some exclusive Absolute Position."[88] Here we have that paradoxical dialectic that lies at the center of Tantric thought within so many traditions in India, a dialectic that can affirm a sense of transcendence even as it asserts unequivocally that "Enlightenment is a state of body, not of mind."[89]

TOWARD AN AMERICAN TANTRA

So what are we to make of all of this? The first thing that we must realize is that these two texts represent only the beginning of the tradition's reflections on the mystical and the erotic. Due to space restrictions, I have only been able to treat the earliest literature, and then, only briefly. In fact, however, the tradition has continued to produce texts that are relevant to the same issues down to the present day.

Of particular interest for our purposes is the volume entitled *Ruchira Tantra Yoga*. Along with *Garbage and the Goddess* and *Love of the Two-Armed Form*, it stands out as one of the three texts that deal most explicitly with the theme of "Sex and Spirit" (recall Franklin's horoscope). Here, Adi Da engages the Asian Tantric and Taoist traditions that he found to be in synch with his earlier sexual discoveries, embracing along the way anthropological insights into the social constructedness of all allegedly "normal" or "natural" sexuality, the integrity and even sacrality of different sexual orientations and gender identities, and the provocative but inescapable insights of oedipal theory. There are real differences, however, between this text and the earlier two, particularly in its heavy use of Sanskrit terms and in its devotional flavor and increased focus on the person of Adi Da himself.

The second point I would like to make involves historical and cultural context, and the third, doctrinal definition. One of the most fruitful ways we might begin to understand this tradition, I think, is by contextualizing both Adi Da and Adidam within American culture and seeing their Tantric practice, not as a literal adoption of Asian practices, but as a self-reflexive adaptation of Tantric ideas and practices for their own institutional needs and modern reflexivities. And by "Tantra" and "Tantric" I most certainly do not mean "simply sex" (as if there is ever such a thing). I mean to invoke rather a particular Asian mode of ontological understanding that refuses to separate the sexual and the spiritual, indeed that sees these two dimensions of human experience as inextricably linked, if not identical on some deep metaphysical level and, more broadly, affirms a paradoxical dialectic between the phenomenal and noumenal dimensions of the universe. Hence, Ramakrishna's Shakta Tantric insistence that, although the religious path begins with the "matting of deception," that is, the sense that the world is something illusory that must be rejected (as we find, for example, in the ascetic traditions of Advaita Vedanta or in traditional Indian renunciation), at a later and more advanced stage, one realizes that the world is in fact a "mansion of fun" (*majar kuti*), a literal embodiment of the divine that is meant to be enjoyed in a humorous spirit. It is this same ontological divinization of the world, accompanied by a set of sexual-ritual, philosophical, and contemplative techniques to embody, express, and effect it, that defines "Tantra" for me in Asian thought, whether we find that ontology in the goddess-universe of Ramakrishna's Bengali Shakta Tantra, the epistemological shock tactics of Tibetan Dzogchen, the rich naturalism of Chinese Taoism, or the ox-herding pictures of Japanese Zen.

Certainly the Indologist, Buddhologist, or Sinologist could detect any number of connections or borrowings between Adidam and traditional Hindu, Buddhist, and Taoist traditions—but the same readers, I think, could not help but notice that much has changed as well. What we might call the tone or rhetorical presentation, for example, is almost completely different, at least in the early texts, where the scripted, literally conversational, and often quite casual genre owes far more to twentieth-century Indian accounts of conversations with modern gurus[90] than it does to any traditional scriptural genre (the *sutra* or traditional commentary, for example). One also almost immediately notices the changed sexual reflexivities of the texts, particularly those revolving around the ethical nodes of gender symmetry, the integrity of alternative sexual orientations such as homosexuality, and their remarkable lack of prudish censorship—no metaphorical bodies here.

The new religious movement self-named Adidam (to consciously distinguish it from Hinduism or Buddhism or anything else) is definitely "Tantric," but it is a distinctly American form of Tantra that is growing differently on different cultural soil. Whether it continues to develop along these lines or some other only the future can tell. In the meantime, it deserves closer attention and critical reflection as a fascinating and sophisticated attempt to integrate human sexuality into the very heart of mystical practice and take the logic of nonduality to its inevitable and natural cultural conclusion, that is, to that world where there is no such thing as a self, much less an Asian or Western one.

A BEGINNING CONCLUSION

The work, then, is always already "accomplished" (*siddha*) and accomplished "every 'where.'" Accordingly, the Dawn Horse of Franklin Jones's original vision did not appear in order to be ridden at all. As a tiny prehistoric horse, it was much too small for that. It appeared in order simply to appear. Like Consciousness itself in Adi Da's system of thought, the Dawn Horse was something prehistoric, literally "before time," prior, primordial, *siddha*, something already perfected, realized, "always already the case." And that, I gather, is the final message of these texts, of this man, and of this community.

As for human sexuality, like everything else in the phenomenal universe it shares in the paradoxical nonduality of reality itself. As such, it is a genuine manifestation or modification of the Real to delight in, *and* it is the "garbage of the goddess" to throw away as non-ultimate or as simply distracting. Brain-based "emanationist" mystical traditions (or Western psychological systems) that identify enlightenment as a product of the hydraulic sublimation of its natural forces in yogic control or institutional celibacy (or make the latter a mark of holiness) are just as mistaken as those "transcendentalist" traditions that deny its intimate connection to the Real altogether: Both have failed to understand the nonduality of *eros*. Granted, through elaborate yogic techniques and contemplative discipline, erotic energies can be harnessed, controlled, recycled through the circle of the mystical body-brain and realized as already participating in the Light that shines infinitely above the crown of the head. In short, they can be ridden. Or so it seems. In truth, however, this is never the case.

In the end, one does not and cannot ride the Dawn Horse. Enlightenment dawns, and the Dawn Horse simply appears. It simply *is*. For Adidam, such has always been the case, and such will always be the case, regardless of whether "you" or "I" or anyone else figures out that the best way to ride the Dawn Horse is to not ride it at all, but simply to let it appear, to cease being a practitioner, to welcome its manifestation as if out of nowhere, which, it turns out, is also a kind of everywhere.

NOTES

I would like to thank Jonathan Condit, Jeremy Morse, and James Steinberg for their astute help with this chapter and The Dawn Horse Press for sharing unpublished material with me over the years.

1. The guru's many names (he has gone through almost a dozen official appellations) are both a fascinating display of an ever-changing personal and doctrinal identity and a real documentary frustration. An entire essay could easily be written on the "history of the name" and the different doctrinal positions or allusions they have encoded. Among them, we might quickly list the following, in roughly the order they appeared:

Franklin Jones (his birth name), Shri Dhyanananda Yogi (his initiation name given to him by Swami Muktananda), Bubba Free John, Heart-Master Da, Da Free John, Avadhoota Da Love-Ananda, Da Kalki, Da Avabhasa, Adi Da, and, most recently, Ruchira Buddha, Avatar Adi Da Samraj. Speaking of the guru as a process of dissolution rather than a source of fixed information, Bubba Free John once referred to himself as a "shape-shifter" and his life as a kind of theatre, an always changing process designed for the needs of the devotees present at that time. Bubba Free John, *Garbage and the Goddess: The Last Miracles and Final Spiritual Instructions of Bubba Free John* (Lower Lake, CA: The Dawn Horse Press, 1974), 310–11.

2. For a pictorial history of this literature and a global map of the communities, consult *See My Brightness Face to Face: A Celebration of The Ruchira Buddha, Avatar Adi Da Samraj, and the First 25 Years of His Divine Revelation Work* (Middletown, CA: The Dawn Horse Press, 1997).

3. Franklin Jones, *The Knee of Listening* (Los Angeles: The Dawn Horse Press, 1973), 9. In a spirit of full disclosure, I should point out that I wrote an appreciative Foreword to the latest edition of this same text.

4. Jones, *The Knee of Listening*, 9.

5. Little has been written on Adidam from a historical-critical, psychological, or sociological perspective. I am aware of only two books that treat this material at any length: Scott Lowe and David Lane, *Da: The Strange Case of Franklin Jones* (Walnut, CA: Mount San Antonio College Philosophy Group, 1996), and Georg Feuerstein, *Holy Madness: The Shock Tactics and Radical Teachings of Crazy-Wise Adepts, Holy Fools, and Rascal Gurus* (New York: Paragon House, 1991). Both draw on the firsthand experiences of the authors within the community (Lowe on the "Garbage and the Goddess" period in 1974) and can function as excellent introductions, particularly to the antinomian tendencies of the tradition.

6. The tradition freely employs capitalization in different ways, particularly as a type of poetic marker in the early texts and as a theological device signaling the displacement of the ego (always, of course, narcissistically capitalized in English) and the nondual grammar of Divinity in the latter source-texts, where almost everything is capitalized within a kind of Monistic Capital.

7. John, *Garbage and the Goddess*, 140; cf. 194.

8. Jones, *The Knee of Listening*, 3–6.

9. John, *Garbage and the Goddess*, v.

10. Da Free John, *Love of the Two-Armed Form: The Free and Regenerative Function of Sexuality in Ordinary Life, and the Transcendence of Sexuality in True Religious or Spiritual Practice*, 2nd ed. (Clearlake, CA: The Dawn Horse Press, 1985), xiii.

11. Ibid., xv.

12. In the ashram, where one should feel free to do and say anything one likes (John, *Love of the Two-Armed Form*, 31) and where no social contract is beyond breaking (John, *Garbage and the Goddess*, 21), the entire rhetoric or emotional complex of "offense" becomes utterly meaningless (John, *Garbage and the Goddess*, 15–16). Indeed, here at least "offense" becomes a type of mystical technique or discipline, as "one of the 'secrets' of spiritual life is continually to violate your own contracts" (John, *Garbage and the Goddess*, 20).

13. John, *Garbage and the Goddess*, viii.

14. Ibid., 19, 296–97, 330, 339, 345, 353.

15. The community interprets such involuntary movements and shouting within an Indian doctrinal context as forms of *kriya*, a Sanskrit term (literally, "activity") referring to the spontaneous movements of the body that are released through yogic practice or the presence of an empowering guru. Looked at comparatively, however, these same behaviors display a remarkable similarity to the spontaneous jerkings, barkings, and shoutings of the early revival movements that swept across the States in the latter part of the eighteenth century and early part of the nineteenth century during the First and Second Great Awakenings (see Ann Taves, *Fits, Trances, and Visions: Experiencing Religion and Explaining Experience from Wesley to James* (Princeton: Princeton University Press, 1999).

16. John, *Garbage and the Goddess*, 102–103.

17. Ibid., 338, 349.

18. Ibid., xiii.

19. Ibid., 30, 330, 366.

20. Ibid., 335.

21. See the third page of the common Introduction to any of the twenty-three source texts.

22. John, *Garbage and the Goddess*, 5.

23. Ibid., 321, 326.

24. Ibid., 8.

25. Ibid., 89.

26. Ibid., 89.

27. Ibid., 99.

28. Ibid., 90.

29. From the very beginning of his teaching (recall that it is 1974), the guru took a generous view of sexual orientation as something that is fundamentally not a moral matter. He qualifies this position somewhat with respect to homosexuality (John, *Love of the Two-Armed Form*, 354–58), but even there he makes a clear and respected place in his community for those individuals who have come to the conclusion, after a period of instruction, that they are homosexual; their freely chosen homosexual relationships may be incorporated into the community as fulfilling all the conditions of a heterosexual marriage (John, *Love of the Two-Armed Form*, 362–63).

30. Ibid., 31.

31. Ibid., 28.

32. Ibid., 7.

33. Ibid., 7–8.

34. Ibid., 10.

35. Ibid., 17.

36. Ibid., 40.

37. Bernard Faure, *The Red Thread: Buddhist Approaches to Sexuality* (Princeton: Princeton University Press, 1998).

38. Jack Kornfield, "Sex and Lives of the Gurus," *Yoga Journal* (1985). See also Katy Butler, "Encountering the Shadow in Buddhist America," *Common Boundary* (May-June 1990): 14–22. I am indebted to Faure for both of these references (*The Red Thread*, 3).

39. Most all of the press reporting took place in April 1985. See "Defectors Voice Several Charges," *Mill Valley Record*, 3 April 1985, 85/15; "'Sex Slave' Sues Guru Pacific Isles Orgies Charged," *San Francisco Chronicle*, 4 April 1985; "Sex Practices Did Not Cease, Marin Cult Officials Admit," *San Francisco Chronicle*, 9 April 1985.

40. For my fullest statement, see my three pieces in G. William Barnard and Jeffrey J. Kripal, eds., *Crossing Boundaries: Essays on the Ethical Status of Mysticism* (New York: Seven Bridges Press, 2002).

41. See especially David Gordon White, *The Alchemical Body: Siddha Traditions in Medieval India* (Chicago: University of Chicago Press, 1996).

42. This, moreover, is the central theme of one of his most recent source-texts, Ruchira Avatara Adi Da Samraj, *Ruchira Avatara Hridaya-Siddha Yoga: The Divine (and not Merely Cosmic) Spiritual Baptism In the Divine Way of Adidam* (Middletown, CA: The Dawn Horse Press, 2000).

43. Adi Da's understanding of "mysticism" and its relationship to "Spirituality" is particularly rich and complex. At certain points in this corpus, he fuses or even equates them, but generally he uses the former category to define those altered sates of consciousness and psychic phenomena that are mediated, and so limited, by the brain (and in some cases may be natural products of this organ) rather than via the Heart, through which Spirituality and Consciousness are most translucently mediated. Informants confirm that "Mysticism" and "Spirituality," in other words, are generally distinguished by the human body structure and its organized meditation of the Divine Spirit-Energy.

44. John, *Garbage and the Goddess*, 81.

45. Ibid., 174.

46. Ibid., 365; cf. 362. Other discussions of conductivity can be found at 90, 97, 173, 320, and 354. Moreover, formal definitions of the term by the community's editors can be found at page 374 and at John, *Love of the Two-Armed Form*, 104 n. 1.

47. John, *Garbage and the Goddess*, 33 n. 1.

48. Ibid., 354 n. 1.

49. John, *Love of the Two-Armed Form*.

50. John, *Garbage and the Goddess*, 242.

51. The community's editors were kind enough to share this text with me in manuscript form.

52. John, *Love of the Two-Armed Form*, xiii.

53. Ibid., 2.

54. Ibid., 1–2.

55. Ibid., 317.

56. Ibid., 3.

57. Ibid., 41.

58. Ibid., 413.

59. Ibid., 41.

60. Ibid., 401.

61. Ibid., 396–97.

62. Ibid., 42.

63. Ibid., 289.

64. Ibid., 293.

65. Ibid., 299.

66. Ibid., 332.

67. Ibid., 310.

68. Ibid., 139. There is a certain tension or double-message in the text on this point, for in other places Da asserts that in sexual communion "we transcend not only ourselves but our lovers" (130), since the ultimate object (or better subject) of the practice is neither one's own body nor one's lover but the Divine Life itself (131).

69. Ibid., 296; cf. 300.

70. Ibid., 231.

71. Ibid., 201.

72. Ibid., 249.

73. Ibid., 248.

74. Ibid., 232.

75. Ibid., 236.

76. Ibid., 297.

77. Avatar Adi Da Samraj, *Ruchira Avatara Hridaya-Tantra Yoga* (forthcoming).

78. John, *Love of the Two-Armed Form*, xx.

79. Ibid., 68; emphasis in original.

80. Ibid., 249.

81. Ibid., 148ff, 234.

82. Ibid., 49.

83. Ibid., 344.

84. Ibid., 423. Traditionally, Tantra was and is to this day often seen in India as a religious path for the married householder (as opposed to the celibate renouncer).

85. Ibid., 426.

86. Ibid., 429.

87. Ibid., 49.

88. Ibid., 407.

89. Ibid., 417.

90. The *Shri-shri-ramakrishna-kathamrta*, the five-volume Bengali classic recording in a script-like fashion (noting speakers, moods, dates, even times) conversations with Ramakrishna over a four-year period (1882–1886), seems to be one of the earliest, if not the earliest, model of these (it was published serially from 1902–1932). What we have here with the "writing guru" (or more often, the speaking guru and the ghost writer or editor) is a method of producing books through the medium of recorded (or at least remembered) conversations. Through this mechanism the traditions can produce small libraries written in an accessible style.

ELEVATED GURUS, CONCRETE TRADITIONS, AND THE PROBLEMS OF WESTERN DEVOTEES

DANIEL GOLD

EVEN CASUAL OBSERVERS are likely to notice differences among the many religious movements established over the last decades by Hindu gurus in the West. In some movements, most members regularly wear Indian dress; in others, most don't. The local branches of some movements appear highly uniform; those of others appear less so. Differences stem in good part from the particular Hindu traditions espoused by the gurus, which assign their own roles to the gurus themselves. From whatever tradition Indian gurus come, however, they can present their Western devotees with two sorts of religious problems.

First there is the problem of the guru's elevated status. Although the term *guru* can refer simply to a respected teacher, in many essays in this volume it refers first of all to a living person taken as a direct embodiment of the divine. For both Indians and Westerners alike, this can be a difficult concept to fathom. Indian devotees, however, are likely to find the concept less foreign and assimilate it more easily into their everyday sense of reality. Western devotees, who usually hold egalitarian preconceptions, may struggle longer with the everyday implications of the guru as an elevated being. Coming to terms with the idea is likely to come at a higher price for Westerners, and disillusionment can be more shattering. That price, however, is one that must be paid. For the role of a living, charismatic teacher—although played out differently in diverse Hindu religious movements—has been central in the great majority of those that have flourished in the West.

Second, there is the problem of the guru's Indianness. In embracing their gurus, Western devotees also necessarily embrace certain aspects of the Hindu traditions that their gurus bring with them. The gurus, however, present Hindu traditions to Western devotees in more and less concrete forms. Most offer some sort of philosophy and with it some internal practices that the majority of prospective devotees should be able to accept. Others also work with a more embedded Indian cultural reality—ritual, say, or image worship—a reality that is attractive to some and puts off others, but may be seen as crucial to a guru's fundamental mission. Outward forms of Hindu religious life regularly found in India are more integral to some imported traditions than others.

The great gurus—the *mahagurus*—treated in this volume thus vary both in the ways they are taken to bring together the human and the divine in their own persons and the levels at which they operate within Hindu religious culture. These variations are then reflected in their movements' developments in the West and their disciples' own attitudes toward adopting some sort of Hindu identity for themselves. Let us first turn to questions of the guru's elevated status.

Here the distinction with the most far-reaching socioreligious implications seems to be this: Is the guru taken to be basically an exceptionally wise human being, a respected teacher of age-old traditions? Or is he or she considered first of all to be an instance of the embodied divine, somehow superhuman and distinct from ordinary mortals? Of the gurus treated in this volume, three seem to fall into the first category, taken by their disciples primarily as respected human teachers. Indeed, Guru Anjali of Yoga Ashram in Amityville, who operated in the West on a smaller scale than a *mahaguru,* is portrayed by Christopher Chapple as particularly unpretentious and humanly sympathetic. Yet it is not just the smaller scale of her mission that kept her personal claims modest. Both Maharishi Mahesh and Bhaktivedanta Swami, too—indisputably *mahagurus* with very large following—are deliberately presented within their movements as human teachers, not divine embodiments. Even though Maharishi Mahesh may be described in superlatives as expert in the science of consciousness and skilled in expounding the Vedas, he is still taken as a scientist and teacher, not as an especially divine being. Indeed, as Cynthia Humes points out, he never "claimed to be anything other than a teacher, one adept in yoga (*yogi*), or a seer of truth (*rishi*)." For him, the term *guru* carried more weight than he has considered seemly to bear. In a similar vein, Bhaktivedanta Swami, described himself as a "postman" delivering the message of his sacred culture. "My only credit," he once said, "is that I haven't changed anything." As *mahagurus* taken to be revered teachers, the two have been understood to have a profound knowledge of tradition, a unique role in propagating it, and access to some very special mantras. Yet even as their enthusiasts insist that the gurus should be eminently respected, they assert no extraordinary metaphysical status for them, even if they sometimes secretly suspect it.

The other gurus treated in this volume might be most aptly taken by their disciples as first of all instances of the embodied divine, a being whose metaphysical status is qualitatively different from that of the rest of us. In these cases, even if the gurus themselves do not regularly make public claims to this effect, they don't disabuse their disciples from doing so. Sometimes these claims are strong and strike an exclusivist note: Satya Sai Baba sees himself not only as the reincarnation of a previous great past saint, but also as an *avatar*, an embodiment of Shiva and Shakti; and for a time, Osho/Rajneesh took the honorific Bhagwan, normally reserved for a divine incarnation (i.e., Bhagavan Ram). Not coincidentally, I think, these two have also been among the *mahagurus* most embroiled in public scandals: Strong assertions may go hand in hand with wide licence. Although Ammachi, like Sai Baba, is also spoken of as an incarnation of the divine, less controversy surrounds her. The claims made about her embodying the divine mother are usually taken in very broad terms and carry little explicit sense of exclusivity.

Devotees have understood the rest, for the most part, as individual enlightened holy persons—about whom Hindu tradition readily admits there can be many at once. Ramana Maharshi, while having come to his own path himself, nevertheless talks about the realized guru who can help the disciple realize the self, implicitly presenting himself as one such. Muktananda and Gurumayi, by contrast, are taken as standing in a guru-disciple lineage of *siddhas*, perfected beings that can transmit something of their divine selves to qualified devotees. This gives them reason to emphasize the necessity of the guru for salvation. Adi Da, too, through his connection with Muktananda, has presented himself in the same *siddha* lineage—although in his current self-understanding he is sooner an exclusive incarnation: claims may grow with a movement's success.

Inevitably, the two categories of respected teacher and embodied divine overlap. Most gurus, however elevated their status, teach from their traditions, and as Christopher Chapple shows us in the introductory sections of his chapter, it is not hard to find scriptural and proverbial references about how the guru—which might be read as *any* religious teacher—should be revered as divine. Nevertheless, a crucial socioreligious distinction between the two types remains: For the respected human teacher, it is primarily the guru's religious culture that mediates the divine, but for the divine embodiment, it is sooner the guru's person itself that does so. The two emphases then lead to differences in the ways in which the *mahagurus'* movements have developed in the West.

In general, when gurus are taken as an embodiment of the divine, their Western organizations present visible continuities with a common kind of traditional Indian ashram, one that is taken as the guru's personal abode. Devotees go to these traditional ashrams to be around a guru and imbibe his or her presence—and often to participate in the good fellowship of other devotees as well. In the present global culture, however, we have *mahagurus* with *maha*-followings that require *maha*-ashrams. But the focus of the new organizations remains the development of ways to keep devotees in touch with the guru and the divine that comes through him or her. At a place such as Gurumayi's *maha*-ashram in South Fallsburg, large groups of people can dwell for a while in a guru's extended physical space, do service for him or her, and may have regular opportunities for brief, routinized *darshan*. Smaller local establishments in this movement and others offer opportunities for group meditations and fellowship in the absence of a guru. Yet these still try to keep a link to the center—if not, as in Siddha yoga, through satellite hookups, than at least, as in Sai Baba's movement, through a regularized liturgy with the guru's stamp. In these more mature movements, the local centers also offer a basis for continuing community; in newer movements, such as that of Ammachi, they tend to play a vital role in the arrangement of the guru's tours.

Institutions developing from a guru presented as a revered teacher of a rich tradition develop in more diverse ways. Not only are these more likely to emphasize the specific cultural resources offered by the movement, but disciples, with the guru's permission, may also feel free to develop their own initiatives. This seems to be especially the case in the development of TM, with its astrological consultations, *yagyas*, and food supplements—in addition to its university and political party. Even as Maharishi extends his broad corporate umbrella over these initiatives, they express the diversity of both his culture and his devotees' enthusiasms. In ISKCON a more specific dimension of Hindu cultural tradition is presented. But it is presented very richly, with ritual worship to Krishna in all its traditional glory, and an elaborate publishing and distribution operation devoted to propagating Krishnaite scripture. In these cases, it is not so much a link to the guru mediating the divine that these institutions offer, as it is some profound riches embedded in Hindu religious culture. Thus, even the manifestly commercial dimensions of these movements differ from those focused on the person of the guru: not Ammachi's dolls—which draw the mind toward the guru—but Maharishi's Ayurvedic treatments and teas; not the questions and answers of Swami Muktananda sold to disciples, but Bhaktivedanta Swami's commentaries on Krishnaite scripture pressed on curious travellers.

The second variable that struck me in reading these essays was characterized initially as the concreteness with which the gurus operate in Indian culture. By this I mean a quality that I see in terms of the *nirguna*/*saguna* distinction of Hindu devotional philosophies, which differentiates between conceptions of ultimate reality as formless (*nirguna*) and having form (*saguna*). In the case of these gurus, though, the difference is not so much in ultimate reality as in the means to realize it, and the two terms are less binary opposites than poles of a continuum. Is what the guru offers for salvation taken as something largely formless, like a mantra or an initiatory power, or does the form in which it is embodied play a vital practical role? This variable thus speaks to the importance of the particulars of Indian culture in the movements.

The cases here are not clear-cut—especially those of Adi Da and Osho/Rajneesh, who both offer extremely creative syntheses. But falling more on the disembodied side, I think, are Ramana's realization of self, Gurumayi's guru *shakti*, and Maharishi's initiatory mantras. To the extent that the essential means are taken to be formless, the more detachable they seem to be from the externals of Indian culture. So it is fairly easy to follow the paths of any of these three gurus without experimenting with Indian food, say, or Indian dress. And many Western devotees do not, but are instead more comfortable with assimilating the spiritual essence in a familiar Western environment. Even many of Maharishi's later Indian imports seem detached from their source and repackaged—like his Ayurvedic teabags—offering the real substance, perhaps, but in a palatable cultural form.

Not so the two cases that seem to me to fall more clearly on the *saguna* side: Bhaktivedanta Swami—offering Krishna culture—and Ammachi, really embodied and there, with her hugs and trances. As respected guru and divine personage respectively, however, the two deal with cultural specifics in different ways. Bhaktivedanta, as teacher, tries consciously to present a version of Gaudiya Vaishnava orthopraxy, albeit with some important allowances for Western sensibilities about gender. Ammachi, by contrast, is very much present in a Hindu cultural idiom, but in no way an orthoprax one. And as a holy person whose authority is taken to transcend traditional Indian cultural norms, she freely mixes them up with Western norms as she sees fit, offering, as Selva Raj describes, a Hindu-style version of Christian communion. In both cases, however, Western devotees—drawn to their gurus in their cultural embeddedness—are on the whole also more likely to be attached to Indian cultural forms than are devotees of the three gurus discussed in the last paragraph. With Ammachi's devotees attracted to her very embodied, if unorthodox, Hindu ways, many experiment with Indian styles, if not always so seriously. Serious Western members of ISKCON, moreover, usually go further. In living the Krishna culture, many do much more than experiment with Indian food and dress, in fact adopting a recognized version of it as their own.

The particularly complex cases presented by Adi Da and Osho/Rajneesh have developed from the encounters of these spiritually daring gurus with Tantric traditions, which put divine realization in active dialectic with embodied reality. Thus, even when Tantric traditions speak of ultimate experiences that are essentially formless (and not all clearly do), these are reached through diverse experiences of the manifest world; different embodied forms can then have their own spiritual significances. It thus follows that Adi Da and Osho, both transcending cultural norms like Ammachi, have created fusions of Eastern and Western traditions that have become more intricately developed than hers.

Of the two, Adi Da, born Franklin Jones on Long Island, in fact seems to fit more closely the model of a conventional Indian guru. Perhaps just because of his American origin, he has been careful to draw attention to his Indian *siddha* guru-lineage. And like many adventurous Indian holy persons he has explored more traditions than one—mostly Indian, but at any rate confined to Asia—and brought them together for his devotees into something of a synthesis.[1]

By contrast, Osho/Rajneesh can appear sooner as an (Western-style) entrepreneur, up front about some of the business aspects of his operation, who arose on his own from India to offer the world alternative therapies for different psycho/spiritual needs. The range of sources and techniques on which he drew was extremely diverse—certainly more so than those of Adi Da—and he made little attempt to synthesize them. In its heyday, his organization could thus appear as a psycho/spiritual "conglomerate" offering an array of certified techniques. Osho's enthusiasts could then display their trust in his brand by wearing clothes in a personal and cultural style of their own choosing, but in a broad spectrum of warm shades that recalled the Indian renunciate's orange.[2] Osho's movement was thus Indian according to one's taste.

For *mahagurus* teaching along more familiar Hindu lines, emphasis on the more ethereal *nirguna* or more concrete *saguna* aspects of Indian culture also have theological underpinnings. These are most apparent in our two *mahagurus* who are respected teachers of tradition, Maharishi Mahesh and Bhaktivedanta Swami. For since the teachers don't claim special authority as divine persons, they strive at least to be rationally consistent. Interestingly, in presenting their teachings to the West, both take a similar approach, attempting to detach them from anything too historically Hindu. But in doing so, they take different tacks.

The *nirguna* Maharishi, like Swami Dayananda a century earlier,[3] looks back to the Vedas as the source of all real knowledge: intellectual, scientific, and cultural. This knowledge is reflected paradigmatically in the whole of Hindu civilization, but is also the essence of the truths known to Western science. So in his view it is no falsehood to scientize Indian traditional knowledge.

The *saguna* Bhaktivedanta, by contrast, sees the essential truth in Krishna consciousness. Although Krishna consciousness flowered in India, it is here less the whole of Hindu culture, but the ideals of Vraj that are taken out and seen as eternal. These ideals can potentially be assimilated anywhere, but they were revealed in very embodied Hindu terms. So even though Western ISKCON members need not ideally embrace all of Hindu culture, those who live the life are likely to act like Hindus in visible cultural ways. If they are to be consistent in practice, if not theory, they must—more than most Western devotees of *mahagurus*—somehow come to terms with a kind of Hindu identity.

Gurus standing on their own divine authority tend to be less concerned about theological consistency, and their disciples—looking first to them, not their traditions—can often harbor easy ambivalence about their religious identities. The gurus are successful because they help evoke an experience, as Tom Forsthoefel points out about Ramana Maharshi, and their disciples understand this experience in their own ways. To the extent that the *mahagurus* do talk global metaphysics, it tends to be perennialist, with a touch of not-unwarranted Hindu spiritual pride. Hindu traditions embody the *sanatana dharma*, the eternal truth, and have nurtured holy persons who can make others realize it. The real truth is Universal but especially Hindu.

So what does all this mean for *mahagurus'* disciples' personal identification with Hinduism? Even if the real truth is beyond any one religion, disciples hear about it from Hindu gurus and tend to think about it in Hindu ways. And they do spiritual practices and have experiences that make sense in terms of their gurus' Hindu-based teachings. Thus, many disciples may have an understanding of the way the world works that might best be characterized as more Hindu than anything else, and would readily admit it. But for many also this may be as far as they can comfortably go. For while Hindu traditions are spiritually inclusive, they also present real social barriers to outsiders, and old religious identities can die hard. One suspects that the *mahagurus* know this; even though their teachings cannot help but be Hindu in spirit, they are frequently not explicitly so in name. Yet in presenting what they offer as being something more than Hindu, the *mahagurus* are being honest to both themselves and their tradition—a tradition that has long been recognized from within as having as its essence the one encompassing eternal truth.

NOTES

1. Daniel Gold, *The Lord as Guru: Hindi Sants in North Indian Tradition* (New York: Oxford University Press, 1987), 55–77; see also Williamson in this volume on Muktananda, Kashmir Shaivism, and Vedanta.

2. For examples of the colored clothes as sectarian identifiers, see Ma Prem Shunyo, *Diamond Days with Osho: The New Diamond Sutra*, 1st ed. (Delhi: Motilal Banarsidass Publishers, 1993), 7–9, 45.

3. On Swami Dayananda and his movement, see Kenneth W. Jones, *Arya Dharm: Hindu Consciousness in 19th-Century Punjab* (Berkeley and Los Angeles: University of California Press, 1976).

CONTRIBUTORS

CHRISTOPHER KEY CHAPPLE is Professor of Theological Studies and Associate Academic Vice President for LMU Extension at Loyola Marymount University in Los Angeles. He has published several books, including: *Karma and Creativity; Nonviolence to Animals, Earth, and Self in Asian Traditions; Reconciling Yogas;* a co-translation of Patanjali's *Yoga Sutra;* and several edited books on religion and ecology, including *Ecological Prospects; Hinduism and Ecology;* and *Jainism and Ecology.* He trained in classical yoga under the direction of Gurani Anjali from 1972–1985 and in 2002 established a university certificate program in Yoga Philosophy.

THOMAS A. FORSTHOEFEL is Associate Professor of Religious Studies at Mercyhurst College in Erie, PA. His work has been published in *Philosophy East and West, Horizons, Journal of Ecumenical Studies,* and *Journal of Vaisnava Studies,* among others. His first book, *Knowing Beyond Knowledge: Epistemologies of Religious Experience in Classical and Modern Advaita* (Ashgate, 2002), explores the nature and scope of "religious knowing" in Indian philosophy. He is currently working on a cross-cultural study of holiness (Orbis Press). Tom is also a poet. A collection of his poems, *The Kiss of God: Being Here on the Path of Becoming,* is currently under review.

DANIEL GOLD is Professor of South Asian Religions in the Department of Asian Studies at Cornell University. His books include *The Lord as Guru* (1987), *Comprehending the Guru* (1988), and *Aesthetics and Analysis in Writing on Religion* (2003).

TAMAL KRISHNA GOSWAMI (1946–2002) was a member and Governing Body Commissioner of the International Society for Krishna Consciousness (ISKCON). He was accepted as a disciple by A. C. Bhaktivedanta Goswami in 1968 in Jaipur, India. He served as ISKCON's first GBC Secretary for India from 1970–1974 and was appointed trustee of the Bhaktivedanta Book Trust.

His publications include *Reason and Belief: Problem-solving in the Philosophy of Religion* (Pundits Press, 1977) and *Prabhupada Antya-lila: The Final Pastimes of Srila Prabhupada* (Institute for Vaishnava Studies, 1988). Long dedicated to faith and intellectual inquiry, he became the premier theologian writing in English for ISKCON. At the time of his death, he was completing his doctorate at Cambridge University.

RAVI M. GUPTA (Radhika Ramana dasa) is a member of the Faculty of Theology at Oxford University and a Junior Research Fellow of Linacre College, Oxford. He holds a D.Phil. in Vaishnava Theology and a master's degree in Religious Studies. His doctoral dissertation focused on the early development of Chaitanya Vaishnava Vedanta, as found in the writings of Jiva Gosvami. Ravi has lectured widely and published numerous articles on Hindu religious and philosophical traditions.

CYNTHIA ANN HUMES is Associate Dean of Faculty and directs Educational Technology Services at Claremont McKenna College. An Associate Professor of Religious Studies, when not conducting administrative tasks, she devotes time to her research interests. Her publications concern the contemporary use of Sanskrit literature, modern ritual in North Indian goddess worship, the political and economic dimensions of Hinduism, issues of gender in world religions, and gurus. Recently, she has co-written a book on the history of the Transcendental Meditation movement in the United States with Dana W. Sawyer, and translated and annotated the popular discourse of Shankaracharya Swami Brahmananda Saraswati.

JEFFREY J. KRIPAL is the J. Newton Rayzor Professor of Religious Studies and Chair of the Department of Religious Studies at Rice University. He is the author of *Roads of Excess, Palaces of Wisdom: Eroticism and Reflexivity in the Study of Mysticism* (Chicago, 2001) and *Kali's Child: The Mystical and the Erotic in the Life and Teachings of Ramakrishna* (Chicago, 1995). His areas of interest include the comparative erotics of mystical literature, the American translations of Hindu and Buddhist Tantric traditions, and the history of western esotericism from ancient gnosticism to the New Age. He is currently writing on the history of the Esalen Institute, the human potential center in Big Sur, California, and its forty-year practice of the "enlightenment of the body."

NORRIS W. PALMER is Associate Professor of Religious Studies at Saint Mary's College of California. His interdisciplinary research interests bring together Anthropology of Religion and Philosophy of Religion to examine multiple sites within South Asian religions, religious pluralism, and comparative ontology. He is currently completing *Pluralism and Religious Identity*, which is an ethnographic study of the construction and negotiation of Hindu identity at one U.S. temple in the context of local and trans-local forces. His interests in larger pedagogical issues are reflected in his work with *Teaching Theology and Religion* for which he is a member of the editorial board and serves as copy editor.

SELVA J. RAJ, who received his PhD in History of Religions from the University of Chicago, is Chair and Stanley S. Kresge Associate of Professor of Religious Studies at Albion College. A Past-President of the Society for Hindu-Christian Studies, he is a Co-Chair of the Comparative Studies in Religion Section of the American Academy of Religion and the current President of the Midwest Region of the American Academy of Religion. His research interests are in the area of ritual exchange between Hindus and Catholics in India, Hindu women saints, tribal religions, and contemporary women's movements in India. Author of several articles, he has co-edited two volumes: (with Corinne Dempsey) *Popular Christianity in India: Riting between the Lines* (State University of New York Press, 2002) and (with William Harman) *Dealing with Deities: The Ritual Vow in South Asia* (State University of New York Press, forthcoming). Currently he is co-editing (with Corinne Dempsey) *Ritual Levity, Ritual Play in South Asian Traditions.*

HUGH B. URBAN is Associate Professor in the Department of Comparative Studies at Ohio State University, Columbus. He is primarily interested in the study of secrecy in religion, particularly in relation to questions of knowledge and power. Focusing on the traditions of South Asia, he is the author of *The Economics of Ecstasy: Secrecy and Symbolic Power in Colonial Bengal*, with an accompanying volume of translations, *Songs of Ecstasy: Tantric and Devotional Songs for Colonial Bengal* (2001). His book *Tantra: Secrecy, Politics, and Power in the Study of Religion* is from the University of California Press.

LOLA WILLIAMSON holds an MS in Communication and an MA in Religions of Asia, both from Florida State University, as well as a Masters in Liberal Studies from Rollins College. She is currently completing her PhD dissertation, "People Who Meditate: An Ethnographic Study of Hinduism-Inspired Meditation Movements in America," through the Department of Languages and Cultures of Asia at the University of Wisconsin-Madison.

INDEX

Abhinavagupta, 150, 165n8, 166nn11,14
Adi Da (b, Franklin Jones), 6, 8, 10, 12,
   165n4, 221, 223–224
  and Adidam, 193–195, 197, 200, 203,
    211–214n5, 216n42
  as American guru, 193–194, 197–198,
    203, 211–212
  and caste, 194–197
  and darshan, 196
  and Dawn Horse, 193, 194, 195–199,
    205, 213
  and gender, 195, 206, 208, 211, 212
  as guru, 193–195, 197, 198–200, 206,
    207, 210, 212, 213n1, 215nn15, 29
  and Hinduism, 193, 194, 200, 203, 208,
    209, 212
  and lineage, 195, 199
  and marriage, 202, 210–211, 215n29,
    217n84
  and Muktananda, 195, 203, 214n1
  names of, 193–194, 214n1
  and sadhana (spiritual practice), 195,
    196, 198, 199, 202, 206, 209
  and sexual communion, 206–211,
    217n68
  and shakti, 204–205
Advaita (nondualism) Vedanta,
  and innovation, 46
  philosophy of, 5–7, 17, 20, 44–45, 48,
    53n38, 64–65, 67, 70, 73, 85, 107,
    197, 200, 212
  and practice, 33, 38–39, 41–42, 49–50,
    197

  and Ramana Maharshi, 6, 37, 39,
    40–42, 45, 47–49, 50–51
  and Satya Sai Baba, 8, 103
  as science, 62–63, 65, 67, 74. *See also*
    Science of Creative Intelligence.
  and Shankaracharya, 40, 58–59, 62–63,
    67
  and Tantra, 10, 12
  and transmission, 6–7, 9, 37, 51, 57–58,
    64–65, 107
  and universalism, 6, 7, 39, 41, 44–46,
    51, 72, 74, 106
ahimsa (nonviolence), 27, 29, 104, 123
Ajeya Bharata Party, 7, 71
Alston, William, 40, 51n8
Ammachi (Mata Amritanandamayi,
    Amma),
  and bhakti (devotionalism), 8–9, 124,
    129, 131
  and caste, 8–9, 135, 138, 142, 143
  as challenging tradition, 123, 138, 143,
    223
  and charitable organizations, 139–145,
    145n23
  and Christianity, 8–9, 130, 131, 134,
    135, 136, 140–141, 142
  commercialism, 222, 139–141
  conflict with family, 125, 127, 142
  and darshan, 9, 129–130, 132–143,
    146n51
  and Devi Bhava, (mood of the god-
    dess), 126–127, 132–136, 140, 142,
    145n33

Ammachi (continued)
  as Divine Mother, Goddess, 9,
    123–124, 126, 129, 221, 131–132,
    136, 137, 143
  ecstatic experiences of, 125–126
  establishment in the United States,
    123, 128, 134, 141, 142, 222
  and gender roles, 127, 138–139
  as Goddess, 131–132, 136, 143
  as guru, 129, 131–132, 140, 142, 143
  and hagiography, 124–125, 126
  and initiation, 127, 134–135
  and innovation, 9, 123, 137–138, 140,
    222
  and Krishna, 124–126, 134, 140
  and miraculous powers, 124–127
  and New Age, 130
  practices of devotees, 127, 128–131, 223
  and shakti, 9, 142
  and Transcendental Meditation, 78n36,
    130, 131, 137
  transnational congregations of, 123,
    127, 139, 142
  and universalism, 8–9, 135, 136
  and Vedanta, 6, 143
Amritanandamayi. See Ammachi
Amrit Desai, 33
Anjali, Gurani, 16, 227
  and bhakti, 19
  and caste, 32–33
  and Christianity, 19, 24, 28,
  and commercialism, 26
  and environmentalism, 28–29
  establishment in the United States, 16,
    18
  and family duties, 29–30
  and gender roles, 24, 25
  as guru/gurani, 16, 18
  and initiation, 19
  and innovation, 23, 28
  and Krishna, 19
  and Mirabai, 19, 20, 22, 23
  philosophy of, 18–25
  and "pillars," (dharmins), 19, 24, 29
  poetic songs, 20, 21, 22, 23
  and sadhana, 18, 19, 27, 29–30
  and universalism, 19, 23–24

Arunachala, 37, 42
Asceticism, 130, 185, 207, 209–210

Batchelor, Steven, 2, 13n1
Bhagavad Gita, 18, 24, 67, 78n32, 79n47,
    82, 93, 155, 165n10
Bhagavata Purana, 81–82, 85, 91, 93n8
bhajans (devotional songs), 99, 110–111,
    114, 116, 131, 133
Bhakti (devotion), 5–9, 19, 143
bhakti yoga, 19
Bhaktivedanta, Swami, AC,
  and bhakti (devotionalism), 84–86, 223
  and caste, 91, 92
  and Chaitanya, 84–86, 90
  as challenging tradition, 85–92, 94n16,
    223, 224
  and commercialism, 91
  establishment in the United States,
    81–83, 87–92, 93n5
  and gender roles, 89–90, 94nn3, 23, 24
  and governance, 88–90, 94n24
  as guru, 86, 88, 91–92, 220, 222
  and initiation, 89–91
  and innovation, 83–86
  and shakti, 84, 93n7
  and transmission, 10, 82–83, 86–88
  and universalism, 39, 91
Bharat(a) ("India"), 3, 8, 71, 75, 104–107
Brahma Sutra, 44
Brahman, 61, 62, 76n14, 84
Brahmananda Saraswati, 58–61, 63–64,
    67, 75, 76n10, 76n17, 228
Brahmin, 10, 39–42, 46, 59–61, 91, 148

Chaitanya, 9, 84–86, 90, 93nn7, 9, 23,
    113, 228
chakra (energy vortice), 150, 153, 165n9,
    204, 209
Chidvilasananda. See Gurumayi
Chopra, Deepak, 68–69
Cox, Harvey, 5, 25–27, 33

darshan (beholding the sacred),
  and attraction, 59
  defined, 9
  mass conveyance, 16

See also Adi Da, Ammachi, Gurumayi,
  Satya Sai Baba
Dawn Horse, 193–194, 196–199, 205,
  213, 214nn2–3,10, 216n42
Devi (the Goddess), 28, 86, 94n23, 124,
  126, 146n55, 200, 205
Devi Bhava (mood of the goddess). *See*
  Ammachi
Dharma (duty, law), 26, 60, 93n5, 104,
  107, 133. *See also* sanatana dharma

Feuerstein, Georg, 31, 35n18,
  189nn15–16, 214n5, 190n27
Foucault, Michel, 170, 177, 185, 189n2,
  190n31, 192n62
Freud, Sigmund, 176, 195, 201–202, 210

Gaudiya, 10, 84–85, 88, 91, 95n29, 223
Gayatri Mantra, 28, 89, 91, 111
Gurudev. *See* Brahmananda Saraswati
Gurudeva, 17, 33
Guru Gita, 15, 30, 32, 145n25, 154
guru kula (school associated with a guru),
  157, 161
Gurumayi,
  and asceticism, 11
  and caste, 148
  and darshan, 147, 222
  emphasis on service (seva), 154, 155
  establishment in the United States,
    149–150, 161–164
  and founding of the SYDA Founda-
    tion, 161
  and gender, 159, 164
  and governance, 148, 159–164
  as guru, 148, 149–150, 154, 155–161,
    163–164
  and Hinduism, 11, 148, 149, 150, 157
  and initiation, 149, 150, 152, 155, 163,
    164, 166nn13, 14, 20. *See also*
    shaktipat
  and innovation/globalization, 11, 148,
    149, 150, 153, 156, 157, 161, 162,
    163
  and lineage, 147–150, 158–161, 164,
    164nn3, 4, 165n5
  and marriage, 11, 154–155

and Nityananda (d. 1961), 147, 148,
  151, 154, 165n5, 167n28
and Nityananda (Subhash), 159,
  167n29
and sadhana, 152, 153–157, 161, 164,
  166n13
and succession controversy, 159–161
and shaktipat, 10, 149–153, 156–158,
  165n8, 165nn10–11
and South Fallsburg ashram, 161, 162
and technology, 148, 149, 153, 156,
  162, 164
and Transcendental Meditation, 157
Griffiths, Bede, 47–49, 53nn40–41

Halbfass, Wilhelm, 38, 51nn2–3, 186, 188,
  192n63
Hare Krishna, dedication, 9, 82–83, 87,
  93n2, 94n24, 95n32
hatha yoga, 5, 125, 166n17
Heelas, Paul, 55, 57, 75n2, 170, 188n1
Hinduism, and definition 2, 4

International Satya Sai Baba Organization
  (ISSBO), 109, 113–115, 119, 121n7
ishta deva (chosen deity), 16, 19
ISKCON (International Society for
  Krishna Consciousness), 222–224,
  227–228. *See also* Swami Bhaktivedanta

Jameson, Fredric, 171, 184, 189n3,
  191nn53,55, 192nn56–57
Jarvis, Jerome W., 59, 64, 66, 77n25

kaivalyam (divine 'isolation' in yoga philosophy), 20, 26
Kali Yuga (the age of strife), 82, 88
Karma, 3, 19, 26, 31, 70, 92, 127, 186
Katz, Steven T., 38–39, 51n5
kayasth (educated clerical caste), 60–61
Krishna, 9–10, 19, 81–86, 88, 90–93n2,
  93n5, 93, 94nn14,18, 95n29, 101,
  109–110, 121n19, 124–126, 130,
  134, 140, 206, 222–224
Krishna Bhava (mood of or identification
  with Krishna). *See* Ammachi

Krishnamurti, 13n3, 30, 46, 203
kundalini (spiritual energy), 149–153, 157, 165n9, 166n22, 199, 205, 207

Lenz, Fred, 30–32
Le Saux, Henri, 47–49
lila (divine 'play'), 102, 117

mahaguru (great guru), 17, 37, 97–98, 142, 145n38, 146n59, 171, 186, 194–195, 203, 220–222, 224–225
defined, 3
Maharishi International University, 65, 77n28
Maharishi Mahesh Yogi, 55, 57–58, 75, 77nn22, 24, 78nn32,41, 131
and Advaita Vedanta, 6, 55, 57, 58, 62–63, 64–65, 67
and Ayur Ved, 58, 67–69
and Beatles, 64, 76n26
and caste, 59, 60–61, 64, 70
and commercialism, 57, 67–70, 73
establishment in the United States, 56–58, 63–67
and gender, 61, 65, 73
as guru, 57, 58, 60–61, 63, 64, 65, 68, 73–75
and hagiography, 59–60
and Hindu Renaissance, 55, 74
and initiation, 63–66, 77n25
and innovation, 57–58, 63–64, 70
as maharishi, 60–63
philosophy of. *See also* Maharishi Mahesh Yogi and Advaita Vedanta
and Natural Law Party, 7, 58, 70–72, 77n26, 222
and New Age, 55–58, 65, 70–74
and "Religion," 66, 73
and Romanticism, 55, 73
and science, 58, 60, 61–62, 65, 67
and Science of Creative Intelligence, 65, 67, 69
and "stress," 58, 65, 70, 72, 78n40
and TM technique, 57, 72
and TM-Sidhi, 58, 66, 67, 68, 70, 72, 75n1, 78n40
and universalism, 55, 57, 62–63

and upaya, 6
and Vedism, 56, 58, 61–62, 66–67, 72
Maharshi, 62
Maharshi, Ramana, 4, 6, 8, 13n4, 17, 195, 221, 225
and Advaitin experience, 39, 42–43, 45, 46, 49, 50, 51
and caste, 39, 40, 41, 42, 46
and darshan, 42
and family, 41
and gender, 40
as guru, 37, 42, 46, 49, 51
and Hinduism, 37, 39, 44
and lineage, 43, 46, 49
ecstatic experiences of, 41–43
and hagiography, 41–42
and perennialism, 37–39, 43, 45–47, 50
philosophy of, 37–38, 40–41, 44, 45, 48
and sadhana, 46
and transmission, 37–39, 51
and universalism, 38, 39, 41, 42, 44, 45, 46, 51
Malnak v Yogi, 66, 69, 77n30, 78n31
math (monastery), 58–60, 76n10, 88, 127
maya (creative power of the divine; illusion), 64, 84–85, 127
Meher Baba, 17–18, 34n5
Mehta, Gita, 186–187, 192n65
Merton, Thomas, 47–48, 53nn38–39
Mirabai, 9, 19, 20, 22, 23
Muktananda, 147–156, 158–164nn2–4, 165nn5, 9, 12, 166nn20, 23, 167nn26, 28, 30, 192n66, 195, 203, 214n1, 221–222, 225n1

Nattier, Jan, 56–57, 76n5
Natural Law Party, 7, 58, 70–71, 77n26
Neem Karoli, 16
Neo-Tantra, 11, 170, 175, 177
nirvana, 186–187
Nisargadatta Maharaj, 46
Nityananda. *See* Gurumayi

Osho,
and capitalism, 170–172, 177–181, 183–185, 187–188, 191nn53, 54, 192n64

establishment in the United States,
   169, 170, 171, 172–173, 178, 180,
   182
and gender, 172
and governance, 170, 171, 179–181,
   182–183, 191n54
as guru, 169, 174, 181, 183, 192n66
and Hinduism, 175, 181
and materialism, 169–171, 177–180,
   187
names of, 169, 171, 181
and Neo-Tantrism, 171, 173–177, 178,
   182, 187, 192n66
and New Age, 170, 177, 182
and Rajneeshpuram, 172, 173,
   179–181
and "religion," 170–171, 174–176,
   181–182, 185, 189n12, 190n33,
   191n37
and sannyasin, 174, 179, 180, 187,
   189n18
and universalism/globalism, 169, 171,
   181, 182, 186
Osho Commune International, 171, 182

Patanjali, 5, 19–20, 25, 66
Plantinga, Alvin, 40, 50–51n8
Prabhupada. See Swami Bhaktivedanta
prakriti (nature), 5, 21, 24, 71
prasad (sanctified offering) 82, 110, 112,
   134
Prasanthi Nilayam, 101, 111–113, 115,
   117, 119, 121n19. See also ashram
prema (love), 84, 104
puja (worship), 63, 78n31, 129, 131, 138,
   142, 156
pujari (ritual officiant), 28–29, 138
purusha (sacred spirit), 5, 19–22, 24,
   75n1

Raam Rajya (reign of Ram/god), 71
raja yoga (royal yoga). See royal yoga
Rajneesh. See Osho
Rajneeshpuram, 172–173, 189n6, 190n36
Ramakrishna, 31–32, 35nn9,15–16,
   44–45, 47, 135, 143, 195, 217n90,
   228

Ram Dass (b. Richard Alpert), 15–16, 26,
   34n1
rishi (seer), 61, 68, 220
Roy, Ram Mohan, 44
royal yoga, 5, 25

sadhana (spiritual practice), 18–19, 27–28,
   32, 46, 85, 101, 113, 126–127,
   152–153, 155–157, 161, 164,
   165nn8,11, 166n13, 195
sadhu (holy one), 60, 147
Sai Baba. See Satya Sai Baba
samadhi (yogic absorption), 26–27, 47, 67
Samkhya (dualistic school of Indian philosophy), 5, 18, 20–22, 24, 30
samsara (cyclic existence), 1, 5, 75, 77n17
samskaras (residual karmic tendencies), 26
sanatana dharma (eternal law or religion),
   74, 91, 225
sangham (fellowship), 10, 148
sannyasa (renunciation), 40, 49, 81, 127
Sarasvati, Dayananda, 44, 224, 225n3
sat guru (perfect, true guru), 127,
   131–132, 137
satsang (association with the good; religious community), 52n31, 116, 130,
   145n24, 164n2, 167n28
satya (truth, the real), 27, 104
Satya Sai Baba, 8, 136, 221
   and caste, 108
   as challenging tradition, 106, 107, 108
   and charitable organizations/service,
      97, 98, 99, 102, 103, 104, 113–116,
      120
   and darshan, 102–103, 113–114
   establishment in the United States, 98,
      108–112, 115–119
   and gender roles, 109–110, 120n1
   as god/avatar, 97, 99, 101–104,
      106–109, 112, 114, 117–120, 120n1
   and governance, 114–116, 119–120
   as guru, 97–100
   and hagiography, 99–102
   and miracles, 99, 100, 101, 103, 108
   and shakti, 101
   and transmission, 97, 98, 102, 103, 105,
      107, 109, 114–119

Satya Sai Baba (*continued*)
and universalism, 101, 104–107, 116,
119
Science of Creative Intelligence, 65, 67,
69, 75n1
seva (service), 104, 130, 155
Shaivism, 150, 166nn16–17, 225n1
shaktipat (descent in shakti; tantric initiation), 10, 149–153, 156–158, 165n8,
165nn10–11, 166nn13–14,16–18
Shankara, 6, 43–45, 48, 51n3, 58, 62, 67,
173
Shankaracharya, 33, 58–63, 75,
76nn10–17, 77n18, 79n50, 228
Shirdi Sai Baba, 100–101, 109–110
Shiva, 41–42, 92, 101, 109, 155, 164n4,
221
siddha (perfected one), 158, 167n28, 193,
197, 205, 213, 216nn41–42, 221, 224
Siddha Yoga, 10–11, 148–164n3,
165nn6,9, 166nn14,17,21,
167nn25,28, 216, 222. *See also*
Gurumayi
siddhi (perfection; power), 76n9, 158, 193.
See also TM-Sidhi
stotras (hymns of praise), 143
SYDA Foundation, 157, 160–161,
163–165, 165nn5,7–9,12,
166nn21,23, 167n27

Transcendental Meditation, 6, 55, 57, 59,
65–66, 69, 74–76, 78nn33,40, 130,
228
Turner, Bryan S., 184–185, 192n60

Universalism, 6, 7–9, 12, 39, 41, 44–46,
51, 72, 74, 106, 135
Upanishads, 6, 20, 24, 44, 58, 84
upaya (skillful means), 7, 92, 166n13,
174

vairagya (renunciation, dispassion), 25, 86
Vaishnava (devotee of, or relating to
Vishnu), 82–84, 88, 92, 94nn18,24,
223, 228
Veda, 58, 67–68, 70–71
Vedic, 6, 8, 20, 56, 62, 64–67, 68, 69, 70,
72–74, 75n1, 78n34, 86, 101, 104
Vivekananda, 4, 35n9, 39, 44, 51, 135,
143, 195

World's Parliament of Religions, 4, 123

Yoga Sutra, 5, 15–16, 18–19, 21, 24–26,
31, 84, 227
Yogananda, Paramahansa, 13n3, 15, 16,
30, 61

Zimmer, Heinrich, 47, 52n31, 52n34